**Date Due**

| OC 19 04 | | | |
|---|---|---|---|
| | | | |
| | | | |
| | | | |
| | | | |
| | | | |
| | | | |
| | | | |
| | | | |
| | | | |
| | | | |

# CHELSEA HOUSE PUBLISHERS

## *Modern Critical Views*

HENRY ADAMS
EDWARD ALBEE
A. R. AMMONS
MATTHEW ARNOLD
JOHN ASHBERY
W. H. AUDEN
JANE AUSTEN
JAMES BALDWIN
CHARLES BAUDELAIRE
SAMUEL BECKETT
SAUL BELLOW
THE BIBLE
ELIZABETH BISHOP
WILLIAM BLAKE
JORGE LUIS BORGES
ELIZABETH BOWEN
BERTOLT BRECHT
THE BRONTËS
ROBERT BROWNING
ANTHONY BURGESS
GEORGE GORDON, LORD BYRON
THOMAS CARLYLE
LEWIS CARROLL
WILLA CATHER
CERVANTES
GEOFFREY CHAUCER
KATE CHOPIN
SAMUEL TAYLOR COLERIDGE
JOSEPH CONRAD
CONTEMPORARY POETS
HART CRANE
STEPHEN CRANE
DANTE
CHARLES DICKENS
EMILY DICKINSON
JOHN DONNE & THE
    17th-CENTURY POETS
ELIZABETHAN DRAMATISTS
THEODORE DREISER
JOHN DRYDEN
GEORGE ELIOT
T. S. ELIOT
RALPH ELLISON
RALPH WALDO EMERSON
WILLIAM FAULKNER
HENRY FIELDING
F. SCOTT FITZGERALD
GUSTAVE FLAUBERT
E. M. FORSTER
SIGMUND FREUD
ROBERT FROST

ROBERT GRAVES
GRAHAM GREENE
THOMAS HARDY
NATHANIEL HAWTHORNE
WILLIAM HAZLITT
SEAMUS HEANEY
ERNEST HEMINGWAY
GEOFFREY HILL
FRIEDRICH HÖLDERLIN
HOMER
GERARD MANLEY HOPKINS
WILLIAM DEAN HOWELLS
ZORA NEALE HURSTON
HENRY JAMES
SAMUEL JOHNSON
BEN JONSON
JAMES JOYCE
FRANZ KAFKA
JOHN KEATS
RUDYARD KIPLING
D. H. LAWRENCE
JOHN LE CARRÉ
URSULA K. LE GUIN
DORIS LESSING
SINCLAIR LEWIS
ROBERT LOWELL
NORMAN MAILER
BERNARD MALAMUD
THOMAS MANN
CHRISTOPHER MARLOWE
CARSON MCCULLERS
HERMAN MELVILLE
JAMES MERRILL
ARTHUR MILLER
JOHN MILTON
EUGENIO MONTALE
MARIANNE MOORE
IRIS MURDOCH
VLADIMIR NABOKOV
JOYCE CAROL OATES
SEAN O'CASEY
FLANNERY O'CONNOR
EUGENE O'NEILL
GEORGE ORWELL
CYNTHIA OZICK
WALTER PATER
WALKER PERCY
HAROLD PINTER
PLATO
EDGAR ALLAN POE

POETS OF SENSIBILITY &
    THE SUBLIME
ALEXANDER POPE
KATHERINE ANNE PORTER
EZRA POUND
PRE-RAPHAELITE POETS
MARCEL PROUST
THOMAS PYNCHON
ARTHUR RIMBAUD
THEODORE ROETHKE
PHILIP ROTH
JOHN RUSKIN
J. D. SALINGER
GERSHOM SCHOLEM
WILLIAM SHAKESPEARE (3 vols.)
    HISTORIES & POEMS
    COMEDIES
    TRAGEDIES
GEORGE BERNARD SHAW
MARY WOLLSTONECRAFT SHELLEY
PERCY BYSSHE SHELLEY
EDMUND SPENSER
GERTRUDE STEIN
JOHN STEINBECK
LAURENCE STERNE
WALLACE STEVENS
TOM STOPPARD
JONATHAN SWIFT
ALFRED LORD TENNYSON
WILLIAM MAKEPEACE THACKERAY
HENRY DAVID THOREAU
LEO TOLSTOI
ANTHONY TROLLOPE
MARK TWAIN
JOHN UPDIKE
GORE VIDAL
VIRGIL
ROBERT PENN WARREN
EVELYN WAUGH
EUDORA WELTY
NATHANAEL WEST
EDITH WHARTON
WALT WHITMAN
OSCAR WILDE
TENNESSEE WILLIAMS
WILLIAM CARLOS WILLIAMS
THOMAS WOLFE
VIRGINIA WOOLF
WILLIAM WORDSWORTH
RICHARD WRIGHT
WILLIAM BUTLER YEATS

*Further titles in preparation.*

*Modern Critical Views*

# NATHANAEL WEST

## Modern Critical Views

# NATHANAEL WEST

Edited with an introduction by

## Harold Bloom

Sterling Professor of the Humanities
Yale University

1986
CHELSEA HOUSE PUBLISHERS
New York
New Haven      Philadelphia

PROJECT EDITORS: Emily Bestler, James Uebbing
ASSOCIATE EDITOR: Maria Behan
EDITORIAL COORDINATOR: Karyn Gullen Browne
EDITORIAL STAFF: Perry King, Bert Yaeger
DESIGN: Susan Lusk

Cover illustration by Liane Fried

Printed and bound in the United States of America

Library of Congress Cataloging in Publication Data

Nathanael West.
    (Modern critical views)
    Bibliography: p.
    Includes index.
    1. West, Nathanael, 1903–1940—Criticism and
interpretation—Addresses, essays, lectures.
I. Bloom, Harold.   II. Series.
PS3545.E8334Z828   1986        813'.52        85–21319
ISBN 0–87754–663–0

**Chelsea House Publishers**
Harold Steinberg, Chairman and Publisher
Susan Lusk, Vice President
A Division of Chelsea House Educational Communications, Inc.
133 Christopher Street, New York, NY 10014

# Contents

Editor's Note . . . . . . . . . . . . . . . . . . . . . . . . . . . . . . . . . . viii

Introduction . . . . . . *Harold Bloom* . . . . . . . . . . . . . . . . . . . . . . 1

Nathanael West . . . . . . *Stanley Edgar Hyman* . . . . . . . . . . . . . 11

Interlude: West's Disease . . . . . . *W. H. Auden* . . . . . . . . . . . . 41

The Mob Tendency:
    *The Day of the Locust* . . . . . . *Alvin B. Kernan* . . . . . . . . . . 49

Late Thoughts on Nathanael West . . . . . . *Daniel Aaron* . . . . . . 61

Days of Wrath and Laughter: West . . . . . . *R. W. B. Lewis* . . . . 69

Nathanael West's
    "Desperate Detachment" . . . . . . *Max F. Schulz* . . . . . . . . . 75

"Abandon Everything!" . . . . . . *Jay Martin* . . . . . . . . . . . . . . . . 89

West's Lemuel and the American Dream . . . . . *T. R. Steiner* . . 99

The Messianic Sexuality of
    *Miss Lonelyhearts* . . . . . . *Miles D. Orvell* . . . . . . . . . . . . . . 111

History and Case History in
    *Red Cavalry* and *The Day of the Locust* . . . . . . *Max Apple* . . . 119

Varieties of Satire in the Art of
    Nathanael West . . . . . . *James F. Light* . . . . . . . . . . . . . . . . 129

The Problem of Language in
    *Miss Lonelyhearts* . . . . . . *Jeffrey L. Duncan* . . . . . . . . . . . . . 145

Dadaist Collage Structure and Nathanael West's
    *Dream Life of Balso Snell* . . . . . . *Deborah Wyrick* . . . . . . . . 157

Personality in the Land of Wish: Popular Motifs
    in Nathanael West's *The Day of the Locust*
    John Keyes . . . . . . . . . . . . . . . . . . . . . . . . . . . . . . . . . . . . . 165

Chronology . . . . . . . . . . . . . . . . . . . . . . . . . . . . . . . . . . . . . . 175

Contributors . . . . . . . . . . . . . . . . . . . . . . . . . . . . . . . . . . . . . 177

Bibliography . . . . . . . . . . . . . . . . . . . . . . . . . . . . . . . . . . . . . 179

Acknowledgments . . . . . . . . . . . . . . . . . . . . . . . . . . . . . . . . . 181

Index . . . . . . . . . . . . . . . . . . . . . . . . . . . . . . . . . . . . . . . . . . . 183

# Editor's Note

This volume reprints what the editor considers to be a representative selection of the best criticism devoted to Nathanael West's fiction. It opens with the editor's "Introduction," which reads *Miss Lonelyhearts* in particular, and West's other novels by extension, as involuntary instances of what Gershom Scholem termed Jewish Gnosticism. The chronological sequence of the book begins by reprinting Stanley Edgar Hyman's pamphlet on West, which remains the best critical overview of West's achievement.

W. H. Auden's darkly witty analysis of the spiritual malaise he called "West's Disease," is followed by Alvin B. Kernan's brilliant reading of *The Day of the Locust* in the full context of the satiric tradition, upon which Kernan is the recognized authority. Daniel Aaron's wise meditation upon West sets him accurately in the context of his literary contemporaries and is followed by a spirited brief analysis of the apocalyptic tendency in West by R. W. B. Lewis. With the study by Max F. Schulz of West's oxymoronic "desperate detachment," another perspective enters, one which compels us to see West as the very involuntary ancestor of the Jewish-American novelists who have arrived in his wake.

Jay Martin, West's biographer, follows with a definitive account of the origins of West's fiction in the composition of *The Dream Life of Balso Snell*. This is supplemented by T. R. Steiner's reading of *A Cool Million*, West's other "minor" novel. A first fuller consideration of West's masterpiece, *Miss Lonelyhearts*, is provided by Miles D. Orvell, whose very different view of "messianic sexuality" in the book contrasts usefully with that given by the editor in his introductory assessment.

Max Apple, a superb comic novelist who is one of West's legitimate heirs, strikingly juxtaposes West with the Soviet Jewish writer Isaac Babel. With James F. Light's essay, we return to the genre of satire, and to its varieties as manifested in West's work. Jeffrey L. Duncan's investigation of *Miss Lonelyhearts* as a vision of the disorder of language is complemented by Deborah Wyrick's account of a conscious Dadaist disordering in the collage structure of *Balso Snell*. In the volume's final essay, John Keyes studies *The Day of the Locust* as a commentary upon the American popular culture of its time. In a sense, that commentary returns us to the problematics of my "Introduction," which reads *Miss Lonelyhearts* as a late, unknowing heir of what might be called the heretical Jewish popular culture of earlier centuries.

# Introduction

## I

Nathanael West, who died in an automobile accident in 1940 at the age of thirty-seven, wrote one remorseless masterpiece, *Miss Lonelyhearts* (1933). Despite some astonishing sequences, *The Day of the Locust* (1939) is an overpraised work, a waste of West's genius. Of the two lesser fictions, *The Dream Life of Balso Snell* (1931) is squalid and dreadful, with occasional passages of a rancid power, while *A Cool Million* (1934), though an outrageous parody of American picaresque, is a permanent work of American satire and seems to me underpraised. To call West uneven is therefore a litotes; he is a wild medley of magnificent writing and inadequate writing, except in *Miss Lonelyhearts* which excels *The Sun Also Rises*, *The Great Gatsby* and even *Sanctuary* as the perfected instance of a negative vision in modern American fiction. The greatest Faulkner, of *The Sound and the Fury*, *As I Lay Dying*, *Absalom, Absalom!* and *Light in August*, is the only American writer of prose fiction in this century who can be said to have surpassed *Miss Lonelyhearts*. West's spirit lives again in *The Crying of Lot 49* and some sequences in *Gravity's Rainbow*, but the negative sublimity of *Miss Lonelyhearts* proves to be beyond Pynchon's reach, or perhaps his ambition.

West, born Nathan Weinstein, is a significant episode in the long and tormented history of Jewish Gnosticism. The late Gershom Scholem's superb essay, "Redemption Through Sin," in his *The Messianic Idea in Judaism*, is the best commentary I know upon *Miss Lonelyhearts*. I once attempted to convey this to Scholem, who shrugged West off, quite properly from Scholem's viewpoint, when I remarked to him that West was manifestly a Jewish anti-Semite, and admitted that there were no allusions to Jewish esotericism or Kabbalah in his works. Nevertheless, for the stance of literary criticism, Jewish Gnosticism, as defined by Scholem, is the most illuminating context in which to study West's novels. It is a melancholy paradox that West, who did not wish to be Jewish in any way at all, remains the most indisputably Jewish writer yet to appear in America, a judgment at once aesthetic and moral. Nothing by Bellow, Malamud, Philip Roth, Mailer, or Ozick can compare to *Miss Lonelyhearts* as an achievement. West's Jewish heir, if he has one, may be Harold Brodkey, whose recent *Women and Angels*, excerpted from his immense novel-in-progress, can be regarded as another powerful instance of Jewish Gnosis, free of West's hatred of his own Jewishness.

Stanley Edgar Hyman, in his pamphlet on West (1962), concluded that, "His strength lay in his vulgarity and bad taste, his pessimism, his nastiness." Hyman remains West's most useful critic, but I would amend this by observing that these qualities in West's writing emanate from a negative theology, spiritually authentic, and given aesthetic dignity by the force of West's eloquent negations. West, like his grandest creation, Shrike, is a rhetorician of the abyss, in the tradition of Sabbatian nihilism that Scholem has expounded so masterfully. One thinks of ideas such as "the violation of the Torah has become its fulfillment, just as a grain of wheat must rot in the earth" or such as Jacob Frank's; "We are all now under the obligation to enter the abyss." The messianic intensity of the Sabbatians and Frankists results in a desperately hysterical and savage tonality which prophesies West's authentically religious book, *Miss Lonelyhearts*, a work profoundly Jewish but only in its negations, particularly the negation of the normative Judaic assumption of total sense in everything, life and text alike. *Miss Lonelyhearts* takes place in the world of Freud, where the fundamental assumption is that everything already has happened, and that nothing can be made new because total sense has been achieved, but then repressed or negated. Negatively Jewish, the book is also negatively American. Miss Lonelyhearts is a failed Walt Whitman (hence the naming of the cripple as Peter Doyle, Whitman's pathetic friend) and a fallen American Adam to Shrike's very American Satan. Despite the opinions of later critics, I continue to find Hyman's argument persuasive, and agree with him that the book's psychosexuality is marked by a repressed homosexual relation between Shrike and Miss Lonelyhearts. Hyman's Freudian observation that all the suffering in the book is essentially female seems valid, reminding us that Freud's "feminine masochism" is mostly encountered among men, according to Freud himself. Shrike, the butcherbird impaling his victim, Miss Lonelyhearts, upon the thorns of Christ, is himself as much an instance of "feminine masochism" as his victim. If Miss Lonelyhearts is close to pathological frenzy, Shrike is also consumed by religious hysteria, by a terrible nostalgia for God.

The book's bitter stylistic negation results in a spectacular verbal economy, in which literally every sentence is made to count, in more than one sense of "count." Freud's "negation" involves a cognitive return of the repressed, here through West's self-projection as Shrike, spit out but not disavowed. The same Freudian process depends upon an affective continuance of repression, here by West's self-introjection as Miss Lonelyhearts, at once West's inability to believe and his disavowed failure to love. Poor Miss Lonelyhearts, who receives no other name throughout the book, has been destroyed by Shrike's power of Satanic rhetoric before the book even opens. But then Shrike has destroyed himself first, for no one could withstand the sustained horror of Shrike's impaling rhetoric, which truly can be called West's horror:

> "I am a great saint," Shrike cried, "I can walk on my own water. Haven't you ever heard of Shrike's Passion in the Luncheonette, or the Agony in the Soda Fountain? Then I compared the wounds in Christ's body to the mouths of a miraculous purse in which we deposit the small change of our sins. It is indeed an excellent conceit. But now let us consider the holes in our own bodies and into what these congenital wounds open. Under the skin of man is a wondrous jungle where veins like lush tropical growths hang along over-ripe organs and weed-like entrails writhe in squirming tangles of red and yellow. In this jungle, flitting from rock-gray lungs to golden intestines, from liver to lights and back to liver again, lives a bird called the soul. The Catholic hunts this bird with bread and wine, the Hebrew with a golden ruler, the Protestant on leaden feet with leaden words, the Buddhist with gestures, the Negro with blood. I spit on them all. Phooh! And I call upon you to spit. Phooh! Do you stuff birds? No, my dears, taxidermy is not religion. No! A thousand times no. Better, I say unto you, better a live bird in the jungle of the body than two stuffed birds on the library table."

I have always associated this great passage with what is central to West: the messianic longing for redemption, through sin if necessary. West's humor is almost always apocalyptic, in a mode quite original with him, though so influential since his death that we have difficulty seeing how strong the originality was. Originality, even in comic writing, becomes a difficulty. How are we to read the most outrageous of the letters sent to Miss Lonelyhearts, the one written by the sixteen-year-old girl without a nose?

> I sit and look at myself all day and cry. I have a big hole in the middle of my face that scares people even myself so I cant blame the boys for not wanting to take me out. My mother loves me, but she crys terrible when she looks at me.
> What did I do to deserve such a terrible bad fate? Even if I did do some bad things I didnt do any before I was a year old and I was born this way. I asked Papa and he says he doesnt know, but that maybe I did something in the other world before I was born or that maybe I was being punished for his sins. I dont believe that because he is a very nice man. Ought I commit suicide?
>
> Sincerely yours,
> Desperate

Defensive laughter is a complex reaction to grotesque suffering. In his 1928 essay on humor, Freud concluded that the above-the-I, the superego, speaks kindly words of comfort to the intimidated ego, and this speaking is humor, which Freud calls "the triumph of narcissism, the ego's victorious assertion of its own invulnerability." Clearly, Freud's "humor" does not include the Westian mode. Reading Desperate's "What did I do to deserve such a terrible bad fate?," our ego knows that it is defeated all the time, or at least is vulnerable to undeserved horror. West's humor has *no* liberating element whatsoever, but is the humor of a vertigo ill-balanced on the edge of what ancient Gnosticism called the *kenoma*, the cosmological emptiness.

## II

Shrike, West's superb Satanic tempter, achieves his apotheosis at the novel's midpoint, the eighth of its fifteen tableaux, accurately titled "Miss Lonelyhearts in the Dismal Swamp." As Miss Lonelyhearts, sick with despair, lies in bed, the drunken Shrike bursts in, shouting his greatest rhetorical setpiece, certainly the finest tirade in modern American fiction. Cataloging the methods that Miss Lonelyhearts might employ to escape out of the Dismal Swamp, Shrike begins with a grand parody of the later D. H. Lawrence, in which the vitalism of *The Plumed Serpent* and *The Man Who Died* is carried into a gorgeous absurdity, a heavy sexuality that masks Shrike's Satanic fears of impotence:

> You are fed up with the city and its teeming millions. The ways and means of men, as getting and lending and spending, you lay waste your inner world, are too much with you. The bus takes too long, while the subway is always crowded. So what do you do? So you buy a farm and walk behind your horse's moist behind, no collar or tie, plowing your broad swift acres. As you turn up the rich black soil, the wind carries the smell of pine and dung across the fields and the rhythm of an old, old work enters your soul. To this rhythm, you sow and weep and chivy your kine, not kin or kind, between the pregnant rows of corn and taters. Your step becomes the heavy sexual step of a dance-drunk Indian and you tread the seed down into the female earth. You plant, not dragon's teeth, but beans and greens. . . .

Confronting only silence, Shrike proceeds to parody the Melville of *Typee* and *Omoo*, and also Somerset Maugham's version of Gauguin in *The Moon and Sixpence*:

> You live in a thatch hut with the daughter of a king, a slim young maiden in whose eyes is an ancient wisdom. Her breasts are golden

speckled pears, her belly a melon, and her odor is like nothing so much as a jungle fern. In the evening, on the blue lagoon, under the silvery moon, to your love you croon in the soft sylabelew and vocabelew of her langorour tongorour. Your body is golden brown like hers, and tourists have need of the indignant finger of the missionary to point you out. They envy you your breech clout and carefree laugh and little brown bride and fingers instead of forks. But you don't return their envy, and when a beautiful society girl comes to your hut in the night, seeking to learn the secret of your happiness, you send her back to her yacht that hangs on the horizon like a nervous racehorse. And so you dream away the days, fishing, hunting, dancing, kissing, and picking flowers to twine in your hair. . . .

As Shrike says, this is a played-out mode, but his savage gusto in rendering it betrays his hatred of the religion of art, of the vision that sought a salvation in imaginative literature. What Shrike goes on to chant is an even more effective parody of the literary stances West rejected. Though Shrike calls it "Hedonism," the curious amalgam here of Hemingway and Ronald Firbank, with touches of Fitzgerald and the earlier Aldous Huxley, might better be named an aesthetic stoicism:

"You dedicate your life to the pursuit of pleasure. No overindulgence, mind you, but knowing that your body is a pleasure machine, you treat it carefully in order to get the most out of it. Golf as well as booze, Philadelphia Jack O'Brien and his chestweights as well as Spanish dancers. Nor do you neglect the pleasures of the mind. You fornicate under pictures by Matisse and Picasso, you drink from Renaissance glassware, and often you spend an evening beside the fireplace with Proust and an apple. Alas, after much good fun, the day comes when you realize that soon you must die. You keep a stiff upper lip and decide to give a last party. You invite all your old mistresses, trainers, artists and boon companions. The guests are dressed in black, the waiters are coons, the table is a coffin carved for you by Eric Gill. You serve caviar and blackberries and licorice candy and coffee without cream. After the dancing girls have finished, you get to your feet and call for silence in order to explain your philosophy of life. 'Life,' you say, 'is a club where they won't stand for squawks, where they deal you only one hand and you must sit in. So even if the cards are cold and marked by the hand of fate, play up, play up like a gentleman and a sport. Get tanked, grab what's on the buffet, use the girls upstairs, but remember, when you throw box cars, take the curtain like a dead game sport, don't squawk.' ". . .

Even this is only preparatory to Shrike's bitterest phase in his tirade, an extraordinary send-up of High Aestheticism proper, of Pater, George Moore, Wilde and the earlier W. B. Yeats:

Art! Be an artist or a writer. When you are cold, warm yourself before the flaming tints of Titian, when you are hungry, nourish yourself with great spiritual foods by listening to the noble periods of Bach, the harmonies of Brahms and the thunder of Beethoven. Do you think there is anything in the fact that their names all begin with a B? But don't take a chance, smoke a 3 B pipe, and remember these immortal lines: *When to the suddenness of melody the echo parting falls the failing day.* What a rhythm! Tell them to keep their society whores and pressed duck with oranges. For you *l'art vivant*, the living art, as you call it. Tell them that you know that your shoes are broken and that there are pimples on your face, yes, and that you have buck teeth and a club foot, but that you don't care, for to-morrow they are playing Beethoven's last quartets in Carnegie Hall and at home you have Shakespeare's plays in one volume.

That last sentence, truly and deliciously Satanic, is one of West's greatest triumphs, but he surpasses it in the ultimate Shrikean rhapsody, after Shrike's candid avowal: "God alone is our escape." With marvelous appropriateness, West makes this at once the ultimate Miss Lonelyhearts letter, and also Shrike's most Satanic self-identification, in the form of a letter to Christ dictated for Miss Lonelyhearts by Shrike, who speaks absolutely for both of them:

> *Dear Miss Lonelyhearts of Miss Lonelyhearts—*
> *I am twenty-six years old and in the newspaper game. Life for me is a desert empty of comfort. I cannot find pleasure in food, drink, or women—nor do the arts give me joy any longer. The Leopard of Discontent walks the streets of my city; the Lion of Discouragement crouches outside the walls of my citadel. All is desolation and a vexation of spirit. I feel like hell. How can I believe, how can I have faith in this day and age? Is it true that the greatest scientists believe again in you?*
> *I read your column and like it very much. There you once wrote: 'When the salt has lost its savour, who shall savour it again?' Is the answer: 'None but the Saviour?'*
> *Thanking you very much for a quick reply, I remain yours truly,*
> *A Regular Subscriber*

"I feel like hell," the Miltonic "Myself am Hell," is Shrike's credo, and West's.

## III

What is the relation of Shrike to West's rejected Jewishness? The question may seem illegitimate to many admirers of West, but it acquires considerable force in the context of the novel's sophisticated yet unhistorical

Gnosticism. The way of nihilism means, according to Scholem, "to free oneself of all laws, conventions, and religions, to adopt every conceivable attitude and to reject it, and to follow one's leader step for step into the abyss." Scholem is paraphrasing the demonic Jacob Frank, an eighteenth century Jewish Shrike who brought the Sabbatian messianic movement to its final degradation. Frank would have recognized something of his own negations and nihilistic fervor in the closing passages that form a pattern in West's four novels:

> His body screamed and shouted as it marched and uncoiled; then, with one heaving shout of triumph, it fell back quiet.
> The army that a moment before had been thundering in his body retreated slowly—victorious, relieved.
>
> *(The Dream Life of Balso Snell)*

> While they were struggling, Betty came in through the street door. She called to them to stop and started up the stairs. The cripple saw her cutting off his escape and tried to get rid of the package. He pulled his hand out. The gun inside the package exploded and Miss Lonelyhearts fell, dragging the cripple with him. They both rolled part of the way down the stairs.
>
> *(Miss Lonelyhearts)*

> "Alas, Lemuel Pitkin himself did not have this chance, but instead was dismantled by the enemy. His teeth were pulled out. His eye was gouged from his head. His thumb was removed. His scalp was torn away. His leg was cut off. And, finally, he was shot through the heart.
> "But he did not live or die in vain. Through his martyrdom the National Revolutionary Party triumphed, and by that triumph this country was delivered from sophistication, Marxism and International Capitalism. Through the National Revolution its people were purged of alien diseases and America became again American."
> "Hail the martyrdom in the Bijou Theater!" roar Shagpoke's youthful hearers when he is finished.
> "Hail, Lemuel Pitkin!"
> "All hail, the American Boy!"
>
> *(A Cool Million)*

> He was carried through the exit to the back street and lifted into a police car. The siren began to scream and at first he thought he was making the noise himself. He felt his lips with his hands. They were clamped tight. He knew then it was the siren. For some reason this made him laugh and he began to imitate the siren as loud as he could.
>
> *(The Day of the Locust)*

All four passages mutilate the human image, the image of God that normative Jewish tradition associates with our origins. "Our forefathers were always talking, only what good did it do them and what did they accomplish? But we are under the burden of silence," Jacob Frank said. What Frank's and West's forefathers always talked about was the ultimate forefather, Adam, who would have enjoyed the era of the Messiah, had he not sinned. West retains of tradition only the emptiness of the fallen image, the scattered spark of creation. The screaming and falling body, torn apart and maddened into a siren-like laughter, belongs at once to the American Surrealist poet, Balso Snell; the American Horst Wessel, poor Lemuel Pitkin; to Miss Lonelyhearts, the Whitmanian American Christ; and to Tod Hackett, painter of the American apocalypse. All are nihilistic versions of the mutilated image of God, or of what the Jewish Gnostic visionary, Nathan of Gaza, called the "thought-less" or nihilizing light.

## IV

West was a prophet of American violence, which he saw as augmenting progressively throughout our history. His satirical genius, for all its authentic and desperate range, has been defeated by American reality. Shagpoke Whipple, the Calvin Coolidge-like ex-President who becomes the American Hitler in *A Cool Million*, talks in terms that West intended as extravagant, but that now can be read all but daily in our newspapers. Here is Shagpoke at his best, urging us to hear what the dead Lemuel Pitkin has to tell us:

> Of what is it that he speaks? Of the right of every American boy to go into the world and there receive fair play and a chance to make his fortune by industry and probity without being laughed at or conspired against by sophisticated aliens.

I turn to today's *New York Times* (March 29, 1985) and find there the text of a speech given by our President:

> But may I just pause here for a second and tell you about a couple of fellows who came to see me the other day, young men. In 1981, just four years ago, they started a business with only a thousand dollars between them and everyone told them they were crazy. Last year their business did a million and a half dollars and they expect to do two and a half million this year. And part of it was because they had the wit to use their names productively. Their business is using their names, the Cain and Abell electric business.

Reality may have triumphed over poor West, but only because he, doubtless as a ghost, inspired or wrote these Presidential remarks. The *Times* reports, sounding as dead-pan as Shrike, on the same page (B4), that the young entrepreneurs brought a present to Mr. Reagan. " 'We gave him a company jacket with Cain and Abell, Inc. on it,' Mr. Cain said." Perhaps West's ghost now writes not only Shagpokian speeches, but the very text of reality in our America.

STANLEY EDGAR HYMAN

# Nathanael West

Nathanael West was born Nathan
Weinstein in New York City on October 17, 1903, the child of Jewish
immigrants from Russia. His mother, Anna Wallenstein Weinstein, came
of a cultivated family, and had been a beautiful girl, courted in Europe by
the painter Maurice Stern. As a housewife she turned stout and bossy.
West's father, Max Weinstein, a building contractor, was slight, kind, and
shy. Of West's two sisters, the elder, Hinda, somewhat resembled the
mother, and the younger, Lorraine (called Laura), was more like the
father. West was particularly devoted to his father, and so close to his
younger sister that in later life he repeatedly said he could never marry less
fine a woman than his sister Laura.

The boy West attended P.S. 81 and P.S. 10, both in Manhattan,
where he showed no academic distinction. He was a thin, awkward, and
ungainly child. Summers he went to Camp Paradox in the Adirondacks,
and a former counselor remembers him as "a quiet chap and not much of a
mixer." Baseball was his passion, although he tended to daydream in the
outfield. When a fly ball hit him on the head and bounced off for a home
run, he got the nickname, "Pep," that stayed with him all his life.

Otherwise West seems to have spent most of his time reading. If his
sisters' recollection can be trusted, he read Tolstoi at ten, and by thirteen
he was familiar with Dostoevski and other Russian literature, Flaubert,
and Henry James. He trained his bull terrier to bite anyone who came into
his room when he was reading. After his graduation from P.S. 10, West
enrolled at De Witt Clinton High School, where he soon distinguished

From *Nathanael West: University of Minnesota Pamphlets on American Writers* 21. Copyright
© 1962 by University of Minnesota.

himself as one of the weakest students in the school. He took no part in any extracurricular activity. In June 1920, West left Clinton without graduating.

In September 1921, West was admitted to Tufts University, on the strength of what now seems to have been a forged transcript from De Witt Clinton. Two months later, as a result of academic difficulties, he withdrew. In February 1922, he was admitted to Brown University as a transfer student from Tufts, this time on the basis of the transcript of the record of another Nathan Weinstein at Tufts. Once enrolled at Brown, West got serious, and managed not only to pass his courses but to graduate in two and a half years.

At Brown, West developed another personality, or showed another side of his personality than the solitary dreamer. He became an Ivy League fashion plate, wearing Brooks Brothers suits and shirts, and a homburg. A college friend, Jeremiah Mahoney, recalls that West looked like a "well-heeled mortuary assistant." Although his manner was reserved, he was friendly and gregarious, generous with his large allowance from his father, and a fairly good banjo player. With girls, he tended to be either too shy or too brash. One summer, West and another college friend, Quentin Reynolds, worked as hod carriers for West's father, and West not only built muscles on his thin frame but got on surprisingly well with the workmen.

West received little or no education in the Jewish religion, and although he was probably ritually circumcised, he was never confirmed in a Bar Mitzvah ceremony. During his years at Brown, West threw off what he could of his Jewishness, and suffered from the rest. "More than anyone I ever knew," his friend John Sanford later reported, "Pep writhed under the accidental curse of his religion." West had nothing to do with any organized Jewish activity on campus, hung around the snobbish Gentile fraternities, and was intensely anxious to be pledged and intensely bitter that he never was. "Nobody ever thought of Pep as being Jewish," a college friend has said, but apparently the Brown fraternities did.

West's great success at Brown was as an aesthete. He dabbled in mysticism, ritual magic, and medieval Catholicism, quoted from obscure saints, discovered Joyce, and for a while was a Nietzschean. S. J. Perelman, a college friend who later married West's sister Laura, recalls that West was the first man on campus to read *Jurgen*. He was equally devoted to Baudelaire, Verlaine, and Rimbaud, Huysmans and Arthur Machen. His personal library was the largest any Brown man had at the time, and he loaned books liberally. Relying on the other Nathan Weinstein's credits in science and economics, West was able to confine himself almost entirely to courses in literature, philosophy, and history. His principal extracurricular activity was working as an editor of *Casements*, the Brown literary magazine. He drew its first cover design, naturally of casements, and contributed a poem, "Death," and an article, "Euripides—a Playwright." The 1924 *Liber Brunensis*, the yearbook, identified West as a genius with an unpredictable future.

After his graduation in 1924, West persuaded his father to send him to Paris, where he spent two happy years and grew a red beard. He returned to New York early in 1926, worked for his father for a while, and then in 1927, through a family connection, got a job as assistant manager at the Kenmore Hotel on East 23rd Street. Put on night duty, he was able to spend the nights reading. He gave rooms to his Brown friends and *their* homeless friends, among them Dashiell Hammett, who finished *The Maltese Falcon* as West's bootleg guest at the Kenmore. In 1928 he progressed to the same job at a fancier hotel, the Sutton on East 56th Street, where he put up other indigent writers, at reduced rates or no charge at all, among them Erskine Caldwell and James T. Farrell. After the stock market crash, which ruined West's father, the Sutton's sun deck became a favored spot for suicides, and West took to calling it "Suicide Leap."

West's first novel, *The Dream Life of Balso Snell*, seems to have been first written in college, but he rewrote it at the Sutton, and in 1931 he managed to get it privately printed in a limited edition of 500 copies. One review appeared, in *Contempo*, but otherwise *Balso Snell* caused no stir whatsoever. The book listed "Nathanael West" as author and thus marked West's official change of name. He had spent much of his class time at Brown doodling "Nathan von Wallenstein Weinstein," which was the named signed to his *Casements* contributions, but even that had turned out to be not Gentile enough. West explained to William Carlos Williams how he got the name: "Horace Greeley said, 'Go West, young man.' So I did." West's anti-Semitism was now considerable. He referred to Jewish girls as "bagels," and avoided them.

In 1931, West took a leave from the Sutton and he and Sanford, another aspiring novelist, rented a shack in the Adirondacks near Warrensburg, New York. Here they wrote in the mornings and fished and hunted in the afternoons. West was working on *Miss Lonelyhearts*, reading each sentence back aloud, producing about a hundred words a day. He rewrote the manuscript five or six times, in the Adirondacks, then back at the Sutton; finally, having quit the Sutton, in a hotel in Frenchtown, New Jersey.

Late in 1932 West and the Perelmans bought a farmhouse in Bucks County, Pennsylvania, and Mrs. Weinstein soon moved in to take over the cooking and try to persuade West to return to the hotel business. In

1933 *Miss Lonelyhearts* was published, and it was reviewed enthusiastically. Unfortunately, the publisher, Horace Liveright, chose that moment to go bankrupt, the printer refused to deliver most of the edition, and by the time West got another publisher to take it over, the reviews were forgotten. Altogether *Miss Lonelyhearts* sold fewer than 800 copies, and West's total income from his first two books and three years of writing came to $780.

In 1932 West had become co-editor with Dr. Williams of a little magazine, *Contact*, and he published articles and chapters of *Miss Lonelyhearts* in it and in *Contempo* in 1933. In August 1933, he became associate editor of a magazine, *Americana*, edited by Alexander King. Before *Americana* expired in November, West managed to publish a Hollywood story, "Business Deal," and some excerpts from *Balso Snell* in it. West then wrote some stories for the slick magazines, but did not succeed in selling any. He applied for a Guggenheim fellowship, with F. Scott Fitzgerald as one of his sponsors, but failed to get it.

West next wrote *A Cool Million* in a hurry, hoping to profit from the reviews of *Miss Lonelyhearts* and make some money. It appeared in 1934, was unfavorably reviewed, sold poorly, and was soon remaindered.

West's personal life in the East was no more successful than his literary career. *Balso Snell* was dedicated to Alice Shepard, a Roman Catholic girl who had gone to Pembroke College with West's sister Laura. He was secretly engaged to her from 1929 to 1932, then publicly engaged, but they never married, although West had bought a marriage license and carried it around with him for several years. His poverty was the explanation given out, but in Sanford's opinion the engagement foundered on the religious difference.

West had been to Hollywood for a few months in 1933, when *Miss Lonelyhearts* was sold to Twentieth Century-Fox and West received a writing contract at $350 a week. He was given little to do, saw his novel made into a Lee Tracy murder thriller, and came back to New York in July disillusioned and bitter. Nevertheless, in 1935, when every other possibility seemed closed to him, West returned to Hollywood and went to work for Republic Studios as a script writer. He switched to RKO Radio in 1938, and also worked for Universal-International Pictures. In the remaining few years of his life, West turned out a number of trivial screenplays, alone or in collaboration, among them *Five Came Back, I Stole a Million*, and *Spirit of Culver*. As a result of his facility as a script writer, West was able to live in comfort and security for the first time since the 1929 crash. He worked a few hours a week dictating to a secretary, and spent most of his weekends on hunting trips, following the season down from Oregon through California into Mexico each year. He acquired two hunting dogs, which slept on his bed, and he explained to people that he needed a house and servants for the dogs.

West made it clear that he despised the "pants pressers" of Hollywood, and he tried to escape in a number of fashions. He collaborated on two plays for Broadway, but the first never got there and the second only lasted two performances, winning from Brooks Atkinson the accolade "nitwit theatre." He became a fellow traveler of the Communist party, signing the call for the American Writers Congress in 1935, joining the Screen Writers Guild, and working strenuously on behalf of Loyalist Spain and other causes. (Earlier, in 1933, he had published a Marxist poem in *Contempo*. Before leaving for California in 1935 he had picketed Orbach's with other Communist sympathizers and was jailed for a few hours "for obstructing traffic.") He was, luckily, unable to get his political orientation explicitly into his fiction.

West published *The Day of the Locust* in 1939, hoping its success would get him out of Hollywood, but despite some good reviews it was a commercial failure, selling fewer than 1500 copies. (West's publisher, Bennett Cerf, explained to him that it failed because women readers didn't like it.)

West's isolation ended suddenly and surprisingly in 1940, when he fell in love with Eileen McKenney, the protagonist of Ruth McKenney's *My Sister Eileen*. They were married in April, and spent a three-month honeymoon in Oregon, hunting and fishing. On West's return he got a higher paid job at Columbia Pictures; later Columbia bought *A Cool Million* and a screen treatment of it on which West had collaborated. The great happy period of West's life, begun in the spring, did not last out the year. On December 22, the Wests were returning from a hunting trip in Mexico, when West, a poor driver, went through a stop sign near El Centro, California. Their station wagon crashed into an automobile. Eileen died instantly, West an hour later on the way to the hospital. He was thirty-seven. His body was shipped to New York and buried in a Jewish cemetery.

Since his death West's reputation has risen continuously. *Miss Lonelyhearts* has sold 190,000 copies in paperback, and *The Day of the Locust* 250,000. Scholarly articles about West, here and abroad, multiply cancerously. *Miss Lonelyhearts* has been made into a play, a more faithful film than the Lee Tracy one, and an opera. In 1946 it was translated into French by Marcelle Sibon as *Mademoiselle Cœur-Brisé*, with an introduction by Philippe Soupault, and it has had a visible effect on later French fiction. Since 1949, all West's books but the first have been published in England.

When the four novels were reissued in this country in one volume in 1957, all the reviews were favorable, and there was general agreement that West was one of the most important writers of the thirties, as American as apple pie. West's picture appeared on the cover of the *Saturday Review*, looking very Jewish.

*The Dream Life of Balso Snell* (1931) is almost impossible to synopsize. A poet named Balso Snell finds the wooden Trojan Horse and has a picaresque journey up its alimentary canal. In the course of his travels he encounters: a Jewish guide; Maloney the Areopagite, a Catholic mystic; John Gilson, a precocious schoolboy; and Miss McGeeney, John's eighth-grade teacher. Each has a story, sometimes several stories, to tell, and their stories merge with their dreams and with Balso's dreams in a thoroughly confusing, and deliberately confusing, fashion. The book ends with Balso's orgasm, still in the bowels of the horse, during a dream of rapturous sexual intercourse with Miss McGeeney. Balso is dreaming the schoolboy's dream, and may have become the schoolboy.

The overwhelming impression the reader gets is of the corruption and repulsiveness of the flesh. In one of John Gilson's fantasies of beating a mistress, he explains his action: "I have a sty on my eye, a cold sore on my lip, a pimple where the edge of my collar touches my neck, another pimple in the corner of my mouth, and a drop of salt snot on the end of my nose." Furthermore, "It seems to me as though all the materials of life—wood, glass, wool, skin—are rubbing against my sty, my cold sore and my pimples." When Balso encounters Miss McGeeney, a middle-aged tweedy woman disguised for the moment as a beautiful naked young girl, she offers him her poetic vision: "Houses that are protuberances on the skin of streets—warts, tumors, pimples, corns, nipples, sebaceous cysts, hard and soft chancres."

In a dream within his dream, Balso is attracted to girl cripples: "He likened their disarranged hips, their short legs, their humps, their splay feet, their wall-eyes, to ornament." He cries tenderly to one of them, Janey the hunchback: "For me, your sores are like flowers: the new, pink, budlike sores, the full, rose-ripe sores, the sweet, seed-bearing sores. I shall cherish them all." One of Balso's beautiful memories in the book is of a girl he once loved who did nothing all day but put bits of meat and gravy, butter and cheese, on the petals of roses so that they would attract flies instead of butterflies and bees.

As the human body is seen as a running sore, Christianity is seen entirely in terms of Christ's wounded and bleeding body. Maloney the Areopagite is writing a hagiography of Saint Puce, a flea who was born, lived, and died in the armpit of Jesus Christ. Maloney's blasphemous idea that Saint Puce was born of the Holy Ghost enables West to mock the mysteries of Incarnation, as the flea's feasting on the divine flesh and blood enables West to mock Eucharist. The Passion is burlesqued by Maloney, who is encountered naked except for a derby stuck full of thorns, trying to crucify himself with thumbtacks, and by Beagle Darwin, a fictional invention of Miss McGeeney's, who does a juggling act, keeping in the air "the Nails, the Scourge, the Thorns, and a piece of the True Cross."

Nor is West's bitterness in the book reserved for Christianity. Judaism comes in for its share. The song in praise of obscene roundness that Balso makes when he starts his journey concludes:

> Round and Ringing Full
> As the Mouth of a Brimming Goblet
> The Rust-Laden Holes
> In Our Lord's Feet
> Entertain the Jew-Driven Nails.

The guide turns out to be not only a Jew, but a Jew who at the mention of such melodious Jewish names as Hernia Hornstein and Paresis Pearlberg finds it necessary to affirm: "I am a Jew. I'm a Jew! A Jew!" Balso answers politely that some of his best friends are Jews, and adds Doughty's epigram: "The semites are like to a man sitting in a cloaca to the eyes, and whose brows touch heaven."

The strength of *Balso Snell* lies in its garish comic imagination. Maloney's crucifixion with thumbtacks is not only a serious theme that West's later work develops, it is also funny, and as a parody of the stance of Roman Catholic mysticism, devastating. The account in John Gilson's journal of his Gidean and Dostoevskian murder of an idiot dishwasher is repulsive but genuinely imagined, and its unconscious sexual motivation is boldly dramatized: stripping for the crime, John notices his genitals tight and hard; afterwards he feels like a happy young girl, "kittenish, cuneycutey, darlingey, springtimey"; when he sees sailors on the street, he flirts and camps and feels "as though I were melting—all silk and perfumed, pink lace." The hunchback Janey is a nightmarish vision of the female body as terrifying, transformed into comedy: she has a hundred and forty-four exquisite teeth, and is pregnant in the hump.

Some of West's language in the book foreshadows his later triumphs. Janey imagines death to be "like putting on a wet [bathing] suit—shivery." John describes his dual nature to his fantasy-mistress, Saniette: "Think of two men—myself and the chauffeur within me. This chauffeur is very large and dressed in ugly ready-made clothing. His shoes, soiled from walking about the streets of a great city, are covered with animal ordure and chewing gum. His hands are covered with coarse woollen gloves. On his head is a derby hat." Sometimes John speaks in a voice we can hear as the youthful West's. He tells Balso: "I need women and because I can't buy or force them, I have to make poems for them. God knows how tired I am of using the insanity of Van Gogh and the adventures of Gauguin as can-openers." John explains his position in a pamphlet, which he sells to Balso for a dollar. In it he confesses: "If it had been possible for me to attract by exhibiting a series of physical charms, my hatred would have been less. But I found it necessary to substitute strange conceits, wise and witty sayings, peculiar conduct, Art, for the muscles, teeth, hair, of my rivals."

The weaknesses of *Balso Snell* are all characteristically juvenile. The principal one is the obsessive scatology, which soon becomes boring. "O Anus Mirabilis!" Balso cries of his rectal entrance to the Trojan Horse, and his roundness song takes off from that anal image. "Art is a sublime excrement," he is told by the Jewish guide (who seems to justify only the first half of Doughty's aphorism). John sees journal-keepers in excremental imagery: "They come to the paper with a constipation of ideas—eager, impatient. The white paper acts as a laxative. A diarrhoea of words is the result." When the idiot dishwasher swallows, John compares it to "a miniature toilet being flushed." As John beats Saniette, he cries: "O constipation of desire! O diarrhoea of love!" He has visions of writing a play that will conclude when "the ceiling of the theatre will be made to open and cover the occupants with tons of loose excrement." Balso speaks "with lips torn angry in laying duck's eggs from a chicken's rectum." James F. Light reports that West was fond of quoting Odo of Cluny's reference to the female as "*saccus stercoris,*" but the book's scatological obsession is clearly not restricted to the female. It is no less than a vision of the whole world as one vast dungheap.

*Balso Snell* is complex and stratified, so much so that at one point we get Janey's thinking as Beagle imagines it in a letter actually written by Miss McGeeney and read by Balso in his dream within a dream. But the book has no form, and consists merely of a series of encounters and complications, terminated rather than resolved by the orgasm. We can sense West's dissatisfaction with it as not fully realized in his re-use of some of its material in later works. Some of *Balso Snell* is extremely schoolboyish, like the guide's aphorism, "A hand in the Bush is worth two in the pocket," or Balso's comment on Maloney's story of the martyrdom and death of Saint Puce: "I think you're morbid. . . . Take cold showers."

When *Miss Lonelyhearts* was published two years later, in 1933,

West told A. J. Liebling that it was entirely unlike *Balso Snell*, "of quite a different make, wholesome, clean, holy, slightly mystic and inane." He describes it in "Some Notes on Miss Lonelyhearts" as a "portrait of a priest of our time who has had a religious experience." In it, West explains, "violent images are used to illustrate commonplace events. Violent acts are left almost bald." He credits William James's *Varieties of Religious Experience* for its psychology. Some or all of this may be Westian leg-pull.

The plot of *Miss Lonelyhearts* is Sophoclean irony, as simple and inevitable as the plot of *Balso Snell* is random and whimsical. A young newspaperman who writes the agony column of his paper as "Miss Lonelyhearts" has reached the point where the joke has gone sour. He becomes obsessed with the real misery of his correspondents, illuminated for him by the cynicism of William Shrike, the feature editor. Miss Lonelyhearts pursues Shrike's wife Mary, unsuccessfully, and cannot content himself with the love and radiant goodness of Betty, his fiancée. Eventually he finds his fate in two of his correspondents, the crippled Peter Doyle and his wife Fay. Miss Lonelyhearts is not punished for his tumble with Fay, but when on his next encounter he fights her off, it leads to his being shot by Doyle.

The characters are allegorical figures who are at the same time convincing as people. Miss Lonelyhearts is a New England puritan, the son of a Baptist minister. He has a true religious vocation or calling, but no institutional church to embody it. When Betty suggests that he quit the column, he tells her: "I can't quit. And even if I were to quit, it wouldn't make any difference. I wouldn't be able to forget the letters, no matter what I did."

In one of the most brilliant strokes in the book, he is never named, always identified only by his role. (In an earlier draft, West had named him Thomas Matlock, which we could translate "Doubter Wrestler," but no name at all is infinitely more effective.) Even when he telephones Fay Doyle for an assignation, he identifies himself only as "Miss Lonelyhearts, the man who does the column." In his namelessness, in his vocation without a church, Miss Lonelyhearts is clearly the prophet in the reluctance stage, when he denies the call and tells God that he stammers, but Miss Lonelyhearts, the prophet of *our* time, is stuck there until death.

Miss Lonelyhearts identifies Betty as the principle of order: "She had often made him feel that when she straightened his tie, she straightened much more." The order that she represents is the innocent order of Nature, as opposed to the disorder of sinful Man. When Miss Lonelyhearts is sick, Betty comes to nourish him with hot soup, impose order on his room, and redeem him with a pastoral vision: "She told him about her childhood on a farm and of her love for animals, about country sounds and country smells and of how fresh and clean everything in the country is. She said that he ought to live there and that if he did, he would find that all his troubles were city troubles." When Miss Lonelyhearts is back on his feet, Betty takes him for a walk in the zoo, and he is "amused by her evident belief in the curative power of animals." Then she takes him to live in the country for a few days, in the book's great idyllic scene. Miss Lonelyhearts is beyond such help, but it is Betty's patient innocence—she is as soft and helpless as a kitten—that makes the book so heartbreaking. She is an innocent Eve to his fallen Adam, and he alone is driven out of Eden.

The book's four other principal characters are savage caricatures, in the root sense of "caricature" as the overloading of one attribute. Shrike is a dissociated half of Miss Lonelyhearts, his cynical intelligence, and it is interesting to learn that Shrike's rhetorical masterpiece, the great speech on the varieties of escape, was spoken by Miss Lonelyhearts in an earlier draft. Shrike's name is marvelously apt. The shrike or butcherbird impales its prey on thorns, and the name is a form of the word "shriek." Shrike is of course the mocker who hands Miss Lonelyhearts his crown of thorns, and throughout the book he is a shrieking bird of prey; when not a butcherbird, "a screaming, clumsy gull."

Shrike's wife Mary is one vast teasing mammary image. As Miss Lonelyhearts decides to telephone Mary in Delehanty's speakeasy, he sees a White Rock poster and observes that "the artist had taken a great deal of care in drawing her breasts and their nipples stuck out like tiny red hats." He then thinks of "the play Mary made with her breasts. She used them as the coquettes of long ago had used their fans. One of her tricks was to wear a medal low down on her chest. Whenever he asked to see it, instead of drawing it out she leaned over for him to look. Although he had often asked to see the medal, he had not yet found out what it represented." Miss Lonelyhearts and Mary go out for a gay evening, and Mary flaunts her breasts while talking of her mother's terrible death from cancer of the breast. He finally gets to see the medal, which reads "Awarded by the Boston Latin School for first place in the 100 yd. dash." When he takes her home he kisses her breasts, for the first time briefly slowing down her dash.

The Doyles are presented in inhuman or subhuman imagery. When, in answer to Fay's letter of sexual invitation, Miss Lonelyhearts decides to telephone her, he pictures her as "a tent, hair-covered and veined," and himself as a skeleton: "When he made the skeleton enter the flesh tent, it flowered at every joint." Fay appears and is a giant: "legs like Indian clubs, breasts like balloons and a brow like a pigeon." When he takes her arm, "It felt like a thigh." Following her up the stairs to his apartment, "he watched the action of her massive hams; they were like two enormous grindstones." Undressing, "she made sea sounds; something flapped like a sail; there was the creak of ropes; then he heard the wave-against-a-wharf smack of rubber on flesh. Her call for him to hurry was a sea-moan, and when he lay beside her, she heaved, tidal, moon-driven." Eventually Miss Lonelyhearts "crawled out of bed like an exhausted swimmer leaving the surf," and she soon drags him back.

If Fay is an oceanic monster, Peter Doyle is only a sinister puppy. In bringing Miss Lonelyhearts back to the apartment at Fay's order, he half-jokes, "Ain't I the pimp, to bring home a guy for my wife?" Fay reacts by hitting him in the mouth with a rolled-up newspaper, and his comic response is to growl like a dog and catch the paper with his teeth. When she lets go of her end, he drops to his hands and knees and continues to imitate a dog on the floor. As Miss Lonelyhearts leans over to help him up, "Doyle tore open Miss Lonelyhearts' fly, then rolled over on his back, laughing wildly." Fay, more properly, accepts him as a dog and kicks him.

The obsessive theme of *Miss Lonelyhearts* is human pain and suffering, but it is represented almost entirely as female suffering. This is first spelled out in the letters addressed to Miss Lonelyhearts: Sick-of-it-all is a Roman Catholic wife who has had seven children in twelve years, is pregnant again, and has kidney pains so excruciating that she cries all the time. Desperate is a sixteen-year-old born with a hole in her face instead of a nose, who wants to have dates like other girls. Harold S. writes about his thirteen-year-old deaf-and-dumb sister Gracie, who was raped by a man when she was playing on the roof, and who will be brutally punished if her parents find out about it. Broad Shoulders was hit by a car when she was first pregnant, and is alternately persecuted and deserted by an unbalanced husband, in five pages of ghastly detail. Miss Lonelyhearts gets only two letters about male suffering, one from a paralyzed boy who wants to play the violin, the other from Peter Doyle, who complains of the pain from his crippled leg and the general meaninglessness of life.

The theme of indignities committed on women comes up in another form in the stories Miss Lonelyhearts' friends tell in Delehanty's. They seem to be exclusively anecdotes of group rape, of one woman gang-raped by eight neighbors, of another kept in the back room of a speakeasy for three days, until "on the last day they sold tickets to niggers." Miss Lonelyhearts identifies himself with "wife-torturers, rapers of small children." At one point he tries giving his readers the traditional

Christian justification for suffering, that it is Christ's gift to mankind to bring them to Him, but he tears up the column.

Ultimately the novel cannot justify or even explain suffering, only proclaim its omnipresence. Lying sick in bed, Miss Lonelyhearts gets a vision of human life: "He found himself in the window of a pawnship full of fur coats, diamond rings, watches, shotguns, fishing tackle, mandolins. All these things were the paraphernalia of suffering. A tortured high light twisted on the blade of a gift knife, a battered horn grunted with pain." Finally his mind forms everything into a gigantic cross, and he falls asleep exhausted.

The book's desperate cry of pain and suffering comes to a focus in what Miss Lonelyhearts calls his "Christ complex." He recognizes that Christ is the only answer to his readers' letters, but that "if he did not want to get sick, he had to stay away from the Christ business. Besides, Christ was Shrike's particular joke." As Miss Lonelyhearts leaves the office and walks through a little park, the shadow of a lamppost pierces his side like a spear. Since nothing grows in the park's battered earth, he decides to ask his correspondents to come and water the soil with their tears. He imagines Shrike telling him to teach them to pray each morning, "Give us this day our daily stone," and thinks: "He had given his reader many stones; so many, in fact, that he had only one left—the stone that had formed in his gut."

Jesus Christ, Shrike says, is "the Miss Lonelyhearts of Miss Lonelyhearts." Miss Lonelyhearts has nailed an ivory Christ to the wall of his room with great spikes, but it disappoints him: "Instead of writhing, the Christ remained calmly decorative." Miss Lonelyhearts recalls: "As a boy in his father's church, he had discovered that something stirred in him when he shouted the name of Christ, something secret and enormously powerful." Unfortunately, he recognizes, it is not faith but hysteria: "For him, Christ was the most natural of excitements."

Miss Lonelyhearts tells Betty he is "a humanity lover," but Shrike more aptly identifies him a "leper licker." "If he could only believe in Christ," Miss Lonelyhearts thinks, "then everything would be simple and the letters extremely easy to answer." Later he recognizes that "Shrike had accelerated his sickness by teaching him to handle his one escape, Christ, with a thick glove of words." He decides that he has had a part in the general betrayal of suffering mankind: "The thing that made his share in it particularly bad was that he was capable of dreaming the Christ dream. He felt that he had failed at it, not so much because of Shrike's jokes or his own self-doubt, but because of his lack of humility." Miss Lonelyhearts concludes that "with him, even the word Christ was a vanity." When he gets drunk with Doyle, he calls on Christ joyously, and goes home with Doyle to bring the glad tidings to both Doyles, to heal their marriage. He preaches "love" to them and realizes that he is only writing another column, switches to preaching Christ Jesus, "the black fruit that hangs on the crosstree . . . the bidden fruit," and realizes that he is only echoing Shrike's poisoned rhetoric.

What Miss Lonelyhearts eventually achieves, since he cannot believe in the real Christ, and refuses to become a spurious Christ, is Peter's condition. He becomes the rock on which the new church will be founded, but it is the church of catatonic withdrawal. After three days in bed Miss Lonelyhearts attains a state of perfect calm, and the stone in his gut expands until he becomes "an ancient rock, smooth with experience." The Shrikes come to take him to a party at their apartment, and against this rock the waves of Shrike dash in vain. When Mary wriggles on Miss Lonelyhearts' lap in the cab, "the rock remained perfect." At the party he withstands Shrike's newest mockery, the Miss Lonelyhearts Game, with indifference: "What goes on in the sea is of no interest to the rock." Miss Lonelyhearts leaves the party with Betty: "She too should see the rock he had become." He shamelessly promises her marriage and domesticity: "The rock was a solidification of his feeling, his conscience, his sense of reality, his self-knowledge." He then goes back to his sickbed content: "The rock had been thoroughly tested and had been found perfect."

The next day Miss Lonelyhearts is burning with fever, and "the rock became a furnace." The room fills with grace, the illusory grace of madness, and as Doyle comes up the stairs with a pistol Miss Lonelyhearts rushes downstairs to embrace him and heal his crippled leg, a miracle that will embody his succoring all suffering mankind with love. Unable to escape Miss Lonelyhearts' mad embrace, terrified by Betty coming up the stairs, Doyle tries to toss away the gun, and Miss Lonelyhearts is accidentally shot. He falls dragging Doyle down the stairs in his arms.

It is of course a homosexual tableau—the men locked in embrace while the woman stands helplessly by—and behind his other miseries Miss Lonelyhearts has a powerful latent homosexuality. It is this that is ultimately the joke of his name and the book's title. It explains his acceptance of teasing dates with Mary and his coldness with Mary; he thinks of her excitement and notes: "No similar change ever took place in his own body, however. Like a dead man, only friction could make him warm or violence make him mobile." It explains his discontent with Betty. Most of all it explains his joy at being seduced by Fay—"He had always been the pursuer, but now found a strange pleasure in have the roles reversed" —and how quickly the pleasure turns to disgust.

The communion Miss Lonelyhearts achieves with Doyle in Delehanty's consists in their sitting silently holding hands, Miss Lonelyhearts pressing "with all the love he could manage" to overcome the revulsion he feels at Doyle's touch. Back at the Doyles, after Doyle has ripped open Miss Lonelyhearts' fly and been kicked by his wife, they hold hands again, and when Fay comes back in the room she says "What a sweet pair of fairies you guys are." It is West's ultimate irony that the symbolic embrace they manage at the end is one penetrating the body of the other with a bullet.

We could, if we so chose, write Miss Lonelyhearts' case history before the novel begins. Terrified of his stern religious father, identifying with his soft loving mother, the boy renounces his phallicism out of castration anxiety—a classic Oedipus complex. In these terms the Shrikes are Miss Lonelyhearts' Oedipal parents, abstracted as the father's loud voice and the mother's tantalizing breast. The scene at the end of Miss Lonelyhearts' date with Mary Shrike is horrifying and superb. Standing outside her apartment door, suddenly overcome with passion, he strips her naked under her fur coat while she keeps talking mindlessly of her mother's death, mumbling and repeating herself, so that Shrike will not hear their sudden silence and come out. Finally Mary agrees to let Miss Lonelyhearts in if Shrike is not home, goes inside, and soon Shrike peers out the door, wearing only the top of his pajamas. It is the child's Oedipal vision perfectly dramatized: he can clutch at his mother's body but loses her each time to his more potent rival.

It should be noted that if this is the pattern of Miss Lonelyhearts' Oedipus complex, it is not that of West, nor are the Shrikes the pattern of West's parents. How conscious was West of all or any of this? I would guess, from the book's title, that he was entirely conscious of at least Miss Lonelyhearts' latent homosexuality. As for the Oedipus complex, all one can do is note West's remarks in "Some Notes on Miss Lonelyhearts": "Psychology has nothing to do with reality nor should it be used as motivation. The novelist is no longer a psychologist. Psychology can become much more important. The great body of case histories can be used in the way the ancient writers use their myths. Freud is your Bulfinch; you can not learn from him."

The techniques West uses to express his themes are perfectly suited to them. The most important is a pervasive desperate and savage tone, not only in the imagery of violence and suffering, but everywhere. It is the tone of a world where unreason is triumphant. Telling Miss Lonelyhearts that he is awaiting a girl "of great intelligence," Shrike "illustrated the word *intelligence* by carving two enormous breasts in the air with his hands." When Miss Lonelyhearts is in the country with Betty, a gas station attendant tells him amiably that "it wasn't the hunters who drove out the deer, but the yids." When Miss Lonelyhearts accidentally collides with a man in Delehanty's and turns to apologize, he is punched in the mouth.

The flowering cactus that blooms in this wasteland is Shrike's rhetoric. The book begins with a mock prayer he has composed for Miss Lonelyhearts, and every time Shrike appears he makes a masterly speech: on religion, on escapes, on the gospel of Miss Lonelyhearts according to Shrike. He composes a mock letter to God, in which Miss Lonelyhearts confesses shyly: "I read your column and like it very much." He is a cruel and relentless punster and wit. In his sadistic game at the party, Shrike reads aloud letters to Miss Lonelyhearts. He reads one from a pathetic old woman who sells pencils for a living, and concludes: "She has rheum in her eyes. Have you room in your heart for her?" He reads another, from the paralyzed boy who wants to play the violin, and concludes: "How pathetic! However, one can learn much from this parable. Label the boy Labor, the violin Capital, and so on . . ." Shrike's masterpiece, the brilliant evocation of the ultimate inadequacy of such escapes as the soil, the South Seas, Hedonism, and art, is a classic of modern rhetoric, as is his shorter speech on religion. Here are a few sentences from the latter: "Under the skin of man is a wondrous jungle where veins like lush tropical growths hang along overripe organs and weed-like entrails writhe in squirming tangles of red and yellow. In this jungle, flitting from rock-gray lungs to golden intestines, from liver to lights and back to liver again, lives a bird called the soul. The Catholic hunts this bird with bread and wine, the Hebrew with a golden ruler, the Protestant on leaden feet with leaden words, the Buddhist with gestures, the Negro with blood."

The other cactus that flowers in the wasteland is sadistic violence. The book's most harrowing chapter, "Miss Lonelyhearts and the Lamb," is a dream or recollection of a college escapade, in which Miss Lonelyhearts and two other boys, after drinking all night, buy a lamb to barbecue in the woods. Miss Lonelyhearts persuades his companions to sacrifice it to God before barbecuing it. They lay the lamb on a flower-covered altar and Miss Lonelyhearts tries to cut its throat, but succeeds only in maiming it and breaking the knife. The lamb escapes and crawls off into the underbrush, and the boys flee. Later Miss Lonelyhearts goes back and crushes the lamb's head with a stone. This nightmarish scene, with its unholy suggestions of the sacrifices of Isaac and Christ, embodies the book's bitter paradox: that sadism is the perversion of love.

Visiting Betty early in the novel, aware "that only violence could make him supple," Miss Lonelyhearts reaches inside her robe and tugs at her nipple unpleasantly. "Let me pluck this rose," he says, "I want to wear it in my buttonhole." In "Miss Lonelyhearts and the Clean Old Man," he and a drunken friend find an old gentleman in a washroom, drag him to a speakeasy, and torment him with questions about his "homosexualistic tendencies." As they get nastier and nastier, Miss Lonelyhearts feels "as he had felt years before, when he had accidentally stepped on a small frog. Its spilled guts had filled him with pity, but when its suffering had become real to his senses, his pity had turned to rage and he had beaten it frantically until it was dead." He ends by twisting the old man's arm until the old man screams and someone hits Miss Lonelyhearts with a chair.

The book's only interval of decency, beauty, and peace is the pastoral idyll of the few days Miss Lonelyhearts spends with Betty in the country. They drive in a borrowed car to the deserted farmhouse in Connecticut where she was born. It is spring, and Miss Lonelyhearts "had to admit, even to himself, that the pale new leaves, shaped and colored like candle flames, were beautiful and that the air smelt clean and alive." They work at cleaning up the place, Betty cooks simple meals, and they go down to the pond to watch the deer. After they eat an apple that has ominous Biblical overtones, Betty reveals that she is a virgin and they go fraternally to bed. The next day they go for a naked swim; then, with "no wind to disturb the pull of the earth," Betty is ceremonially deflowered on the new grass. The reader is repeatedly warned that natural innocence cannot save Miss Lonelyhearts: the noise of birds and crickets is "a horrible racket" in his ears; in the woods, "in the deep shade there was nothing but death—rotten leaves, gray and white fungi, and over everything a funereal hush." When they get back to New York, "Miss Lonelyhearts knew that Betty had failed to cure him and that he had been right when he had said that he could never forget the letters." Later, when Miss Lonelyhearts is a rock and leaves Shrike's party with Betty, he tries to create a miniature idyll of innocence by taking her out for a strawberry soda, but it fails. Pregnant by him and intending to have an abortion, Betty remains nevertheless in Edenic innocence; Miss Lonelyhearts is irretrievably fallen, and there is no savior who can redeem.

The book's pace is frantic and its imagery is garish, ugly, and compelling. The letters to Miss Lonelyhearts are "stamped from the dough of suffering with a heart-shaped cookie knife." The sky looks "as if it had been rubbed with a soiled eraser." A bloodshot eye in the peephole of Delehanty's glows "like a ruby in an antique iron ring." Finishing his sermon to the "intelligent" girl, Shrike "buried his triangular face like the blade of a hatchet in her neck." Miss Lonelyhearts' tongue is "a fat thumb," his heart "a congealed lump of icy fat," and his only feeling "icy fatness." Goldsmith, a colleague at the paper, has cheeks "like twin rolls of smooth pink toilet paper." Only the imagery of the Connecticut interlude temporarily thaws the iciness and erases the unpleasant associations with fatness and thumb. As Miss Lonelyhearts watches Betty naked, "She looked a little fat, but when she lifted something to the line, all the fat disappeared. Her raised arms pulled her breasts up until they were like pink-tipped thumbs."

The unique greatness of *Miss Lonelyhearts* seems to have come into the world with hardly a predecessor, but it has itself influenced a great many American novelists since. *Miss Lonelyhearts* seems to me one of the three finest American novels of our century. The other two are F. Scott Fitzgerald's *The Great Gatsby* and Ernest Hemingway's *The Sun Also Rises*. It shares with them a lost and victimized hero, a bitter sense of our civilization's falsity, a pervasive melancholy atmosphere of failure and defeat. If the tone of *Miss Lonelyhearts* is more strident, its images more garish, its pace more rapid and hysterical, it is as fitting an epitome of the thirties as they are the twenties. If nothing in the forties and fifties has similarly gone beyond *Miss Lonelyhearts* in violence and shock, it may be because it stands at the end of the line.

*A Cool Million*, subtitled "The Dismantling of Lemuel Pitkin," is a comic, even a parody, novel, to some extent a reversion to the world of *Balso Snell*. It tells the story of Lemuel Pitkin, a poor but honest Vermont boy, as he attempts to make his way in the world. As he confronts each experience with the old-fashioned virtues of honesty, sobriety, good sportsmanship, thrift, bravery, chivalry, and kindness, he is robbed, beaten up, mutilated, cheated, and victimized. In an interwoven subplot, Elizabeth Prail, a neighbor who similarly represents decent American girlhood, is sexually mistreated: raped, beaten by a sadist, kidnapped by white slavers and sold into prostitution, turned out to walk the streets, and so forth. Meanwhile their town banker, "Shagpoke" Whipple, a former President of the United States, creates an American fascist movement and takes over the country.

The total effect is that of a prolonged, perhaps overprolonged, jape. The stages of the action are the stages of Lem's dismantling: thrown into jail in a frame-up, he loses all his teeth because the warden believes teeth to be the source of moral infection; rescuing a banker and his daughter from a runaway horse, Lem loses an eye; kidnapped by agents of the Communist International, he is involved in an automobile collision and loses a thumb; trying to save Betty from rape, he is caught in a bear trap that the villain has planted, which costs him a leg, and while unconscious in the trap he is scalped by a Harvard-educated Indian. He is eventually hired as stooge for a vaudeville act and demolished during each performance; when he is hit with a mallet, "His toupee flew off, his eye and teeth popped out, and his wooden leg was knocked into the audience." Eventually Lem is shot down onstage while making a speech for American fascism. As a result of his martyrdom Whipple's Leather Shirts triumph, and Pitkin's Birthday becomes a national holiday, on which the youth of America parade singing "The Lemuel Pitkin Song."

What form the book has comes from these ritual stages of dismemberment, but in a truer sense *A Cool Million* is formless, an inorganic stringing together of comic set-pieces, with the preposterous incidents serving merely to raise the various topics West chooses to satirize. Thus Betty's residence in Wu Fong's brothel sets off pages of comic description, first of the brothel as a House of All Nations, then, when Wu Fong is converted by the "Buy American" campaign of the Hearst newspapers, into an all-American establishment. West joyously describes the regional costumes and decor of each girl at considerable length, concluding with the cuisine: "When a client visited Lena Haubengrauber, it was possible for him to eat roast groundhog and drink Sam Thompson rye. While with Alice Sweethorne, he was served sow belly with grits and bourbon. In Mary Judkins' room he received, if he so desired, fried squirrel and corn liquor. In the suite occupied by Patricia Van Riis, lobster and champagne wine were the rule. The patrons of Powder River Rose usually ordered mountain oysters and washed them down with forty-rod. And so on down the list: while with Dolores O'Riely, tortillas and prune brandy from the Imperial Valley; while with Princess Roan Fawn, baked dog and firewater; while with Betty Prail, fish chowder and Jamaica rum. Finally, those who sought the favors of the 'Modern Girl,' Miss Cobina Wiggs, were regaled with tomato and lettuce sandwiches and gin."

The introduction of a Pike County "ring-tail squealer" and "rip-tail roarer" gives West an opportunity to improvise tall talk and anecdotes concluding: "His bones are bleachin' in the canyon where he fell." The Indian chief who scalps Lem is a Spenglerian philosopher and critic of our gadget civilization, and his speech to the tribe to rouse them for the warpath is a long comic diatribe, culminating in: "But now all the secret places of the earth are full. Now even the Grand Canyon will no longer hold razor blades." Later Lem and Whipple join up with a traveling show exhibiting a Chamber of American Horrors, and West gives himself a chance to describe some of the horrors of American life. In one exhibit, all the materials are disguised: "Paper had been made to look like wood, wood like rubber, rubber like steel, steel like cheese, cheese like glass, and, finally, glass like paper." In another, function is disguised: "The visitor saw flower pots that were really victrolas, revolvers that held candy, candy that held collar buttons and so forth." West here is entirely indiscriminate. The accompanying pageant of American history consists of sketches "in which Quakers were shown being branded, Indians brutalized and cheated, Negroes sold, children sweated to death," as though these acts were on the order of disguising paper to look like wood.

It is at once comic and depressing, the fitting work of a man Robert M. Coates has called "the most thoroughly pessimistic person I have ever known." If its indictment of American material civilization does not go very deep, its awareness of the precariousness of American freedom does, and the book is perhaps strongest as a political warning. Writing just after the accession of Hitler, West felt the vulnerability of America to totalitarianism disguised as superpatriotism, and he makes it disturbingly convincing. Whipple's bands of the mindless and disaffected, got up in fringed deerskin shirts, coonskin caps, and squirrel rifles, are the same joke as Lena Haubengrauber's clients washing down roast groundhog with Sam Thompson rye, but here it images our nightmare. Recruiting on street corners, Whipple alternates appeals to destroy the Jewish international bankers and the Bolshevik labor unions with shouts of "Remember the Alamo! Remember the Maine!" and "Back to the principles of Andy Jackson and Abe Lincoln!"

In his final tribute to the martyred Lemuel Pitkin at the end of the book, as his storm troops parade down Fifth Avenue, Whipple makes it clear that the true enemy from which his National Revolutionary party has delivered the country is "sophistication." Lem's life represented the expectations of American innocence, frustrated by "sophisticated aliens," and the revolution has been made by those who share Lem's expectations. As such it is the revolt of the frustrated and tormented lower middle class, a fantasy foreshadowing of the riot at the end of *The Day of the Locust*. To become the Horst Wessel of American fascism, in West's ugliest joke, Lem has stepped out of a Norman Rockwell cover for the *Saturday Evening Post*.

What makes this cautionary tale convincing in *A Cool Million* is West's sense of the pervasiveness of American violence. It is like the savagery of Russian life in Leskov or Gorki. We see Betty Prail at twelve, the night her family's house burns down and her parents are killed in the fire. When the firemen finally arrive, drunk, they do nothing to put out the fire. Instead they loot the house while the chief rapes Betty, leaving her naked and unconscious on the ground. She is then sent to an orphan asylum, and put out at fourteen to be a maid in the household of Deacon Slemp, where in addition to her other duties she is enthusiastically beaten twice a week on the bare behind by the Deacon, who gives her a quarter after each beating.

In this world where firemen are looters and rapists and church elders perverts and hypocrites, policemen appear only to beat up the victims of crimes. When Lem is first seized by the police, on his way to the big city to make his fortune, a patrolman clubs him on the head, one detective kicks him in the stomach, and a second kicks him behind the ear; all three actions unrelated to any of the remarks they make to Lem, but rather, natural reflexes. When Lem faints from the wound he received from stopping the runaway horse, he is found by a policeman, who establishes communication by kicking him in the groin. The brutal image of the police in the book is always the raised truncheon, the doubled fist, the foot drawn back.

The weaknesses of the book are perhaps the inevitable weaknesses of the form, jokes that do not come off and failures of tone. Sometimes the book is almost unbelievably corny and heavy-handed. When he is in this mood, West will even have someone address a Chinese in pidgin and be answered in flawless English.

The uncertainty of tone is mainly in regard to sex. When West is openly vulgar, he is fine, but on occasion he seems to smirk, and then he is less fine. A scene between Lem, captured by Wu Fong's men, dressed in a tight-fitting sailor suit, and set up as a homosexual prostitute in the brothel, and his client, a lisping Indian maharajah, is perhaps the most extreme failure. The first rape of Betty by the drunken fire chief is disturbing and effective, but her thousandth rape is boring and meaningless, as comedy, social comment, or even titillation. Betty is almost invariably unconscious when raped, an oddly necrophiliac touch, and sometimes the details lead us to expect a salacious illustration on the next page.

West's last book, *The Day of the Locust* (1939), is a novel about a young painter named Tod Hackett, working at a Hollywood movie studio as a set and costume designer, and some people he encounters. These are principally Faye Greener, a beautiful young girl whom he loves; her father Harry, an old vaudeville comic; Earle Shoop, Faye's cowboy beau; Miguel, Earle's Mexican friend who breeds fighting cocks; Abe Kusich, a dwarf racetrack tout; and Homer Simpson, an innocent from the Midwest also in love with Faye. In the course of the novel Harry dies, and Faye and her friends go to live with Homer. The action is climaxed by a wild party at Homer's, after which Faye and Miguel end up in bed. This results, the next day, in Homer's demented murder of a boy, which in turn precipitates a riot in the streets, on which the book ends. The title comes from the plague of locusts visited on Pharaoh in the Book of Exodus.

Like the characters in *Miss Lonelyhearts*, the characters in *The Day of the Locust* tend to be symbolic abstractions, but here with some loss of human reality. Tod, who never quite comes to life (mainly, I think, because of West's efforts to keep him from being autobiographical), represents The Painter's Eye. All through the book he is planning a great canvas, "The Burning of Los Angeles," which will sum up the whole violent and demented civilization. It is to show the city burning at high noon, set on fire by a gay holiday crowd, who appear carrying baseball bats and torches: "No longer bored, they sang and danced joyously in the red light of the flames." In the foreground, Tod and his friends flee the mob in various characteristic postures: Faye naked and running rather proudly, throwing her knees high; Homer half-asleep; Tod stopping to throw a stone at the crowd. Meanwhile the flames lick avidly "at a corinthian column that held up the palmleaf roof of a nutburger stand."

Faye is nothing like the Fay of *Miss Lonelyhearts* (as the Betty of *A Cool Million* is nothing like the Betty of *Miss Lonelyhearts*—West was overeconomical of names). Faye is seventeen, "a tall girl with wide, straight shoulders and long, swordlike legs." She has "a moon face, wide at the cheek bones and narrow at chin and brow," her hair is platinum-blonde, her breasts are "placed wide apart and their thrust" is "upward and outward," her buttocks look "like a heart upside down." She dresses like a child of twelve, eats an apple with her little finger curled, and has a brain the size of a walnut.

Like Betty in *Miss Lonelyhearts*, Faye represents Nature, but now Nature's appearance of innocence is seen as deceptive, and Faye is as far as can be from Betty. Tod looks at an inviting photograph of her, lying "with her arms and legs spread, as though welcoming a lover," and thinks: "Her invitation wasn't to pleasure, but to struggle, hard and sharp, closer to murder than to love. If you threw yourself on her, it would be like throwing yourself from the parapet of a skyscraper. You would do it with a scream. You couldn't expect to rise again. Your teeth would be driven into your skull like nails into a pine board and your back would be broken. You wouldn't even have time to sweat or close your eyes." What then is Tod's conclusion? "If she would only let him, he would be glad to throw himself, no matter what the cost." Luckily, she never lets him.

All experience rolls off Faye. She smells to Tod like "buckwheat in flower"; when she leans toward him, drooping slightly, "he had seen young birches droop like that at midday when they are over-heavy with sun." When she announces her intention of becoming a call girl, Tod decides that "her beauty was structural like a tree's, not a quality of her mind or heart. Perhaps even whoring wouldn't damage it for that reason." A spell of whoring does not in fact damage it, and when Tod sees her later: "She looked just born, everything moist and fresh, volatile and perfumed." In her natural acceptance of the world of sexuality, she is, as Homer tells Tod proudly, "a fine, wholesome child."

This vision of Nature emphasizes its infuriating invulnerability, and Tod not only wants to smash himself on it, but in other moods, to smash Faye. He thinks: "If he only had the courage to throw himself on her. Nothing less violent than rape would do. The sensation he felt was like that he got when holding an egg in his hand. Not that she was fragile or even seemed fragile. It wasn't that. It was her completeness, her egglike self-sufficiency, that made him want to crush her." Seeing her again, Tod feels: "Her self-sufficiency made him squirm and the desire to break its smooth surface with a blow, or at least a sudden obscene gesture, became irresistible." When Faye disappears at the end of the book, Tod cannot decide whether she has gone off with Miguel or gone back to being a call girl. "But either way she would come out all right," he thinks. "Nothing could hurt her. She was like a cork. No matter how rough the sea got, she would go dancing over the same waves that sank iron ships and tore away piers of reinforced concrete." Tod then produces an elaborate fantasy of waiting in a parking lot to knock Faye unconscious and rape her, and he steps from that into the riot of the book's last scene.

The men around Faye are in their different fashions as mindless as she. Her father, Harry Greener, after forty years in vaudeville and burlesque, no longer has any personality apart from his clowning role. "It was his sole method of defense," West explains. "Most people, he had discovered, won't go out of their way to punish a clown." West invents a superb clown act for him, presented in the form of an old clipping from the Sunday *Times*, but the clowning we see in the book is a more poignant sort, his comic act peddling home-made silver polish.

Faye's cowboy, Earle Shoop, is an image of virile idiocy. "He had a two-dimensional face that a talented child might have drawn with a ruler and a compass. His chin was perfectly round and his eyes, which were wide apart, were also round. His thin mouth ran at right angles to his straight, perpendicular nose. His reddish tan complexion was the same color from hairline to throat, as though washed in by an expert, and it completed his resemblance to a mechanical drawing." His conversation consists of "Lo, thar," "Nope," and "I was only funning."

The Mexican, Miguel, is an image of pure sensuality: "He was toffee-colored with large Armenian eyes and pouting black lips. His head was a mass of tight, ordered curls." When Faye responds to him, "his skin glowed and the oil in his black curls sparkled." Early in the book we see him rhumba with Faye, until jealousy drives Earle to smash him over the head with a stick. Later he tangos with her, a tango that ends in bed. "Mexicans are very good with women," Tod decides, as the moral of the episode.

Homer is the most completely abstracted character in the book. As Mary Shrike in *Miss Lonelyhearts* is entirely reduced to Breasts, so Homer is entirely reduced to an image of Hands, enormous hands independent of his body. We see him waking in the morning: "Every part was awake but his hands. They still slept. He was not surprised. They demanded special attention, had always demanded it. When he had been a child, he used to stick pins into them and once had even thrust them into a fire. Now he used only cold water." We see him plunge his hands into the washbasin: "They lay quietly on the bottom like a pair of strange aquatic animals. When they were thoroughly chilled and began to crawl about, he lifted them out and hid them in a towel." In the bath: "He kept his enormous hands folded quietly on his belly. Although absolutely still, they seemed curbed rather than resting." When Homer cuts his hand opening a can, "The wounded hand writhed about on the kitchen table until it was carried to the sink by its mate and bathed tenderly in hot water."

When Faye cries at their first meeting, Homer makes "his big hands dance at the end of his arms," and "several times his hands moved forward to comfort her, but he succeeded in curbing them." As he and Faye sit and eat: "His hands began to bother him. He rubbed them against the edge of the table to relieve their itch, but it only stimulated them. When he clasped them behind his back, the strain became intolerable. They were hot and swollen. Using the dishes as an excuse, he held them under the cold water tap of the sink." When Faye leaves, Homer is too bashful to say anything affectionate, but: "His hands were braver. When Faye shook good-bye, they clutched and refused to let go." After she leaves, "His hands kept his thoughts busy. They trembled and jerked, as though troubled by dreams. To hold them still, he clasped them together. Their fingers twined like a tangle of thighs in miniature. He snatched them apart and sat on them."

This garish and remarkable image is built up throughout the book to embody all of Homer's repressed violence; the hands are strangler's hands, rapist's hands. For reasons impossible to imagine or justify, West let it all go to waste. When Homer's violence finally does break out, when Faye's leaving has driven him out of his mind, he kills a boy who has hit him in the face with a stone by stomping him to death, never touching him with his hands.

The most grotesque character in this gallery of grotesques is the dwarf, Abe Kusich. When Tod first meets him, he is wearing perfect dwarf headgear, a high green Tyrolean hat. Unfortunately, "the rest of his outfit didn't go well with the hat. Instead of shoes with long points and a leather apron, he wore a blue, double-breasted suit and a black shirt with a yellow tie. Instead of a crooked thorn stick, he carried a rolled copy of the *Daily Running Horse*." His tiny size is made pathetic in an image of his catching Tod's attention by tugging at the bottom of his jacket, but it is accompanied by an unbelievable pugnacity, verbal and physical. He is a small murderous animal like Homer's hands, and he too finally erupts into violence, responding to a kick in the stomach from Earle by squeezing Earle's testicles until he collapses.

West's earlier title for *The Day of the Locust* was *The Cheated*, and the latent violence of the cheated, the mob that fires Los Angeles in Tod's picture, and riots in the flesh at the end of the book, is its major theme. The cheated are recognizable by sight in Hollywood: "Their clothing was somber and badly cut, bought from mail-order houses." They stand on the streets staring at passers-by, and "when their stare was returned, their eyes filled with hatred." They are the people who have "come to California to die." At one point Tod wonders "if he weren't exaggerating the importance of the people who come to California to die. Maybe they weren't really desperate enough to set a single city on fire, let alone the whole country." His ultimate discovery is that they are.

Some of the cheated come to Harry's funeral, "hoping for a dramatic incident of some sort, hoping at least for one of the mourners to be led weeping hysterically from the chapel." As he stares at them, "it seemed to Tod that they stared back at him with an expression of vicious, acrid boredom that trembled on the edge of violence." In the book's last scene, the cheated line up by the thousands outside Kahn's Persian Palace Theatre for the première of a new picture. The mob terrifies Tod, and he now recognizes it as a demonic collective entity, unstoppable once aroused except by machine guns. In one of West's rare Marxist slantings, the mob includes no workingmen, but is entirely "made up of the lower middle classes." Tod concludes:

"It was a mistake to think them harmless curiosity seekers. They were savage and bitter, especially the middle-aged and the old, and had been made so by boredom and disappointment.

"All their lives they had slaved at some kind of dull, heavy labor, behind desks and counters, in the fields and at tedious machines of all sorts, saving their pennies and dreaming of the leisure that would be theirs when they had enough. Finally that day came. They could draw a weekly income of ten or fifteen dollars. Where else should they go but California, the land of sunshine and oranges?

"Once there, they discovered that sunshine isn't enough. They get tired of oranges, even of avocado pears and passion fruit. Nothing happens. They don't know what to do with their time. They haven't the mental equipment for leisure, the money nor the physical equipment for pleasure. Did they slave so long just to go on an occasional Iowa picnic? What else is there? They watch the waves come in at Venice. There wasn't any ocean where most of them came from, but after you've seen one wave you've seen them all. The same is true of the airplanes at Glendale. If only a plane would crash once in a while so that they could watch the passengers being consumed in a 'holocaust of flame,' as the newspapers put it. But the planes never crash.

"Their boredom becomes more and more terrible. They realize that they've been tricked and burn with resentment. Every day of their lives they read the newspapers and went to the movies. Both fed them on lynchings, murder, sex crimes, explosions, wrecks, love nests, fires, miracles, revolutions, wars. This daily diet made sophisticates of them. The sun is a joke. Oranges can't titillate their jaded palates. Nothing can ever be violent enough to make taut their slack minds and bodies. They have been cheated and betrayed. They have slaved and saved for nothing."

As the marching Leather Shirts were West's fantasy of American fascism, the vicious mob of the cheated lower middle class is his fantasy of American democracy, and it is overpowering and terrifying. The rest of Hollywood, the cheaters, have no more cultural identity than the "cheated," but their plight is comic or pathetic rather than menacing. They inhabit the Chamber of American Horrors, come to life. They live in "Mexican ranch houses, Samoan huts, Mediterranean villas, Egyptian and Japanese temples, Swiss chalets, Tudor cottages, and every possible combination of these styles." Tod sees "a miniature Rhine castle with tarpaper turrets pierced for archers. Next to it was a little highly colored shack with domes and minarets out of the *Arabian Nights*." The house Homer rents is Irish peasant style: "It had an enormous and very crooked stone chimney, little dormer windows with big hoods and a thatched roof that came down very low on both sides of the front door. This door was of gumwood painted like fumed oak and it hung on enormous hinges. Although made by machine, the hinges had been carefully stamped to appear hand-forged. The same kind of care and skill had been used to make the roof thatching, which was not really straw but heavy fireproof paper colored and ribbed to look like straw." The living room is "Spanish," with red and gold silk armorial banners and a plaster galleon; the bedrooms "New England," with spool beds made of iron grained like wood.

The people are as spurious as the houses and things. An old Hollywood Indian called Chief Kiss-My-Towkus speaks a language of "Vas you dere, Sharley?" Human communication is impossible anywhere in Hollywood. At a party of movie people, the men go off to talk shop and at least one woman assumes that they are telling dirty jokes. Harry and Faye are unable to quarrel in words, but have bitter wordless battles in which he laughs insanely, she sings and dances. Even Faye's sensual gesture of wetting her lips with her tongue as she smiles is meaningless. At first Tod takes it to be an invitation, and dreams: "Her lips must taste of blood and salt." Eventually he discovers the truth: "It was one of her most characteristic gestures and very effective. It seemed to promise all sorts of undefined intimacies, yet it was really as simple and automatic as the word thanks. She used it to reward anyone for anything, no matter how unimportant."

One of the clues West gives to his conception of the nature and destiny of his characters is subtly dropped in a comic scene. Tod and Homer meet a neighbor of Homer's, Maybelle Loomis, and her eight-year-old son, Adore, whom she has trained as a performer. He is dressed as an adult, his eyebrows are plucked, and he sings a salacious song with a mechanical counterfeit of sexuality: "When he came to the final chorus, his buttocks writhed and his voice carried a top-heavy load of sexual pain." In a more personal display, Adore makes horrible faces at Homer, and Mrs. Loomis apologizes: "He thinks he's the Frankenstein monster." Adore is the Frankenstein monster, and it is he who is killed by Homer in the book's last scene. But Homer too is the Frankenstein monster, getting out of bed "in sections, like a poorly made automaton," and his hands are progeny monsters. Earle is a lesser monster, a wound-up cowboy toy, and Miguel is a phallic Jack-in-the-box. More than any of them, Faye is a Frankenstein monster, a mechanical woman self-created from bits of vanished film heroines, and her invulnerability is the invulnerability of the already dead. Here is the novel's deepest indictment of the American civilization it symbolizes in Hollywood: if the rubes are cheated by the image of an artificially colored orange, Tod is more deeply cheated by a zombie love; our dreams are fantasies of death.

In his article, "Some Notes on Violence," published in *Contact* in 1932, West writes: "What is melodramatic in European writing is not necessarily so in American writing. For a European writer to make violence real, he has to do a great deal of careful psychology and sociology. He often needs three hundred pages to motivate one little murder. But not so the American writer. His audience has been prepared and is neither surprised nor shocked if he omits artistic excuses for familiar events." The action of *The Day of the Locust* is the releasing of springs of violence that have been wound too tight: Abe's sexual maiming of Earle, Miguel smashing Abe against the wall in retaliation, Homer's brutal murder of Adore, the riot of the cheated. All of these are directly or indirectly inspired by Faye: Earle and Abe and Miguel are competing for Faye, Faye has made Homer insane, Homer's act triggers the mob's insanity.

The party scene consists of a progressive stripping of Faye. She receives her five male guests wearing a pair of green silk lounging pajamas with the top three buttons open. By the time she dances with Miguel all the buttons are open. In the succeeding fight her pajamas are badly torn, and she takes off the trousers, revealing tight black lace drawers. When Homer finds her in bed with Miguel, she is naked. It beautifully represents a metaphoric stripping of Faye in the course of the book. Darwin writes that we observe the face of Nature "bright with gladness," and forget the war to the death behind its innocent appearance. Faye is that bright glad face of Nature, and the stripping gradually reveals the violence and death her beauty conceals. The novel is a great unmasking of a death's head.

West's literary techniques in *The Day of the Locust* develop organically out of his themes. The imagery for Hollywood is wild and surrealist. Tod's friend Claude Estee, a successful screen writer, has a lifesize rubber dead horse, bloated and putrefying, in his swimming pool. The supermarket plays colored spotlights on the food: "The oranges were bathed in red, the lemons in yellow, the fish in pale green, the steaks in rose and the eggs in ivory." As Tod walks through the movie lot looking for Faye, it becomes the nightmare of history: stepping through the swinging door of a Western saloon, he finds himself in a Paris street; crossing a bridge marked "To Kamp Komfit," he finds himself in a Greek temple; he walks on, "skirting the skeleton of a Zeppelin, a bamboo stockade, an adobe fort, the wooden horse of Troy, a flight of baroque palace stairs that started in a bed of weeds and ended against the branches of an oak, part of the Fourteenth Street elevated station, a Dutch windmill, the bones of a dinosaur, the upper half of the Merrimac, a corner of a Mayan temple." "A dream dump," he concludes. "A Sargasso of the imagination!"

"Having known something of the Hollywood West saw at the time he was seeing it," Allan Seager has written, "I am of the opinion that *Locust* was not fantasy imagined but fantasy seen." Although West probably invented the specific details of the dead horse and the pale green supermarket fish, the fireproof paper thatch and his old favorite the Trojan Horse, there is a sense in which Seager's remark is true: these things are no more garish than what West actually did see in Hollywood. West's technique in the book is often, as Seager suggests, what the artists call *objets trouvés*: he finds in reality the symbol he needs, rather than creating it. When *The Day of the Locust* appeared, I recall thinking how masterfully West had invented the bloody sex-drenched details of the cockfight that leads up to the book's final party. Having since been to cockfights, I now know that every symbolic detail was realistically observed, and the object of my admiration in connection with the scene is no longer West's brilliance of invention but his brilliance of selection.

The humor of the book arises out of its themes, the incongruities of Hollywood and its lack of a cultural identity. Standing on the porch of his plantation mansion, Claude Estee cries, "Here, you black rascal! A mint julep," and a Chinese servant promptly brings a Scotch and soda. What do the Gingos, an Eskimo family brought to Hollywood to make retakes of an Arctic film, eat? Naturally, smoked salmon, white fish, and marinated herring, bought at Jewish delicatessens. The spoken language in the book is a tribute to the delicacy of West's ear. It includes Harry Greener's vaudeville jargon: "Joe was laying up with a whisker in the old Fifth Avenue when the stove exploded. It was the broad's husband who blew the whistle." Along with it there is the very different belligerent idiom of Abe Kusich, shouting "No quiff can give Abe Kusich the fingeroo and get away with it," calling Earle a "pee-hole bandit," or boasting after he has incapacitated him, "I fixed that buckeroo." At the same time there is the witty and epigrammatic conversation of Claude and Tod. Typically, Claude describes Mrs. Jenning's brothel as "a triumph of industrial design," Tod answers that he nevertheless finds it depressing, "like all places for deposit, banks, mail boxes, tombs, vending machines," and Claude then improvises on that set theme. Claude is clearly West's ideal vision of himself: "He was master of an involved comic rhetoric that permitted him to express his moral indignation and still keep his reputation for worldliness and wit."

Some of the images in the book are as powerful as any in *Miss Lonelyhearts*. One is bird blood. We see it first as Earle plucks some quail: "Their feathers fell to the ground, point first, weighed down by the tiny drop of blood that trembled on the tips of their quills." It reappears magnified and horrible as the losing cock's beak breaks: "A large bubble of blood rose where the beak had been." Another powerful image is of Homer crying, at first making a sound "like that of a dog lapping gruel," then in his madness sobbing "like an ax chopping pine, a heavy, hollow, chunking noise." A third image is the scene of male communion between Tod and Homer, resembling that between Miss Lonelyhearts and Doyle, and like it a prelude to violence. Tod and Homer leave the party to sit out on the curb, and Homer sits inarticulate, with a "sweet grin on his face," then takes Tod's hand and makes "trembling signals of affection."

The book's most vivid sustained image, perhaps more powerful than anything in *Miss Lonelyhearts*, is the riot, which is nightmarishly sexual as well as threatening. Swept along by the mob, Tod is thrown against a young girl whose clothes have been half torn off. With her thigh between his legs, she clings to him, and he discovers that she is being attacked from behind by an old man who has a hand inside her dress and is biting her neck. When Tod frees her from the old man, she is seized by another man, as Tod is swept impotently by. In another part of the crowd, they are talking with delight of a pervert who ripped up a girl with a pair of scissors, as they hug and pinch one another. Tod finally kicks off a woman trying to hang on to him, and escapes with no more than his leg broken, and a vision of the mob for his painting as "a great united front of screwballs and screwboxes."

Despite this and other very powerful scenes, I think that *The Day of the Locust* ultimately fails as a novel. Shifting from Tod to Homer and back to Tod, it has no dramatic unity, and in comparison with *Miss Lonelyhearts*, it has no moral core. Where Miss Lonelyhearts' inability to stay in Betty's Eden is heartbreaking, Tod's disillusion with Faye is only sobering, and where the end of the former is tragic, the end of this, Tod in the police car screaming along with the siren, is merely hysteric.

There is humor but little joy in West's novels, obsessive sexuality but few consummations (except for that sit-up-and-lie-down doll Betty Prail). The world West shows us is for the most part repulsive and terrifying. It is his genius to have found objective correlatives for our sickness and fears: our maimed and ambivalent sexuality, our terror of the idiot mass, our helpless empathy with suffering, our love perverted into sadism and masochism. West did this in convincing present-day forms of the great myths: the Quest, the Scapegoat, the Holy Fool, the Dance of Death. His strength lay in his vulgarity and bad taste, his pessimism, his nastiness. West could never have been the affirmative political writer he sometimes imagined, or written the novels that he told his publisher, just before his death, he had planned: "simple, warm and kindly books." We must assume that if West had lived, he would have continued to write the sort of novels he had written before, perhaps even finer ones.

In his short tormented life, West achieved one authentically great novel, *Miss Lonelyhearts*, and three others less successful as wholes but full of brilliant and wonderful things. He was a true pioneer and culture hero, making it possible for the younger symbolists and fantasists who came after him, and who include our best writers, to do with relative ease what he did in defiance of the temper of his time, for so little reward, in isolation and in pain.

# W. H. AUDEN

# Interlude: West's Disease

Nathanael West is not, strictly speaking, a novelist; that is to say, he does not attempt an accurate description either of the social scene or of the subjective life of the mind. For his first book, he adopted the dream convention, but neither the incidents nor the language are credible as a transcription of a real dream. For his other three, he adopted the convention of a social narrative; his characters need real food, drink and money, and live in recognizable places like New York or Hollywood, but, taken as feigned history, they are absurd. Newspapers do, certainly, have Miss Lonelyhearts columns; but in real life these are written by sensible, not very sensitive, people who conscientiously give the best advice they can, but do not take the woes of their correspondents home with them from the office, people, in fact, like Betty of whom Mr. West's hero says scornfully:

> Her world was not the world and could never include the readers of his column. Her sureness was based on the power to limit experience arbitrarily. Moreover, his confusion was significant, while her order was not.

On Mr. West's paper, the column is entrusted to a man the walls of whose room

> were bare except for an ivory Christ that hung opposite the foot of the bed. He had removed the figure from the cross to which it had been fastened and had nailed it to the walls with large spikes. . . . As a boy in his father's church, he had discovered that something stirred in him when he shouted the name of Christ, something secret and enormously

powerful. He had played with this thing, but had never allowed it to come alive. He knew now what this thing was—hysteria, a snake whose scales were tiny mirrors in which the dead world takes on a semblance of life, and how dead the world is . . . a world of doorknobs.

It is impossible to believe that such a character would ever apply for a Miss Lonelyhearts job (in the hope, apparently, of using it as a stepping-stone to a gossip column), or that, if by freak chance he did, any editor would hire him.

Again, the occupational vice of the editors one meets is an overestimation of the social and moral value of what a newspaper does. Mr. West's editor, Shrike, is a Mephisto who spends all his time exposing to his employees the meaninglessness of journalism:

> Miss Lonelyhearts, my friend, I advise you to give your readers stones. When they ask for bread don't give them crackers as does the Church, and don't, like the State, tell them to eat cake. Explain that man cannot live by bread alone and give them stones. Teach them to pray each morning: 'Give us this day our daily stone.'

Such a man, surely, would not be a Feature Editor long.

A writer may concern himself with a very limited area of life and still convince us that he is describing the real world, but one becomes suspicious when, as in West's case, whatever world he claims to be describing, the dream life of a highbrow, lowbrow existence in Hollywood, or the American political scene, all these worlds share the same peculiar traits—no married couples have children, no child has more than one parent, a high percentage of the inhabitants are cripples, and the only kind of personal relation is the sadomasochistic.

There is, too, a curious resemblance among the endings of his four books.

> His body broke free of the bard. It took on a life of its own; a life that knew nothing of the poet Balso. Only to death can this release be likened—the mechanics of decay. After death the body takes command; it performs the manual of disintegration with a marvelous certainty. So now, his body performed the evolutions of love with a like sureness. In this activity, Home and Duty, Love and Art were forgotten. . . . His body screamed and shouted as it marched and uncoiled; then with one heaving shout of triumph, it fell back quiet.

> He was running to succor them with love. The cripple turned to escape, but he was too slow and Miss Lonelyhearts caught him. . . . The gun inside the package exploded and Miss Lonelyhearts fell, dragging the cripple with him. They both rolled part of the way down the stairs.

'I am a clown,' he began, 'but there are times when even clowns must grow serious. This is such a time. I . . .' Lem got no further. A shot rang out and he fell dead, drilled through the heart by an assassin's bullet.

He was carried through the exit to the back street and lifted into a police car. The siren began to scream and at first he thought he was making the noise himself. He felt his lips with his hands. They were clamped tight. He knew then it was the siren. For some reason this made him laugh and he began to imitate the siren as loud as he could.

An orgasm, two sudden deaths by violence, a surrender to madness, are presented by West as different means for securing the same and desirable end, escape from the conscious Ego and its make-believe. Consciousness, it would seem, does not mean freedom to choose, but freedom to play a fantastic role, an unreality from which a man can only be delivered by some physical or mental explosion outside his voluntary control.

There are many admirable and extremely funny satirical passages in his books, but West is not a satirist. Satire presupposes conscience and reason as the judges between the true and the false, the moral and the immoral, to which it appeals, but for West these faculties are themselves the creators of unreality.

His books should, I think, be classified as Cautionary Tales, parables about a Kingdom of Hell whose ruler is not so much the Father of Lies as the Father of Wishes. Shakespeare gives a glimpse of this hell in *Hamlet*, and Dostoievsky has a lengthy description in *Notes from the Underground*, but they were interested in many hells and heavens. Compared with them, West has the advantages and disadvantages of the specialist who knows everything about one disease and nothing about any other. He was a sophisticated and highly skilled literary craftsman, but what gives all his books such a powerful and disturbing fascination, even *A Cool Million*, which must, I think, be judged a failure, owes nothing to calculation. West's descriptions of Inferno have the authenticity of first-hand experience: he has certainly been there, and the reader has the uncomfortable feeling that his was not a short visit.

All his main characters suffer from the same spiritual disease which, in honor of the man who devoted his life to studying it, we may call West's Disease. This is a disease of consciousness which renders it incapable of converting wishes into desires. A lie is false; what it asserts is not the case. A wish is fantastic; it knows what is the case but refuses to accept it. All wishes, whatever their apparent content, have the same and unvarying meaning: "I refuse to be what I am." A wish, therefore, is either innocent and frivolous, a kind of play, or a serious expression of guilt and despair, a hatred of oneself and every being one holds responsible for oneself.

Our subconscious life is a world ruled by wish but, since it is not a world of action, this is harmless; even nightmare is playful, but it is the task of consciousness to translate wish into desire. If, for whatever reason, self-hatred or self-pity, it fails to do this, it dooms a human being to a peculiar and horrid fate. To begin with, he cannot desire anything, for the present state of the self is the ground of every desire, and that is precisely what the wisher rejects. Nor can he believe anything, for a wish is not a belief; whatever he wishes he cannot help knowing that he could have wished something else. At first he may be content with switching from one wish to another:

> She would get some music on the radio, then lie down on her bed and shut her eyes. She had a large assortment of stories to choose from. After getting herself in the right mood, she would go over them in her mind as though they were a pack of cards, discarding one after another until she found one that suited. On some days she would run through the whole pack without making a choice. When that happened, she would either go down to Fine Street for an ice-cream soda or, if she were broke, thumb over the pack again and force herself to choose.
>
> While she admitted that her method was too mechanical for the best results and that it was better to slip into a dream naturally, she said that any dream was better than none and beggars couldn't be choosers.

But in time, this ceases to amuse, and the wisher is left with the despair which is the cause of all of them:

> When not keeping house, he sat in the back yard, called the patio by the real estate agent, in a broken down deck chair. In one of the closets he had found a tattered book and he held it in his lap without looking at it. There was a much better view to be had in any direction other than the one he faced. By moving his chair in a quarter circle he could have seen a large part of the canyon twisting down to the city below. He never thought of making this shift. From where he sat, he saw the closed door of the garage and a patch of its shabby, tarpaper roof.

A sufferer from West's Disease is not selfish but absolutely self-centered. A selfish man is one who satisfies his desires at other people's expense; for this reason, he tries to see what others are really like and often sees them extremely accurately in order that he may make use of them. But, to the self-centered man, other people only exist as images of what he is or of what he is not, his feelings towards them are projections of the pity or the hatred he feels for himself and anything he does to them is really done to himself. Hence the inconsistent and unpredictable behavior of a sufferer from West's Disease: he may kiss your feet one moment and kick you in the jaw the next and, if you were to ask him why, he could not tell you.

In its final stages, the disease reduces itself to a craving for violent physical pain—this craving, unfortunately, can be projected onto others—for only violent pain can put an end to wishing *for* something and produce the real wish of necessity, the cry "Stop!"

All West's books contain cripples. A cripple is unfortunate and his misfortune is both singular and incurable. Hunchbacks, girls without noses, dwarfs, etc., are not sufficiently common in real life to appear as members of an unfortunate class, like the very poor. Each one makes the impression of a unique case. Further, the nature of the misfortune, a physical deformity, makes the victim repellent to the senses of the typical and normal, and there is nothing the cripple or others can do to change his condition. What attitude towards his own body can he have then but hatred? As used by West, the cripple is, I believe, a symbolic projection of the state of wishful self-despair, the state of those who will not accept themselves in order to change themselves into what they would or should become, and justify their refusal by thinking that being what they are is uniquely horrible and uncurable. To look at, Faye Greener is a pretty but not remarkable girl; in the eyes of Faye Greener, she is an exceptionally hideous spirit.

In saying that cripples have this significance in West's writing, I do not mean to say that he was necessarily aware of it. Indeed, I am inclined to think he was not. I suspect that, consciously, he thought pity and compassion were the same thing, but what the behavior of his "tender" characters shows is that all pity is self-pity and that he who pities others is incapable of compassion. Ruthlessly as he exposes his dreamers, he seems to believe that the only alternative to despair is to become a crook. Wishes may be unreal, but at least they are not, like all desires, wicked:

> His friends would go on telling such stories until they were too drunk to talk. They were aware of their childishness, but did not know how else to revenge themselves. At college, and perhaps for a year afterwards, they had believed in Beauty and in personal expression as an absolute end. When they lost this belief, they lost everything. Money and fame meant nothing to them. They were not worldly men.

The use of the word *worldly* is significant. West comes very near to accepting the doctrine of the Marquis de Sade—there are many resemblances between A Cool Million and Justine—to believing, that is, that the creation is essentially evil and that goodness is contrary to its laws, but his moral sense revolted against Sade's logical conclusion that it was therefore a man's duty to be as evil as possible. All West's "worldly" characters are bad men, most of them grotesquely bad, but here again his artistic instinct seems at times to contradict his conscious intentions. I do not think, for example, that he meant to make Wu Fong, the brothel-keeper, more sympathetic and worthy of respect than, say, Miss Lonelyhearts or Homer Simpson, but that is what he does:

> Wu Fong was a very shrewd man and a student of fashion. He saw that the trend was in the direction of home industry and home talent and when the Hearst papers began their "Buy American" campaign, he decided to get rid of all the foreigners in his employ and turn his establishment into a hundred percentum American place. He engaged Mr. Asa Goldstein to redecorate the house and that worthy designed a Pennsylvania Dutch, Old South, Log Cabin Pioneer, Victorian New York, Western Cattle Days, Californian Monterey, Indian and Modern Girl series of interiors. . . .
>
> He was as painstaking as a great artist and in order to be consistent as one he did away with the French cuisine and wines traditional to his business. Instead, he substituted an American kitchen and cellar. When a client visited Lena Haubengrauber, it was possible for him to eat roast groundhog and drink Sam Thompson rye. While with Alice Sweethorne, he was served sow belly with grits and bourbon. In Mary Judkins' rooms he received, if he so desired, fried squirrel and corn liquor. In the suite occupied by Patricia Van Riis, lobster and champagne wine were the rule. The patrons of Powder River Rose usually ordered mountain oysters and washed them down with forty-rod. And so on down the list. . . .

After so many self-centered despairers who cry in their baths or bare their souls in barrooms, a selfish man like this, who takes pride in doing something really well, even if it is running a brothel, seems almost a good man.

There have, no doubt, always been cases of West's Disease, but the chances of infection in a democratic and mechanized society like our own are much greater than in the more static and poorer societies of earlier times.

When, for most people, their work, their company, even their marriages, were determined, not by personal choice or ability, but by the class into which they were born, the individual was less tempted to develop a personal grudge against Fate; his fate was not his own but that of everyone around him.

But the greater the equality of opportunity in a society becomes, the more obvious becomes the inequality of the talent and character among individuals, and the more bitter and personal it must be to fail, particularly for those who have some talent but not enough to win them second or third place.

In societies with fewer opportunities for amusement, it was also easier to tell a mere wish from a real desire. If, in order to hear some music, a man has to wait for six months and then walk twenty miles, it is easy to tell whether the words, "I should like to hear some music," mean what they appear to mean, or merely, "At this moment I should like to forget myself." When all he has to do is press a switch, it is more difficult. He may easily come to believe that wishes can come true. This is the first symptom of West's Disease; the later symptoms are less pleasant, but nobody who has read Nathanael West can say that he wasn't warned.

ALVIN B. KERNAN

# The Mob Tendency:
# "The Day of the Locust"

The central character of Nathanael
West's *The Day of the Locust* (In *The Complete Works of Nathanael West*,
New York, 1957, pp. 257–421), is a young painter, Tod Hackett, who has
been brought to Hollywood to design costumes for one of the studios, and
his problems as a painter of Hollywood parallel exactly the problems of
West and other writers as satirists, who are driven to more and more
bizarre styles to catch the disordering tendencies of dullness. When Tod
leaves the Yale School of Fine Arts, his masters are the realists Winslow
Homer and Thomas Ryder; he paints such solid, orderly, familiar subjects
as "a fat red barn, old stone wall or sturdy Nantucket fisherman." But
once in Hollywood he abandons realism and turns, "despite his race,
training and heritage" to the caricaturists Goya and Daumier in search of
an adequate style to portray the fantastic world of the Golden West. As he
sees more of Hollywood, the fantastic turns to the nightmarish, and Tod
begins

> to think not only of Goya and Daumier but also of certain Italian artists
> of the seventeenth and eighteenth centuries, of Salvator Rosa, Francesco
> Guardi and Monsu Desiderio, the painters of Decay and Mystery. Look-
> ing downhill now, he could see compositions that might have actually
> been arranged from the Calabrian work of Rosa. There were partially
> demolished buildings and broken monuments, half-hidden by great, tor-
> tured trees, whose exposed roots writhed dramatically in the arid ground,
> and by shrubs that carried, not flowers or berries, but armories of spikes,
> hooks and swords.

From *The Plot of Satire*. Copyright © 1965 by Yale University. Yale University Press.

For Guardi and Desiderio there were bridges which bridged nothing, sculpture in trees, palaces that seemed of marble until a whole stone
portico began to flap in the light breeze.

(Ch. 18)

After a tour of such churches as the "Tabernacle of the Third Coming"
where the "Crusade against Salt" is preached, Tod is forced to reject Goya
and Daumier altogether because they treat their subjects with too much
pity and without enough respect for their "awful anarchic power." Tod
turns at last to Alessandro Magnasco and thinks how well he "would
dramatize the contrast between . . . drained-out, feeble bodies and . . .
wild, disordered minds."

Tod's master painting, "The Burning of Los Angeles," is a huge
satiric canvas in which he uses the techniques of the painters of Decay
and Mystery and creates those grotesque images which Pope sees as
characteristic of the bathetic style:

Across the top, parallel with the frame, he had drawn the burning city,
a great bonfire of architectural styles, ranging from Egyptian to Cape
Cod colonial. Through the center, winding from left to right, was a long
hill street and down it, spilling into the middle foreground, came the
mob carrying baseball bats and torches. For the faces of its members, he
was using the innumerable sketches he had made of the people who
come to California to die; the cultists of all sorts, economic as well as
religious, the wave, airplane, funeral and preview watchers—all those
poor devils who can only be stirred by the promise of miracles and then
only to violence. A super "Dr. Know-All Pierce-All" had made the
necessary promise and they were marching behind his banner in a great
united front of screwballs and screwboxes to purify the land. No longer
bored, they sang and danced joyously in the red light of the flames.

In the lower foreground, men and women fled wildly before the
vanguard of the crusading mob. Among them were Faye, Harry, Homer,
Claude and himself. Faye ran proudly, throwing her knees high. Harry
stumbled along behind her, holding on to his beloved derby hat with
both hands. Homer seemed to be falling out of the canvas, his face
half-asleep, his big hands clawing the air in anguished pantomime.
Claude turned his head as he ran to thumb his nose at his pursuers. Tod
himself picked up a small stone to throw before continuing his flight. . . .
the tongues of fire . . . licked even more avidly at a corinthian column
that held up the palmleaf roof of a nutburger stand.

(Ch. 27)

Both Pope's advice to the Profund Poet and "The Burning of Los
Angeles" serve as expanded glosses on the root meaning of the word
"satire." The Latin root, the adjective *satura*, originally seems to have

meant "filled or charged with a variety of things"—a hodgepodge, a farrago. In the course of time this adjective came to be used to form a noun which designated the type of poetry written by Lucilius, Horace, Persius, and Juvenal. Its meaning was then gradually extended to cover any piece of writing "which contains a sharp kind of irony or ridicule or even denunciation." Though largely forgotten, the root meaning of "satire" remains functional, for the world of satire is always a fantastic jumble of men and objects. Whatever particular form dullness may take in a given satire, it moves always toward the creation of messes, discordancies, mobs, on all levels and in all areas of life. Pope in *Peri Bathous* shows vulgarity creating disorder in poetry and language, and in *The Dunciad* he shows Dulness manufacturing confusion in grammar, literature, thought, the theater, education, religion, politics, and the human personality. Dulness' genius for disorder assumes the visible shape of the routs, straggling processions, and ever-growing mobs which her sons form throughout the poem, until at last, in Book IV, they achieve the ultimate mythic shape of the mob, Chaos and Uncreation, the primal mess from which the Cosmos was once constructed by the Creating Word.

As a moralist Nathanael West would seem to be about as far from Pope as it is possible to get. The neoclassical values of tradition, culture, common sense, and Nature are so diminished for West that he could once write, wryly but accurately, that "there is nothing to root for in my work and what is even worse, no rooters." But the particular form of dullness which is the disintegrating force in *The Day of the Locust* still seeks out and expresses itself in those jumbles and mobs which it finds so "naturally" in *The Dunciad*, or which new wealth and lack of taste create in Petronius' *Satyricon*, or which pedantry, ignorance, and the burning desire for fame discover so regularly in that greatest image of confusion, Swift's *Tale of a Tub*. A poet like Pope will often dramatize the mob tendency of dullness in a single line, using, or purposely misusing, some rhetorical device such as zeugma or antithesis: "Or lose her heart, or necklace, at a ball"—"Puffs, Powders, Patches, Bibles, Billet-doux." In a novelist like West the crowding effect is not so obviously rhetorical or so concentrated; it is built up in blocks of semirealistic description of scenes, characters, and actions. But the effect is still to show dullness' disorganization of all the fundamental patterns of sense.

The dynamics of *The Day of the Locust* are focused in Tod's painting, "The Burning of Los Angeles." In the background is the mob which exerts a downward and outward pressure on the people below and on the picture as a whole. The mob is made up of "the people who come to California to die." These are the retired farmers from the midwest, the "senior citizens" tired of ice and snow, the housewives and clerks and small merchants dissatisfied with their dull, dreary lives in some small town, who come to California for sunshine, orange juice, and excitement. But these people are already sophisticates in violence.

> Every day of their lives they read the newspapers and went to the movies. Both fed them on lynchings, murder, sex crimes, explosions, wrecks, love nests, fires, miracles, revolutions, wars.
>
> (Ch. 27)

Only disappointment can follow, and they quickly discover that you can get enough orange juice and sunshine, that one wave in the ocean looks much like another, and that airplanes almost never crash and consume their passengers in a "holocaust of flame." As simpler entertainments fail, these people, dressed in their dark mail-order suits, begin to loiter on street corners staring with hard, bold gazes at the brighter passersby. Themselves empty of talent; lacking beauty, vitality, and intelligence; and completely without compassion, the people who come to California to die search more and more wildly for the life that is not in themselves. They attend funerals waiting for the collapse of a mourner or some other show of strong emotion, they follow movie stars hoping that their person-alities will magically be changed by proximity to beauty and dynamism, they take up fad diets which promise health and vigor if they avoid meat and cooked vegetables, they learn "Brain-Breathing, The Secret of the Aztecs" in a search for contact with mysterious powers which will bring them to life. But nothing works, for "Nothing can ever be violent enough to make taut their slack minds and bodies. They have been cheated and betrayed. They have slaved and saved for nothing." As this realization comes home to them, their expressions change to "vicious, acrid bore-dom" that trembles on the "edge of violence," and their fury at being cheated becomes "an awful, anarchic power" that can "destroy civilization."

Before the destroying mob in "The Burning of Los Angeles" runs a group of fugitives made up of the principal characters of the novel. These men and women are imperfect, but each has some one virtue which the mob lacks. Faye Greener is completely emptyheaded, but she has a breathtaking beauty, "structural like a tree's, not a quality of her mind or heart"; her father Harry Greener is a clever vaudeville actor, a master of the art of staying alive in a world fraught with dangers; Claude Estee is a writer and a talented wit; Tod Hackett a painter; and Homer Simpson a simple man capable of and needing love and kindness. But they are not complete people. It seems as if some god with a wry sense of humor had decided to give them only one virtue apiece while withholding the auxiliary virtues needed to make the gift meaningful.

The relationship of these people to the mob in the background is not simple. They are in one way, as the picture suggests, the victims of the mob, pursued and destroyed because they are different and talented. In another sense they are the purveyors of excitement to the mob, the representatives of all those people in the "entertainment industries" who make a living manufacturing the fake "amour and glamor" needed by the tired barber in Purdue who has spent his day cutting hair. But these people with their single talents, while contemptuous of the mob which follows them, "run before" in another sense, for they too are people who have come to California to die. They too seek vicarious pleasure or strange experiences to compensate for lives which, despite their gifts, are still inadequate. Because they have money or are cleverer and more attractive, their escapes into fantasy are more expensive and glossed over with a show of indifference and sophistication. But they are still escapes. Claude Estee puts a dead horse made of inflated rubber at the bottom of his swimming pool, and he and his friends visit a fancy bawdy house to see pornographic films with such titles as "Le Prédicament de Marie, ou La Bonne Distraite." He lives in an exact reproduction of an old southern mansion where he stands on the porch trying to look like a Civil War colonel and calling "Here, you black rascal! A mint julep," to a Chinese servant who comes up with a scotch and soda. Faye Greener's beauty is so overwhelming that she can be described only as a Botticelli Venus, "smiling a subtle half smile uncontaminated by thought . . . just born, everything moist and fresh, volatile and perfumed." Yet because her beauty is joined with no other virtue, she cannot find her life in the world and seeks it instead in daydreams built on Hollywood plots. In her dream world she becomes a rich-young-girl cruising on her father's yacht in the South Seas. Engaged to a Russian count, she falls in love with a young sailor, and they alone are saved in the inevitable shipwreck. They swim to a desert island where she is attacked by a huge snake while bathing, etc., etc.

The major portion of *The Day of the Locust* is made up of a panorama in which each of these talented people "dies" in some fashion. Harry Greener literally dies of a bad heart, exhausted and feeling cheated because he never became the great actor he thought he was. Homer Simpson's dreams of love sour into hate. He ends by killing a most unpleasant small boy and is in turn torn apart by an excitement-seeking mob. Claude and Faye survive physically, but their abilities, thwarted, lead only to sterility and emptiness. Tod Hackett ends as a wailing mad-man after being caught in the maelstrom of the mob.

This is West's image of Hollywood, but, as Richard Gehman says, "West used Hollywood as a microcosm . . . because . . . everything that is wrong with life in the United States is to be found there in rare purity, and because the unreality of the business of making pictures seemed a most proper setting for his 'half-world'." The same point is made in *The Day of the Locust* where the people who come to California to die are described as the "cream of America's madmen" which is skimmed from a milk "just as rich as violence." West is not condemning all of American life but isolating and exposing in grotesque forms a peculiar danger or brand of dullness within it. This is, specifically, the peculiar emptiness of many people and lives, and the search for compensation in vicarious excitement and glamor. This appetite is always fed and sharpened by sensational newspapers, lurid writing, impossibly romantic movies, enthu-siastic religions, health fads, and quackery of all kinds which trade on dullness, fear, and hatred. These substitutes for life, West shows, are necessarily illusions, and because they are such, they—like Jonson's al-chemy or the contemporary half-world created by television and Madison Avenue—cannot but fail in the end to satisfy the impossible desires they have fed and fanned. When the inevitable drop to reality comes and it is discovered that sunshine, orange juice, and waves are not really very exciting, the cheated fools will turn to mobs and destroy civilizations to revenge themselves and "get a little fun out of life."

West offers no specific cure for these empty lives. In fact, like many satirists, he deliberately leaves any positive, reforming element out of his work in order to intensify the shrillness of the siren announcing disaster.

> If I put into *The Day of the Locust* any of the sincere, honest people who work . . . [in Hollywood] and are making such a great, progressive fight, those chapters couldn't be written satirically and the whole fabric of the peculiar half-world which I attempted to create would be badly torn by them . . . I believe there is a place for the fellow who yells fire and indicates where some of the smoke is coming from without actually dragging the hose to the spot.

I doubt if West really had any cure, except the dynamite blast of satire, for the deep-seated ills which he isolates, but he did diagnose the disease and predict its course with remarkable accuracy. Because he believed in no traditional value systems, he could only denote the disease in pragmatic and symbolic terms. He could not say, for example, that men were wrong to try to escape from unsatisfactory lives because each man is created by

God as a part of a great plan; nor could he argue that every man has his allotted work in society which, properly done, will be richly rewarding and serve the best interests of the society and the individual. But he could show again and again that while the phony may momentarily satisfy some desire for the impossible, that it can only disappoint more painfully, and dangerously, in the end. Eggs bathed in a rich cream-colored light in the supermarket can only turn out to be plain eggs when you get them home, and romantic dreams of passion and adventure lived in the darkness of the Bijou can only make more unsatisfactory the ordinary lives which inevitably begin again at the sidewalk.

The particular horror of West's satiric world is that in their search for romance the people who have come to California to die, and those who pander to their appetites, create such a grotesquely phony and pitifully illusionary world. Whatever they put their hand to is unreal, and unreality begins to build on unreality—furniture "painted to look like unpainted pine," or movie indians cracking jokes in fake German accents, "Vas you dere Sharley?" As the fake encrusts itself on the fake, obeying no law except the need for the novel, the result can only be fantastic disorder, combinations of things unrelated, great jumbles, and the division of those things which properly belong together. The search for glamor creates the strange dress of the Angelenos:

> Their sweaters, knickers, slacks, blue flannel jackets with brass buttons were fancy dress. The fat lady in the yachting cap was going shopping, not boating; the man in the Norfolk jacket and Tyrolean hat was returning, not from a mountain, but an insurance office; and the girl in slacks and sneaks with a bandanna around her head had just left a switchboard, not a tennis court.
>
> (Ch. 1)

A dwarf in a high green Tyrolean hat, black shirt, and yellow tie may be an amusing, harmless kind of disorder, but the disintegration of architecture and a city into a dream world sounds a more serious note:

> Only dynamite would be of any use against the Mexican ranch houses, Samoan huts, Mediterranean villas, Egyptian and Japanese temples, Swiss chalets, Tudor cottages, and every possible combination of these styles that lined the slopes of the canyon.
>
> When he noticed that they were all of plaster, lath and paper, he was charitable and blamed their shape on the materials used. Steel, stone and brick curb a builder's fancy a little, forcing him to distribute his stresses and weights and to keep his corners plumb, but plaster and paper know no law, not even that of gravity.
>
> On the corner of La Huerta Road was a miniature Rhine castle

with tarpaper turrets pierced for archers. Next to it was a little highly colored shack with domes and minarets out of the *Arabian Nights.*

(Ch. 1)

The dreams that know no law, not even such impersonal laws as gravity and complementary colors, also ignore the simple laws of chronology and distance. The movies which feed this hunger for romance make cheap pretenses and a jumbled heap—"a Sargasso of the imagination" —out of the long history of human efforts to achieve a civilization. Tod Hackett wanders through the "dream dump" of a studio lot, moving from a giant *papier mâché* sphinx across a manmade desert to the front of the Last Chance Saloon, from where he can see a conical grass hut in a jungle compound, a charging Arab on a white stallion, a truck loaded with snow and sled dogs, a Paris street, a Romanesque courtyard, and a group of people in riding costume eating cardboard food on a fiber lawn in front of a cellophane waterfall. Crossing a bridge, he comes to a "Greek temple dedicated to Eros. The god himself lay face downward in a pile of old newspapers and bottles." Tod moves on through a

tangle of briars, old flats and iron junk, skirting the skeleton of a Zeppelin, a bamboo stockade, an adobe fort, the wooden horse of Troy, a flight of baroque palace stairs that started in a bed of weeds and ended against the branches of an oak, part of the Fourteenth Street elevated station, a Dutch windmill, the bones of a dinosaur, the upper half of the Merrimac, a corner of a Mayan temple, until he finally reached the road.

(Ch. 18)

After this we can only ask, "What road?"

Not only does the search for dreams mangle history, making it impossible to believe in it or see in it such simple patterns even as enduring human courage or ingenuity; it fragments and jumbles the human character as well. *The Day of the Locust* is populated with strange inhuman mixtures and the broken wholes of men. A small child brought to Hollywood to win fame and fortune combines a childish innocence with phony adult manners, learned from the movies, such as bowing low and clicking his heels together when introduced. He moves his small body in a suggestive manner while dancing and singing sexy songs, which he does not understand. Men yearn to be women and croon lullabies to imaginary babies they pretend are real, and then they pretend to be men again. An incredibly beautiful young woman speaks always in the most vulgar tones and voices the most trivial of clichés. A "dried-up little man with the rubbed features and stooped shoulders of a postal clerk" pretends that he is a southern colonel and at the same time dresses in ivory shirts, black ties, red-checked trousers, and enormous rust-colored shoes.

This division of human nature becomes most apparent in Homer Simpson, the quiet hotel clerk who has wandered to Hollywood looking for health and for the love of which he is capable but can never find. He is described as large and muscular yet not looking strong or fertile. "He was like one of Picasso's great sterile athletes, who brood hopelessly on pink sand, staring at veined marble waves." He sleeps whenever he can, seeking in unconsciousness the peace he cannot find in the world. The disintegration of self which he has suffered is clearest in the disjunctive, awkward movements of his body, and particularly in his hands, which have become separated from the rest of his being:

> He got out of bed in sections, like a poorly made automaton, and carried his hands into the bathroom. He turned on the cold water. When the basin was full, he plunged his hands in up to the wrists. They lay quietly on the bottom like a pair of strange aquatic animals. When they were thoroughly chilled and began to crawl about, he lifted them out and hid them in a towel.
>
> (Ch. 8)

Beaten by a world where he cannot find or take what he needs, he retreats in on himself and coils back into the position of Uterine Flight. Then, in the final scene of the book, this kindly but ineffective man, frenzied by finding nothing but hatred and violence in people where he hoped for love and gentleness, turns into a savage murderer who stamps to death the small boy who throws a stone at him. Homer's simple dream of love and peace is more acceptable than the dreams of most of the people who come to California to die, but West's point would seem to be that Homer's is still a dream which, because it is not realistic and is therefore hopeless, leads to the same fragmentation and violence that grows from the more grotesque dreams of fame, passion, and adventure. The retreat into sleep to find peace is finally as fatal a dream as the visit to the movies to find love.

In *The Day of the Locust*, as in most satires, there is no consistent story and, therefore, by the usual standards, no plot. The narration does come back frequently to the life of a few major characters, and we are most often led on our tour of Hollywood by Tod Hackett. But the total effect is of phantasmagoria now thrusting forward a vaudeville act filled with brawny acrobats tossing a helpless clown about; then a shift to the charge of an army of extras up a plaster Mont St. Jean at Waterloo for the glory of Grotenstein Productions. We stop to watch a lizard emerge from a tin can and trap flies, pass on to a funeral, a scene on Hollywood Boulevard, and move in to look at the furnishings of a house. We attend the showing of a blue film in which all the members of a household attempt to seduce the maid, who is attempting to seduce the young daughter, and then move on to the Church of Christ Physical "where holiness was attained through the constant use of chestweights and spring grips." As disjunct as these scenes may seem to be, each shows the dream seekers searching for satisfaction and achieving only the flimsiest illusion, which in turn creates what is at first an amusing and then a terrifying disorder. This recurring movement from dream through illusion to disorder is the basic action of the novel. As these madmen search more and more feverishly for what is missing in their lives they turn all they touch to a mob. Clothing, furniture, architecture, history, the human personality are jumbled into monstrous collages, and under the pressure of the need for excitement and dreams every relationship, every ritual occasion, every social meeting turns to bedlam, babel, riot. A funeral becomes a sideshow as an Eskimo family, the Four Gingos, grunts in time to a record of Bach's chorale, "Come Redeemer, Our Savior," and the sensation-seekers pour in from the street to look at the corpse. A church service turns to a scene in a madhouse as a man "from one of the colonies in the desert near Soboba Hot Springs where he had been conning over his soul on a diet of raw fruit and nuts" explodes in anger against the wicked world:

> The message he had brought to the city was one that an illiterate anchorite might have given decadent Rome. It was a crazy jumble of dietary rules, economics, and Biblical threats. He claimed to have seen the Tiger of Wrath stalking the walls of the citadel and the Jackal of Lust skulking in the shrubbery, and he connected these omens with "thirty dollars every Thursday" and meat eating.
>
> (Ch. 19)

The search for amusement creates cock-fights in which one bird cuts another to pieces and then eats its eyes. A typical "party" ends with a dwarf, frantic with lust for the cold Venus, Faye Greener, being kicked in the stomach when he tries to break in between two dancers.

> The dwarf struggled to his feet and stood with his head lowered like a tiny ram. . . . He charged between Earle's legs and dug upward with both hands. Earle screamed with pain . . . then groaned and started to sink to the floor, tearing Faye's silk pajamas on his way down.
>     Miguel grabbed . . . [the dwarf] by the throat. . . . Lifting the little man free, Miguel shifted his grip to his ankles and dashed him against the wall, like a man killing a rabbit against a tree. He swung the dwarf back to slam him again.
>
> (Ch. 23)

The pressure toward disorder evident in each of these scenes is embodied in the episodic form of the novel, and it takes its final form in the great mob scene with which the book ends. Here, as in the scene of chaos and uncreation with which *The Dunciad* closes, all forms of dullness are gathered together to express their ultimate nature and to achieve the final shapelessness toward which they have been constantly moving. The crowd begins to gather to see the moving-picture stars arrive at a premiere at Khan's Persian Palace—"Mr. Khan a Pleasure Dome Decreed." As the people who came to California to die come up to the crowd they look "diffident, almost furtive," but once they enter it all their inhibitions are released and they become arrogant and pugnacious. The inevitable panders are present to stir the mixture more violently and amuse the folks at home who couldn't make it this year. Colored lights flash madly about, and a radio announcer stands above the crowd asking, in a high, hysterical voice broadcast over a national network and amplified for the benefit of those present, "can the police hold them? Can they? It doesn't look so, folks." The mob grows every moment, shoving, bulging, pushing, breaking out of any lines authority attempts to impose on it. Within, it mills about, stumbling and swirling and releasing the most primitive powers, hatred, lust, dislike for anyone different, and the desire to break and kill to avenge a life of emptiness.

Only a spark is needed to touch the mob off and release its full destructive power, and this comes when Homer Simpson, who has wandered into the crowd in a state of shock resulting from the loss of his own dream, kills the small boy who is tormenting him. One form of riot releases another: the rumor sweeps through the crowd that a pervert has attacked a child, and it explodes, surging and churning over all barriers. Homer is torn apart, Tod's leg is broken, an old man attacks a young girl pinned helpless by other bodies, men and women are crushed and trampled down. Here is "The Burning of Los Angeles," the great Vortex of Dulness sucking all down into nothingness, the final expression of the mob tendency.

Broken by the mob's awesome power, the satirist Tod Hackett goes mad. Taken to a police car, he begins to imitate the siren as loudly as he can. In the end the only style which the satirist can turn to is the wail sounding all the fires, bombings, accidents, and violences of a world which has tried to cure emptiness with illusion.

---

[The Profound Poet should] consider himself as a *Grotesque* Painter, whose Works would be spoil'd by an Imitation of Nature, or Uniformity of Design. He is to mingle Bits of the most various, or discordant kinds, Landscape, History, Portraits, Animals, and connect them with a great deal of *Flourishing*, by *Heads* or *Tails*, as it shall please his Imagination, and contribute to his principal End, which is to glare by strong Oppositions of Colours, and surprize by Contrariety of Images. . . . His Design ought to be like a Labyrinth, out of which no body can get you clear but himself.

*(Peri Bathous*, Ch. V)

DANIEL AARON

# Late Thoughts on Nathanael West

The revival of interest in Nathanael West, now of some fifteen years' duration, continues to mount. In the reappraisal of the literary 'thirties, West has caught up with and overtaken most of the triple-decked Naturalists whose solemn and often infelicitous documentations no longer are devoured with relish. Over thirty years ago, West decided that

> Lyric novels can be written according to Poe's definition of a lyric poem. The short novel is a distinct form especially fitted for use in this country. . . . Forget the epic, the master work. In America fortunes do not accumulate, the soil does not grow, families have no history. Leave slow growth to the book reviewers, you have only time to explode. Remember William Carlos Williams' description of the pioneer women who shot their children against the wilderness like cannonballs. Do the same with your novels.

West wrote these words when, as Angel Flores observed about the same time, "the current vanguard taste" insisted "on directing literature towards the casehistory, gravymashpotato tradition," and only a few mavericks like F. Scott Fitzgerald (an admirer of *Miss Lonelyhearts*) shared West's dislike for the long-winded Scandinavian novel.

To see West, however, as a misunderstood and neglected "taker-outer" shouldered into obscurity by the more celebrated "putter-inners" is to exaggerate his singularity. Besides doing an injustice to a number of discerning critics who read his books with delight and appreciation such a view detaches him from a small but distinct group of literary kinsmen.

From *The Massachusetts Review* 6 (Winter–Spring 1965). Copyright © 1965 by *The Massachusetts Review*, Inc.

Being a radical in the 1930's (and West was a faithful subscriber to Party manifestoes) did not necessarily mean that one had to write ritualistic proletarian novels or Whitmanesque exhortations to revolt. There was another kind of writing, Edward Dahlberg called it "implication literature," tinged with "just as deep a radical dye." West belonged to that select company of socially committed writers in the Depression decade who drew revolutionary conclusions in highly idiosyncratic and undoctrinaire ways: in the eerie episodes of Dahlberg's *Bottom Dogs* and *From Flushing to Calvary*, in the nightmarish poems of Kenneth Fearing, and in the pointed buffoonery of S. J. Perelman. Like these writers, West supported the objectives of the Left while retaining the verbal exuberance, the unplayful irony, the nocturnal surrealist fancies associated with a certain school of expatriate writing in the 'twenties.

Had West (and the same might be said of Fearing), been merely an unaffiliated rebel, an inveterate non-joiner suspicious of causes and unburdened by any social philosophy, his satire and humor would hardly have been condoned by the Communists. The 1930's was not a good time for antinomians, as the career of the brilliant E. E. Cummings attests. Orthodox Party intellectuals detected no ideological heresies in the fiction of West or the poetry of Fearing, and they never attacked them as they did a number of other literary deviationists, but neither did they regard these masters of the grotesque and the macabre as the proper models for the proletarian literature of the future. Their dark vision of society, their twisted wry comedy, their recognition of an ineradicable evil denser and more durable than the capitalist blight, violated the spirit of Socialist Realism. It was all well and good to depict the hells of bourgeois capitalism, imperialism, and fascism, but in the last reel, the glow of the Heavenly City ought to be revealed.

Literary experimentation in Left circles came more and more to be identified with cultism and individual self-indulgence. The whole point of radical satire might be lost if the writer subordinated social purpose to literary effect. When James Agee, writing in *The New Masses* in 1937, asserted that Left artists and Surrealists were both revolutionaries and "that there are no valid reasons why they should be kept apart," he was told by a Communist critic that he stood on very dangerous ground:

> Certainly the proletarian movement has made use of much that was in the early part of the century regarded as experimental. But it is the strength of proletarian art that it can take to itself only that which it can use. Under the mandate of its approach to life and the necessity to communicate, it cannot lose itself in blind alleys. It has learned from experimental art when that experimentation actually devised effective

modes of expression or rediscovered what was fine and effective in the art of remoter times. But when experimentation lapsed into cultism, the health was gone out of it.

Just what has Gertrude Stein to offer? Is not her whole attempt to divorce language from meaning a cul-de-sac? And just how will a living art, based upon realities so pressing that even former Dadaists have been forced to face them, gain from the mumbo-jumbo of the latter day transitionists?

Revolution is not made in the hazy caverns of the subconscious, not by any mystic upsurge of the human spirit. This is not to deny that the dream life of man is real; but to contemplate dream states for their own sake and isolated from the rest of reality is a sickness which we cannot afford. . . .

All who rebel are by no means revolutionary in our sense of the word. If the proletarian movement took to its bosom all who call themselves revolutionary, there would be no disciplined movement either in politics or the arts—only confusion and betrayal.

Now West could not be accused of divorcing dreams from reality, but the literary and artistic streams that fed his bizarre imagination—the French school of the *fin de siècle*, Dostoievsky, squalid pulp fiction, the comic strip, the cinema—set him apart from the Proletarians who saw no revolutionary significance in myths and dreams. For this reason, despite such discerning readers as Josephine Herbst, Edmund Wilson, Fitzgerald, William Carlos Williams, Angel Flores and others, the Movement never took West to its bosom. In misconstruing his humor and failing to explore his baleful Wasteland, it committed both a political and an aesthetic blunder.

MISS LONELYHEARTS: "VARIETIES OF RELIGIOUS EXPERIENCE"

In "Some Notes on Miss L.," Nathanael West disclosed that his novel could be considered as a classical case history "of a priest of our time who has a religious experience." The portrait of Miss Lonelyhearts was "built on all the cases in James' *Varieties of Religious Experience* and Starbuck's *Psychology of Religion*. The psychology is theirs not mine. . . . Chapt. I—maladjustment. Chapt. III—the need for taking symbols literally is described through a dream in which a symbol is actually fleshed. Chapt. IV—deadness and disorder; see Lives of Bunyan and Tolstoy. Chapt. VI—self-torture by conscious sinning; see life of any saint. And so on."

It would be handy if West had left an annotated copy of his William James for his biographers, and yet anyone who reads *Miss Lonelyhearts* in the light of the *Varieties* will understand what West meant when he declared that if the novelist is no longer the psychologist, psychology has provided him with a vast quantity of case histories which "can be used in the way the ancient writers used their myths. Freud is your Bullfinch; you can learn from him." Undoubtedly Freud helps as an interpreter of Miss Lonelyhearts' subliminal self, but William James, as he acknowledged, supplied the structure of the novel. West, I think, drew most heavily from two chapters: "The Religion of Healthy-Mindedness" and "The Sick Soul," but his hero displays all of the classical symptoms of the conversion experience described throughout James' book.

According to James,

> There are people for whom evil means only a maladjustment with *things*, a wrong correspondence of one's life with the environment. Such evil as this is curable, on principle at least, upon the natural plane, for merely by modifying either the self or the things, or both at once, the two terms may be made to fit, and all go merry as a marriage bell again. But there are others for whom evil is no mere relation of the subject to particular outer things, but something more radical and general, a wrongness or vice in his essential nature, which no alteration of the environment, or any significant rearrangement of the inner self, can cure, and which requires a supernatural remedy.

James hazarded the generalization (which Santayana was to elaborate in his novel, *The Last Puritan*) that it was the "Germanic races" rather than the Latin who capitalized the S in sin and conceived of it as "something ineradicably ingrained in our natural subjectivity, and never to be removed by any superficial piecemeal operation."

Miss Lonelyhearts, it will be remembered, is the son of a Baptist minister, "the New England puritan" with a high forehead, long fleshless nose, and bony chin. He can find no consolation in the faith of the "healthy-minded" for whom evil is merely a disease and a preoccupation with evil an additional manifestation of the sickness. His "healthy-minded" sweetheart, Betty, attributes his "anhedonia" (dreariness, discouragement, dejection, disgust) to some physical ailment. "What's the matter?" she asks him. "Are you sick?" And Miss Lonelyhearts lashes back: "What a kind bitch you are. As soon as anyone acts viciously, you say he's sick. Wife torturers, rapers of small children, according to you they're all sick. No morality, only medicine. Well, I'm not sick. I don't need any of your damned aspirin. I've got a Christ complex, etc."

The conversion process is already under way. Before the unregenerate man can attain saintliness, he must go through the stages of "depression, morbid introspection, and sense of sin." Preparatory to the bliss of grace is "the pitch of unhappiness so great that all the goods of nature may be entirely forgotten," and when the sufferer happens to be a neurotic with a very low threshold of pain, his agony is almost unbearable. His anguish takes the forms of self-loathing, extreme exasperation, self-mistrust, self-despair. Miss Lonelyhearts' despair is patterned on the melancholia of Tolstoy overwhelmed by a heightened awareness of objective evil. And just as John Bunyan was sickened by the depths of his own iniquity, so Miss Lonelyhearts writhes in the presence of his own corruption and his inability to control it.

Miss Lonelyhearts' conversion during a bout of fever is quite similar to many of those recorded by William James, and although his brief interlude of ecstasy and his ridiculous death are presented almost farcically, there is no reason to conclude that West was denying the value of saintliness in his modern *Pilgrim's Progress*. The torments of the misfits and the grotesques in *Miss Lonelyhearts* may be exacerbated by sordid social conditions—it is, in a technical sense, a Depression novel—but is West really saying that the plight of Sick-of-it-all, Broken-hearted, Broad-shoulders, and Disillusioned-with-tubercular-husband could have been solved by the expropriation of the expropriators? To the healthy-minded Communist, West's lonely madman could only be judged as a dupe ministering to the duped. But the novel, as I read it, implicitly enforces rather the conclusion of William James than that of Karl Marx.

The healthy-minded, James remarks at the end of his chapter on "The Sick Soul," reject as "unmanly and diseased" the "children of wrath and cravers of a second birth." But James predicts that if the days of killing and torture ever return, "the healthy-minded would at present show themselves the less indulgent of the two." Healthy-mindedness, however adequate it is for certain cheery temperaments, fails "as a philosophical doctrine, because the evil facts which it refuses positively to account for are a genuine portion of reality, and they may after all be the best key to life's significance, and possibly the only openers of our eyes to the deepest levels of truth." *Miss Lonelyhearts* is a profane assertion of this idea.

## WEST AND POLITICAL SATIRE

The Horatio Alger hero in West's third novel, *A Cool Million* (1934), comes of age during the Great Depression, and after a slap-stick sequence of nasty and brutal misadventures (he loses his scalp, one eye, a leg, all of his teeth, and finally his life) he winds up as a Fascist martyr. Some of

West's admirers have detected Dostoievskian profundities in his "Tattered Tom" parody, but *A Cool Million* is the most dated and the most tiresome of his novels, a sour joke that the author cannot sustain. What redeems it (besides its flashes of lurid comedy) is West's initial conception; the ruthlessly innocent American Boy, one of Norman Rockwell's wholesome caricatures, who moves dreamily through a Hieronymus Bosch landscape, survives one outrage after another and dies still loyal to his benighted code. Here is a text on the perversion of healthy-mindedness in "the days of killing and torture."

A *Cool Million* made even less stir among the literary radicals than *Miss Lonelyhearts* did, and the reasons were not entirely aesthetic. Party intellectuals and their literary supporters tended to be as doctrinaire about the right and wrong uses of humor as they were about a good many other matters, and *A Cool Million*, through Marxist glasses, was as ideologically unfocused as its predecessor. To Kyle Crichton, "humorist" and columnist in the *New Masses* who wrote under the pen-name of Robert Forsythe, merely to have a sense of humor was not enough—especially when the working class was being slaughtered by Fascists, betrayed by Trotskyites, and deceived by the hirelings of Hearst and Morgan. Satire of the Perelman-Benchley-Donald Ogden Stewart variety, favored by the *New Yorker* magazine, merely diverted a segment of the society that was beyond redemption. "It is the old dada stuff," Forsythe complained, "the irrelevant incongruous type of humor; you start with one thing and end up with something utterly different and silly." The purpose behind his own humor, he went on to say, was to make the working classes "realize that they had nothing to fear from their so-called betters." To Perelman, whose *New Yorker* pieces (*Strictly from Hunger*, 1937) provoked these remarks, Forsythe concluded:

> if you really want to do something with that great talent in humor, learn at what point it is necessary to stick the stiletto in and twist it around! If there is a loud scream of anguish, you will know you've written some-thing. If it's hilarious to the people it helps, it's humor.

Forsythe's commentary makes it easier to understand why West's humor and satire were not highly esteemed in the *New Masses*. He knew how to twist the stiletto all right, but his writing also smacked of that "crazy" humor Forsythe disliked.

West had dedicated *A Cool Million* to his brother-in-law, a gesture both fraternal and literary, for Perelman, the author of "Dawn Ginsburg's Revenge" and creator of Ming Toy Epstein, was himself a master of the Victor "Tom Swift" Appleton style. Both possessed a talent for blending

the esoteric, the technical, and the commonplace into absurd and brilliant combinations, and neither was at his best (despite their left-wing
affiliations) when he was being studiedly political and dealing with what
the Party would call "real issues." In a zany mood, Perelman could paint a
dadaist portrait of the author of *Miss Lonelyhearts* that is a masterpiece of
nonsense. His pieces in the *New Masses*, however, lacked the spontaneity
and outrageousness of his best work, perhaps because the policies of the
magazine checked his usual extravagance. They point up the dilemma of
the humorist who is required to be funny about unfunny things, in this
case anti-semitism, xenophobia, and lynchings.

Mr. Kenneth Burke, who has at one time or another managed to
say something important about almost every literary problem, touched on
this matter in one of his reviews. In 1935 Burke was serving as a superior
if unappreciated aesthetician for the Marxists, and in a discussion of Kyle
Crichton's humor, he extracted some significant principles from Crichton's
topical and jejune commentaries.

Burke defined three kinds of humorist: the "comic exorcist," the
"universal satirist," and the "satiric propagandist." The first, and most
acceptable to the Establishment, divert society's attentions from the por-
tentous to the inconsequential by changing "the scale of things, turning
major terrors into minor annoyances." They are much sought after by
magazines like the *New Yorker*, he says, because "with the help of such
magazines, the Vague Shapes of Historical Calamity are whisked away, to
be displaced by odd discomforts, reassuring in their tininess." The "universal satirist" is unselectively critical, sees all mankind as foolish or
swinish or worse, and is engaged in a general and universal denigration.
Unlike the first two types, the "satiric propagandist" is not allowed to
swivel his guns in all directions. If the "comic exorcist" hates no one and
the "universal satirist" hates everyone, the "satiric propagandist" has "a
clear alignment of friends and foes" and exempts the former from his
wrath. He neither wishes to reduce grave problems to triviality nor to
magnify them to such a degree that no solution seems possible. Selecting
his targets according to a particular social platform, he sees capitalism as a
system that organizes "the anti-social, giving it efficiency, voice, and
authority, and consolidating it with the help of the educative, legislative,
and constabulary forces."

This very selectivity, as Burke realizes, presents a danger, because
the man engaged in "political excoriation," especially the self-righteous
moralist, hesitates to trust his wit and humor alone. He becomes in effect
an editorialist for a party and feels obliged to keep wig-wagging his
message to readers whose response is partly determined by their familiarity

with the ephemeral events and personalities he deals with. He dare not stray beyond the fences of their prejudices or play games with their gods, and his shuttling back and forth "between the serious and the mock serious" is both politically and aesthetically disquieting.

Into which of the Burkean categories does Nathanael West fall? Plainly he is an exorcist of a kind, for all comedy is cathartic; and clearly he tried to become on occasion a "satiric propagandist." A Cool Million is an anti-capitalist satire, its well-defined targets obvious in 1934 to any Communist, Fellow-traveler or even liberal. It is hardly an example, however, of the socially conscious fiction the Left-Wing was calling for, and it displays the Westian idiosyncrasies that kept him from becoming an acceptable political marksman for the Party: pessimism, an impatience with codes, and an inability to accommodate revolutionary parables to his gothic imagination.

At his most authentic, West is the "universal satirist." His humor is savage and sad, in contrast to Perelman's brash spoofing, and it springs, I think, from his tragi-comic view of the world, from his wry awareness of the disparity between secular facts and his suppressed religious ideals. His slapstick ends in a scream; the self-hatred of his characters, their efforts—sometimes grotesque and always painful—to find answers or relief, only curdles his pity. In A Cool Million, as in his other novels, the real culprit is not capitalism but humanity.

R. W. B. LEWIS

# Days of Wrath
# and Laughter: West

We might well begin with Faulkner's *The Hamlet* (1940), where the unmistakable figure of Satan unloosed is named Flem Snopes, where the victory of the Antichrist over the novel's world is virtually complete, and where laughter is indeed a major instrument for coping with the awfulness. But this antipastoral masterpiece has such a variety of fictional tones and narrative modes that an effective analysis of it would pull us off course. We will do better to begin with Nathanael West's *The Day of the Locust*, and its hardminded comic portrait of the imminent destruction of America by a holocaust of hate. The Satanic character in West's novel, the harnesser of all that hatred, goes in fact unnamed; but we know that he will be an even greater scoundrel, making even wilder promises, than the lesser demagogues we have seen throughout the book serving the bitter frustrations of the aging California citizenry. He will be a successor as well to West's earlier Antichrists, the editor Shrike in *Miss Lonelyhearts* (1933) and Shagpoke Whipple in *A Cool Million* (1934). The realm of the California super-promiser, however, seems larger than that of Shrike and Shagpoke; for if there is not, unarguably, an increase in West's imaginative power from *Miss Lonelyhearts* to *The Day of the Locust*, there is an observable increase in the range of the horror always comically explored.

The world of *Miss Lonelyhearts* is an airlessly tight little island—Manhattan Island, in fact, plus a short stretch of countryside; a world so narrowed, in a novella so compressed, that its rhythms and tensions

From *Trials of the Word*. Copyright © 1965 by R. W. B. Lewis. Yale University Press.

(which themselves are eschatological in nature and have to do with the last things) are well-nigh uncontainable. The novella moves unfalteringly between nightmare and actuality, its tone between horror and jesting; which is West's exemplary way of apprehending *our* world as under the dominion of a contemporary Antichrist. The human condition thus apprehended is characterized by a sort of absolute dis-order, by a dislocation observable pre-eminently in the relations of love, in almost every heterosexual and homosexual variety; but also a dislocation in man's other crucial relations—his relation to things, to words, to the rituals of life, to his own perennial aspirations. Human life, as depicted in *Miss Lonelyhearts*, has become a grotesque parody of itself; and the name of the book's Antichrist, Shrike, has the merit not only of meaning a toothbeaked bird of prey, but also of being as it were a parody of the name Christ, or Christ almost spelled backward. It is Shrike who rules over and preys upon an urban scene composed of the heartless, the violent, and the wretched. And it is Shrike who pits himself against the would-be imitator of Christ, the hapless columnist we know only by his pen name Miss Lonelyhearts, and whom Shrike torments in particular by spoken parodies of the Eucharist—that holy *communion* after which Miss Lonelyhearts so yearns. The central image of the novella, indeed, is a parody of the Gospel encounter between Christ and the Devil—in this case between a man, on the one hand, whose soul is sickened by a human misery he cannot assuage; and, on the other, the spokesman of ice-cold and yet witty and intellectually brilliant inhumanity. In speech after speech, Shrike tempts and taunts Miss Lonelyhearts with vistas of grandeur, channels of escape, resources of compensation; until he drives the columnist to attempting the final absurd miracle. In a ludicrously ill-timed and feverish effort to embrace and hence to redeem by love at least one individual human victim—a crippled homosexual named Pete Doyle—Miss Lonelyhearts is accidentally shot and killed; and in the abrasively ironic eschatology of this novella, the field is left to the further machinations of the Antichrist. But Shrike, consummate satirist though he be, is at the same time an object of satire—that is, of West's satire—and the field of his triumph is no more than a frozen chaos.

The enlargement of setting in *A Cool Million* is suggested by this: that Miss Lonelyhearts is shot (in an obscure rooming house) not even by a man but, as though in its supreme revolt, by a thing, by the freakish explosion of a gun wrapped in a newspaper; while Lemuel Pitkin, whose gradual "dismantling" is half of the theme of *A Cool Million*, is shot by a hired assassin, "Operative 6348XM," during a huge political rally staged in New York by the National Revolutionary Party. The satire in *A Cool*

*Million* is cruder and broader than in *Miss Lonelyhearts*; and West is not himself implicated in that which he satirizes, as he had been earlier. Still, while *A Cool Million* plays comical havoc with the Horatio Alger tradition and the American daydream of the easy surge upward to fame and fortune, it is also this country's most vigorous narrative vision of the political apocalypse—far more penetrating, for example, than the rather hastily contrived image which appeared the following year in Sinclair Lewis' *It Can't Happen Here*. The devil as the editor Shrike is succeeded in *A Cool Million* by the devil as national political Fuehrer: by Shagpoke Whipple, a more ambitious and amiable and even more completely fraudulent figure than his predecessor. The "mantling" of Shagpoke, former President and future dictator of the United States, is the other half of the book's theme; his loudmouthed and evidently interminable reign is just beginning as the story ends. On the national holiday commemorating young Lemuel's assassination, Whipple spells out his triumphant program to shouting thousands at a Fifth Avenue parade:

> The National Revolutionary Party [has] triumphed, and by that triumph this country was delivered from sophistication, Marxism and International Capitalism. Through the National Revolution its people were purged of alien diseases and America became again America.

This is a fine example of what Richard Hofstadter has defined as the paranoid style in American politics: a style historically based, as Mr. Hofstadter points out, on a most intensive apocalyptic outlook—a belief in some evil worldwide conspiracy, an identification of a wild conglomeration of elements as agencies of the Antichrist (communism, eastern capitalism, intellectual sophistication, and so on), a conviction of approaching disaster unless counteraction is swiftly taken. West's complex achievement in *A Cool Million* is to satirize this apocalyptic temper in such a way as to show that it is itself the source of the potential catastrophe. But Mr. Hofstadter was talking primarily not about the political debaucheries of the 1930s, the actual scene of *A Cool Million*, but about the presidential campaign of 1964; and it is because that phenomenon is still so close to us that one finds it harder to laugh at Shagpoke's speech or at Shagpoke than it used to be. Yet, even as we are once again astonished at the capacity of life to follow slavishly in the wake of art, and as our admiration for West's prophetic power deepens into downright awe, we also become aware that the perspective in *A Cool Million* is exactly right. For in West's perspective of rough-hewn satire, the squalid reality of American fascism—the absurdities that pervade its spurious nostalgia and its venomous racism, its radical ignorance and contradictory assortment of fears—gets utterly exposed. What passes among the brutalized citizenry as the New Jerusalem is revealed to be a catastrophic vulgarity. And the very real menace, even as it is uncovered and defined, is in part overcome (insofar as a work of art can ever overcome anything) through the restoration of sanity by laughter.

But *The Day of the Locust*, as I have already said, is West's supreme Book of Revelations. This beautifully composed novel makes dreadfully and hilariously evident in the superb dance of its elements a threat beyond that of *A Cool Million*: a threat to the very roots of life in America, a threat as it were to the human nature of American humanity. It is a threat incarnate in a certain mass of people—bored, frustrated, vindictive, and moribund—who have come to California impelled by a dream of their own obscene millennium, by a sterile lust for some experience of violence that might exhilarate and revivify. They are disappointed—"nothing [could] ever be violent enough to make taut their slack minds and bodies"—and with a devouring sense of having been betrayed, they await the summons to provide out of themselves the violence denied. The summons begins to be audible in the animal roaring of a mob rioting outside a Hollywood theater as the novel ends.

Against that tremendous force of hatred—and for West, since love is the sign of spiritual grace, hatred, its polar opposite, is the defining quality of apostasy and damnation—West poses the allied powers of art and comedy. His hero is a young painter named Tod Hackett, presently employed as a set designer in Hollywood; a tougher-spirited Miss Lonelyhearts and a more self-protective Lemuel Pitkin. It is Tod who takes to studying the dead ferocity of the invaders, seeking them out in odd nooks and corners of the city, driven by a profound fascination with their "awful anarchic power" and determined to represent them on canvas. He finds them gathered, more than anywhere else, in the temples and churches, the lunatic-fringe cults of California; for one of the most terrible of the truths and prophecies disclosed in *The Day of the Locust* is the organic connection in America between radical religiosity, an extreme Protestantism gone finally insane, and the organized impulse of hatred and destruction.

> As [Tod] watched these people writhe on the hard seats of their churches, he thought of how well Alessandro Magnasco would dramatize the contrast between their drained-out feeble bodies and their wild disordered minds. He would not satirize them as Hogarth and Daumier might, nor would he pity them. He would paint their fury with respect, appreciating its awful, anarchic power, and aware that they had it in them to destroy civilization.

Nathanael West does not precisely satirize them either; despite its carefully wrought poetic intensity, *The Day of the Locust* stays closer to a palpable historical reality than his other fictions. The tone and movement of the novel are comic, nonetheless, and both are suited to a world in which, due to the utter instability of its outward forms, everything is on the verge of giving way.

The scene upon which the locusts descend is a scene made up of masqueraders and impostors; of movie actors dressed up as French and British generals and of ordinary citizens dressed up as Tyrolean hunters. Even plants and natural phenomena are fictitious: cactus plants are made of rubber and cork; a hill on a movie set, as it collapses, spills the nails and rips the canvas of which it is composed. A world so grotesquely insubstantial is ripe for conquest; and yet within its atmosphere, the wrath to come can be contemplated with just that drunken and hazily amused equanimity that Tod Hackett expresses when, lying on his back in a clump of wild mustard, he thinks about the invasion of California by "the cream of America's madmen" and feels certain that "the milk from which it had been skimmed was just as rich in violence. The Angelenos would be first, but their comrades all over the country would follow. There would be civil war." That antic Armageddon, however, takes place not quite in the actual rioting and lynching and sexual assaults of the final scene; but, rather, in an interpretive work of art, in the painting (and it is to be a great painting, West clearly wants us to believe) Tod Hackett is meticulously projecting on the last page, even as he is being mauled and half-crushed by the frenzied mob.

Thus superimposed in thought above the actual disorders, the painting—it will be called "The Burning of Los Angeles"—will eventually explain and comment upon the apocalypse it describes by the patterned juxtaposition of its elements. It will show a "mob carrying baseball bats and torches" down a long hill street, a mob that includes "the cultists of all sorts" whom Tod had been observing—"all those poor devils who can only be stirred by the promise of miracles, and then only to violence." Now, "no longer bored, they sang and danced joyously in the red light of the flames," following the leader who "had made the necessary promise"; "they were marching behind his banner in a great united front of screwballs and screwboxes to purify the land." Elsewhere on the canvas, various postures suggest various responses to that savage absurd Puritanism: a girl running naked in smiling mindless panic; a man named Claude turning to thumb his nose; Tod himself pausing to throw stones at the mob like a small boy. Nose thumbing and stone throwing are commendable acts of derision; but Tod's major response is of course his painting, just as West's major response is the novel that contains it. And both painting and novel fulfill their purpose by portraying these maddened humans, whirling forward in their orgiastic dance, as devils who are yet poor devils, seized by a fury of hatred which is as silly as it is explosive.

MAX F. SCHULZ

# Nathanael West's "Desperate Detachment"

Nathanael West is reputed to have remained detached from the grotesqueries of Hollywood during the many years he worked there and from the follies of the human world for the thirty-seven years he lived in it. Yet West's novels make it clear that in the deeper reaches of his mind he was obsessed with man's nightmarish dual nature: his neurotic isolation and his social impulse, his self-deception and his self-mockery. Unlike Singer, and so many of the current Jewish-American writers, West was unable to rest content in the human suspension between heavenly aspirations and earthly limitations, belief and skepticism, order and disorder. He portrays life in his novels as a conflict of inadequate imperatives offered to man by society and culture as guides to live by. Conflict supposes not equipoise between codeterminants but supremacy of one over another. In that sense each novel, despite its basic satirical intention, represents a search for absolutes. "Reality! Reality! If I could only discover the Real," John Gilson calls for in his "journal." "A Real that I could know with my senses." In the astringent disillusionment of West's hope of finding something real to believe in—"A Real that would wait for me to inspect it as a dog inspects a dead rabbit"—each novel ends as a mocking denunciation of a false dream: the bardic dream (*The Dream Life of Balso Snell*), the Christ dream (*Miss Lonelyhearts*), the Horatio Alger dream (*A Cool Million*), and the Hollywood dream (*The Day of the Locust*). West's bitter cognizance of betrayal is pervasive. The thoroughgoing nature of his sense of the fraudulence and destructiveness of life is brilliantly, almost excessively, portrayed by the Trojan Horse correlative

From *Radical Sophistication: Studies in Contemporary Jewish-American Novelists*. Copyright © 1969 by Max F. Schulz. Ohio University Press.

in *The Dream Life of Balso Snell*. Synonymous in Western thought with falsity and the end of a civilization, the wooden horse—specifically its alimentary canal—becomes the hallucinatory terrain over which Balso Snell wanders. Thus West clearly identifies man's dream world with sham and *fin de siècle*. He uneasily describes its death rattle, while trying desperately to dissociate himself with a comic ploy from emotional involvement in its agony. Unfortunately for the complete success of his stories, he was unable to control his own sense of outrage and despair. His shriek of laughter, as Victor Comerchero notes, "keeps breaking into a sob."

The first work of a writer is more likely to rely on literary analogues than later works which draw directly on experience for their substance. Such is the case with the four novels of West. *The Dream Life of Balso Snell* satirizes the ineffectuality of the imagination by way of an inexhaustible stream of allusions to and parodies of English writers from Dryden to Joyce, and from Dostoevsky to the French Symbolists and Dadaists, as well as much miscellaneous Western thought. The novel is a book perversely bent on proclaiming the illusoriness of books. West is reported to have told Liebling "that he had written *Balso* as a protest against writing books." That is ostensibly its general satirical aim. In fact, the novel strikes out thematically in a variety of directions, foreshadowing most of the preoccupations of West in his subsequent novels. Of these I wish to look at one to demonstrate West's ambivalent involvement in the despairing world that he depicts.

An essential thematic antithesis in the story pits romantic love against the procreative instinct. Like the nympholeptic shepherd-king in Keats's *Endymion* (and like Samuel Perkins, the subject of a biography by Mary McGeeney), Balso Snell swoons in and out of a dream within his dream as he mentally pursues Miss McGeeney, his thoughts struggling "to make the circle of his sensory experience approach the infinite." The prevailing situation is one of incompatibility. Lust encounters conditions of courtly love, and sacred love the wiles of the seducer. "Oh, I loved a girl once," Balso Snell laments:

> All day she did nothing but place bits of meat on the petals of flowers. She choked the rose with butter and cake crumbs, soiling the crispness of its dainty petals with gravy and cheese. She wanted to attract flies, not butterflies or bees.

This perverse merger of the fleshly and the ethereal becomes inextricably ambiguous in the witty biography of Saint Puce, the flea "who was born, lived, and died, beneath the arm of our Lord." In his daily sensations of supping on Christ, whose body provided him with both meat and drink, Saint Puce enacted perpetual Holy Communion.

As the ironic tone of these two examples indicates, West will not allow the mystery of the "Two-become-One" to remain intact. For him the contraries reconciled are always coming undone. Like Fra Lippo Lippi he forever sees "the garden and God there / A-making man's wife"; and this lesson of "The value and significance of flesh" he "can't unlearn ten minutes afterward."

If the spiritual cannot exist without the incarnate, through substance then must we confirm our substancelessness. Thus West fashions his own infernal mystery. The ideal vanishes into solid flesh. "Who among us can boast that he was born three times, as was Dionysius?" B. Hamlet Darwin asks caustically.

> Or who can say, like Christ, that he was born of a virgin? . . . Alas! none of us . . . You who were born from the womb, covered with slime and foul blood, 'midst cries of anguish and suffering.
>
> At your birth, instead of the Three Kings, the Dove, the Star of Bethlehem, there was only old Doctor Haasenschweitz who wore rubber gloves and carried a towel over his arm like a waiter.
>
> And how did the lover, your father, come to his beloved? . . . Did he come in the shape of a swan, a bull, or a shower of gold? No! But with his pants unsupported by braces, came he from the bathroom.

Unfortunately for West's peace of mind, as the savage despair of the passage suggests, he found no satisfaction in this reduction of the infinite into the corporeal either. In an acrid satire of fleshly desire the story (and dream) concludes with Balso having a nocturnal emission. (The entire story represents the strenuously intellectual efforts of Balso's body to have a wet dream.) Even sex, the urge to procreate, ends as a pointless solo exercise in release of tension, likened to "the mechanics of decay." At the instant of emission, West exultantly informs us that Balso's "body broke free of the bard" and "took on a life of its own" "that knew nothing of the poet Balso." Despite this freedom from the false constraints of the categorizing imagination, not life, not the organic, but death and the mechanical describe the evolutions of the body. The basic metaphor used is that of an army performing "the manual of disintegration," maneuvering automatically "with the confidence and training of chemicals acting under the stimulus of a catalytic agent." Release is described in terms of a mortally wounded soldier: "His body screamed and shouted as it marched . . . then with one heaving shout of triumph, it fell back quiet . . . victorious." Thus the "miracle was made manifest" in the One, West says sardonically.

The One that is all things and yet no one of them: the priest and the god, the immolation, the sacrificial rite, the libation offered to ancestors, the incantation, the sacrificial egg, the altar, the ego and the alter ego, as well as the father, the child, and the grandfather of the universe, the mystic doctrine, the purification, the syllable "Om," the path, the master, the witness, the receptacle, the Spirit of Public School 186, the last ferry that leaves for Weehawken at seven.

In the diminishing manner of the burlesque stanzas of Byron's *Don Juan*, this catalogue of the body's regality ("the Spirit of Public School 186"!) underscores the skepticism with which West assents to the enthronement of matter.

Worse, yet, mind returns in the form of false literary sentiment to adulterate further the autonomous reality of the body. In a brilliant analysis of its style, Victor Comerchero shows how Balso's imagined copulation with Mary McGeeney is a parody of the melting, swooning seduction of eighteen-century sentimental literature, of the stereotype passion of pulp fiction, of the hard-boiled back-seat wrestle of the realistic school, of the decadent *fin de siècle* dreams of encounters with an oriental *femme fatale*, and of the Molly Bloom monologue at the conclusion of Joyce's *Ulysses*. Saturninely, if comically, West reveals that even Balso's "dreams have been corrupted by literature. When he dreams, even a wet dream, it is a literary one." Driven by sexual desire, Balso Snell in his dream exploration of the nature of mind and matter may have discovered complacently that the body reigns supreme; but West's interpretation of the same event is less optimistic. In acrid disillusionment he concludes (corroborated by the dream context of the narrative) that Balso's solution to the hopeless bifurcation of life is as chimerical as the empty constructs of the mind, which man fools himself into believing are a pledge of meaningful order in the world.

"If there is a vision of love" in West's fiction, Josephine Herbst has remarked, "it is etched in the acid of what love is not." *The Dream Life of Balso Snell* presents a satyr's conception of love, *Miss Lonelyhearts* that of the whorehouse madam turned church-choir mistress. From cynical exploiter of his correspondents' cries for help, Miss Lonelyhearts metamorphoses into a Christlike savior of these lost and lonely souls of modern civilization.

West's point of view, however, is more subtle and complex in *Miss Lonelyhearts* than in his other three novels. His virulent skepticism is forever testing the validity of a thought and seeking the motive behind an action. Thus, he constantly and ambivalently undercuts his effort to find a pattern in existence. The horrifying lives of Miss Lonelyhearts' readers unquestionably move the columnist to sincere desire to succor them. But his conversion from hard-boiled columnist to soft-souled evangelist is compromised at every turn. The psychology of sex—the twentieth-century substitute for previous centuries' religious faith—is the instrument of his betrayal of others as well as of himself. More often than not he is depicted as selfishly demanding rather than selflessly giving of his love. His impulse toward the Divine Love of man and "all God's creation" advocated by Father Zossima in *The Brothers Karamazov*, which he has been reading, manifests itself in sexual cruelty, self-loathing seduction, latent homosexuality, and religious hysteria. Like infernal stations of the cross in his outrageous progress toward saintly love of humanity, he bloodily bungles (in a dream) the sacrifice of a lamb, viciously tugs at the nipples of his fiancée's breasts, brutally twists the arm of an old homosexual, calculatingly attempts to seduce his boss's wife, distastefully submits to the sexual advances of a correspondent, ardently holds hands with her crippled husband, eventually strikes the housewife seductress in the face again and again, and finally achieves union with Christ while in a fever.

Throughout this inverse way of the pilgrim, religious ardor is confused with sexual desire, love with lust, and lust with violence and destruction. Miss Lonelyhearts' addresses of love to Betty, Mary Shrike, and Mrs. Doyle are associated with a Mexican War obelisk that like a giant phallus "lengthening in rapid jerks," and "red and swollen in the dying sun," seems "about to spout a load of granite seed" of death. The arm of the "clean old man," who was pulled from the stall of a public restroom and accused by Miss Lonelyhearts of being a pervert, becomes "the arm of all the sick and miserable, broken and betrayed, inarticulate and impotent . . . of Desperate, Broken-hearted, Sick-of-it-all, Disillusioned-with-tubercular-husband." In its effort to create order out of the entropy about him, Miss Lonelyhearts' sensibility, ill from its encounter with Fay Doyle, nightmarishly grapples with the contents of a pawnshop window, "the paraphernalia of suffering." Out of this jumble of articles it attempts to construct a phallus. Failing in this, it works to form the paraphernalia into a gigantic cross on the shore of an ocean, but

> . . . every wave added to his stock faster than he could lengthen its arms. His labors were enormous. He staggered from the last wave line to his work, loaded down with marine refuse—bottles, shells, chunks of cork, fish heads, pieces of net.

The linkage of Christ with the sea has strong libidinous overtones ([there are instances] where Christ and a phallic snake and Christ and a fish are also joined). The prior encounter with Fay Doyle is described in marine terms. Her undressing in the dark is heard by Miss Lonelyhearts as "sea sounds":

> Something flapped like a sail; there was the creak of ropes; then he heard the wave-against-a-wharf smack of rubber on flesh. Her call to him to hurry was a sea-moan, and when he lay beside her, she heaved, tidal, moon-driven.

And in language that foreshadows his subsequent building of the cross, he staggers out of bed fifteen minutes later "like an exhausted swimmer leaving the surf." In short, moved by the inadequacy of sex to steady his nerves and allay his self-hatred, he sublimates his eroticism in Christian humility, as a complementary form of therapy.

West could not formulate the ambivalence of his hope for a religious solution to life more clearly. As if the condemnation of *agapé* is not vehement enough, Miss Lonelyhearts' religious conversion, as Victor Comerchero demonstrates conclusively, has a homosexual origin, further underlining West's "mythic, mocking, agonizing" suspicion that "true compassion" is unendurable in this decaying world. In the plight of Miss Lonelyhearts West portrays a devastating debasement of the Ulysses and Sirens motif. And the blasphemously blind universe that he envisions, in which "the Miss Lonelyhearts are the priests of twentieth-century America," receives full confirmation when Miss Lonelyhearts interprets his fever as a religious experience and climbs out of bed to embrace the crippled Doyle, whom he believes "God had sent him so that Miss Lonelyhearts could perform a miracle and be certain of his conversion." But West in his heart of hearts knew that God was dead. Miss Lonelyhearts never quite qualifies for membership in Graham Greene's pantheon of tainted saints. West's faith is at once too strong of desire and too weak of belief. Miss Lonelyhearts' need for a confirmatory miracle italicizes this profound skepticism. And the consequences of his desire for certainty are ironically devastating on both the sacramental and psychological levels of the narrative. He rushes to embrace the cripple and heal his leg. Doyle, however, is terrified by Miss Lonelyhearts' mad charge and by Betty's sudden appearance at the bottom of the stairs. As they grapple, a pistol Doyle is carrying accidentally fires, killing Miss Lonelyhearts. Locked in each other's arms they roll down the stairs. The symbolic union of the two men at the end is no doubt on one level expressive of Miss Lonelyhearts' spiritual yearnings; but their embrace, as Stanley Edgar Hyman observes, is also homosexual, the one ironically penetrating "the body of the other with a bullet," "while the woman stands helplessly by." The disparity in the novel between the simple narrative affirmation of religious faith and the underlying metaphoric insinuation of Oedipal obscenities adumbrates the tortured ambiguity of West's imagination—its attraction to a Christ dream that it could not believe in.

In *A Cool Million* and *The Day of the Locust*, West explores the *Zeitgeist* of the cheaters and the cheated on native grounds. The dreams are now distinctly the home-grown variety found sprouting in the land of opportunity. "America takes care of the honest and industrious and never fails them as long as they are both," Nathan "Shagpoke" Whipple expounds from his perch on a cracker barrel. "The story of Rockefeller and of Ford is the story of every great American," he tells Lemuel Pitkin, "and you should strive to make it your story. Like them, you were born poor and on a farm. Like them, by honesty and industry, you cannot fail to succeed." The rest of *A Cool Million* is West's saturnine retort. Not from rags to riches but to the same old shirtsleeves, not from log cabin to White House but to the same old mortgaged farm house—this is the just reward of the barefoot, but honest and industrious, American boy. With acrid irony West equates business enterprise with the imagination, foresight, and aggressiveness of Wu Fong's white slavery emporium; and economic success with unapprehended chicanery and thievery. The American capitalistic system is posited on the productive ideal that the building of a better mousetrap is always good for the community. West's answer is to demonstrate that the folklore of Horatio Alger is more likely to be destructive of the individual than to be beneficial to society. And so he gives us the allegory of Lemuel's inexorable dismemberment on the barricades of capitalism: *sans* teeth, eye, thumb, scalp, and leg. To the memory of this derelict of the American way of life, the fascistic "Leather Shirt" followers of Shagpoke Whipple shout at the conclusion in a national holiday celebration of Lemuel's birthday, "All hail, the American Boy!"

Victor Comerchero contends that because of the broadly comic tone of *A Cool Million*, a reversion to the tone of *The Dream Life of Balso Snell*, it fails to engage the reader. Consequently one tends to miss the serious point of the novel; "one is so amused by America as West presents it that one is neither frightened nor angered by it." In his effort to set up a critical issue, a straw man, so to speak, Comerchero exaggerates the difficulty posed by the blurred focus of the book's tone. The plain fact is that few readers (critical commentators, that is) have missed the central warning of the novel. Comerchero's observation, however, about the strange refusal of the story to take itself seriously is penetrating. The "personal involvement" that he suggests as an explanation has more than a grain of truth in it, as this essay, I hope, makes clear. But Comerchero does not, unfortunately, make anything more of this insight.

With what in the story is West involved? One cannot see the temperament and agony of West in either Lemuel Pitkin or Shagpoke Whipple, as one can in Balso Snell, Miss Lonelyhearts, and Tod Hackett. Hence the disturbing reserve of the story, by way of its excessiveness, does not derive from West's effort to dissociate himself from the central characters. Closer to the simple truth, probably, is that West, like his great predecessor Swift, is engaged in a lover's quarrel with a world that does not live up to his expectations. The broadly vulgar style in which he tells the story is, of course, on one level a parody of the crass, didactic prose of the Horatio Alger tale. Not so much the economic system, however, as the noisome aura of sanctity which enshrouds it is the object of his attack. After all, in writing his books, West himself hoped to turn an honest dollar. That hope was appropriately enough strongest with *A Cool Million*. The pious cant of a Shagpoke Whipple celebrates the manufacturing process and the pursuit of gain as the golden ends of human activity. The result is that the manufactured article deteriorates into a by-product and man is lost sight of altogether, transformed into a helpless ministrant to his own inexorable dehumanization. In the "Chamber of American Horrors, Animate and Inanimate Hideosities," West brilliantly pictures the debasement of taste and of sensibility produced by this carnival atmosphere. Here the flotsam of an industrial civilization buttressed by a false ethic is accorded the revered permanence of museum exhibits. Man's Hippocratic ideal is enshrined in the patent medicine offerings of the drugstore: in a "Hercules wearing a small, compact truss" and in "a copy of Power's 'Greek Slave' with elastic bandages on all her joints." Technical know-how is displayed in the cheap imitative tricks of paper "made to look like wood, wood like rubber, rubber like steel, steel like cheese, cheese like glass, and, finally, glass like paper." So the inconstant and the deceptive are memorialized with sneaking admiration as a tribute to American technological genius.

In Greenfield Village, Henry Ford's monument to Americana, there is an ash heap meticulously encased and labeled as having come from behind Thomas Edison's Menlo Park laboratory. Gazing at this dump pile, one can never be quite sure of the degree of fetish worship and, contrariwise, of sly humor that it represents. Nor can one categorically isolate West's attitude in *A Cool Million*. Shagpoke Whipple, the homespun American philosopher, wins our sufferance; but Shagpoke the politician, the America-firster, terrifies us. Lemuel, the innocent pawn, evokes our pity; but Lemuel the fool, the classic rube, equally arouses our derision. The names that West chooses for his characters are invariably witty wordplays, adding an extra dimension to our understanding of that person. Lemuel Pitkin's last name is close in sound to pipkin. Whether we are right to associate pipkin with Lemuel, we cannot avoid the scathing sense of the diminutive in his name; hence in comparison to his namesake Lemuel Gulliver, his misfortunes are seen as a diminuendo echo of the Brobdingnag gulling suffered by Gulliver on *his* Whittingtonian travels in search of fame and fortune.

The big lie is certain. Less evident is the source of the lie: the ideals of the American Way of Life? the naïveté of such simpletons as Lemuel? the "sophisticated aliens" decried by Whipple? or the ingrained evil of an economic system? The tone of *A Cool Million* reflects West's own uncertainty of what to finger. For all his pessimism he was not a little bitten with the American dream of a new Eden in the wilderness, as Betty's and Miss Lonelyhearts' nostalgic interlude on the farm in Connecticut hints—a surprising performance for seemingly so confirmed an urban novelist. There is also his love of the Bucks County countryside and of hunting and fishing. And there is the prophet's fervent need to believe in something, which in West is strung taut by the contrary pull of the cynical side of his nature. It is no wonder in his daily life that he strove to divorce himself from the furious indignation which drove his artistic vision.

With *The Day of the Locust*, West's view of life approaches Swift's in the fourth book of *Gulliver's Travels*. Spectators and performers alike feel the lash of his derision. Attracted by its semblance of life, Midwesterners come to Hollywood only to be tricked into death by a diet of sophisticate sex. They gyrate from movie premiere to movie premiere, as much automatons as the celluloid celebrities they push and shove to glimpse. The cinematic promise of ripe love and of a richer, fuller life never materializes. Faye Greener is a pathetic imitation of the Hollywood sex goddess, her thoughts and mannerisms a pastiche of Grade B movies. Both Homer Simpson and Tod Hackett (note the puns on death and havoc in the latter's name) discover in her ever fresh lure of sexuality a fey, receding will-o-the-wisp. Her appearance promises love, but it proves no more rewarding than the suggestive accents and movements of a screenland heroine. Each one's desire for renewal of person is eventually betrayed by her beauty, "whose invitation wasn't to pleasure, but to struggle, hard and sharp, closer to murder than to love." The mechanically destructive recoil of the mob at the end of the novel reflects West's view of what happens to man when his hopes end as tattered scarecrows of reality. The adulatory pursuit of celebrities blurs sinisterly into the sexual violence that underlies emotional hunger. Spasms surge periodically through the crowd. Smutty remarks pass freely from stranger to stranger. Men hug passing complacent women. With such senseless eroticism, the mob apes the dark underside of the lives of its screen heroes and heroines. Death is inextricably linked to love. Human energy is easily diverted from a life instinct to a death impulse. Thus the adoration of the premiere mob is manifested as the blight of locusts, just as the alteration of the primordial hills of southern California into travesties of exotic architecture is another manifestation of the locust's presence.

The Westian novel is concerned at its center with the instability of existence, which derives basically from a metaphysical reaction to the modern world picture of everything being in flux. What more frighteningly askew world of metamorphosis can one imagine than the one of architecture, aesthetics, music, and mathematics Miss McGeeney tells us that Samuel Perkins discovered "in the odors of a woman's body." In these terms the Hollywood setting of *The Day of the Locust* provides West with the most perfect of the correlatives he has used to set forth his vision of life. As is proper in the city dedicated to the making of movies—to the creation of shapes that alter before one's eyes—the guises and gestures of the celluloid world of shadowy change, of make-believe, become the status quo. A fat lady in yachting cap converts into a housewife going shopping; a man in Norfolk jacket and Tyrolean hat, an insurance agent returning from his office; and a girl in slacks and sneakers with a bandanna around her head, a receptionist leaving a switchboard. The painted canvas, plaster, and lath sets on the back lots of the film studios reappear as the Mexican ranch houses, Samoan huts, Mediterranean villas, Egyptian and Japanese temples, Swiss chalets, and Tudor cottages that line Pinyon Canyon at the end of Vine Street. Repeatedly the Westian man transmutes into a woman. John Gilson as Raskolnikov, after murdering a dishwasher, caresses his breasts "like a young girl who has suddenly become conscious of her body on a hot afternoon." He imitates "the mannered walk of a girl showing off before a group of boys," flirts with some sailors, going "through all the postures of a desperate prostitute," and "camping" for all it is worth. Lemuel is transformed momently into a male prostitute in Wu Fong's establishment. And Miss Lonelyhearts exhibits more than one symptom of the homosexual. The many periods in history endlessly shift their outlines. Searching for Faye, who has a bit part in the movie "Waterloo," Tod Hackett wanders through a kaleidoscope of time and place and of the artifices of civilization:

> The only bit of shade he could find was under an ocean liner made of painted canvas with real lifeboats hanging from its davits. He stood in its narrow shadow for a while, then went on toward a great forty-foot papier mâché sphinx that loomed up in the distance. He had to cross a desert to reach it, a desert that was continually being made larger by a fleet of trucks dumping white sand. . . .

He skirted the desert, making a wide turn to the right, and came to a western street with a plank sidewalk. On the porch of the "Last Chance Saloon" was a rocking chair. He sat down on it and lit a cigarette.

From there he could see a jungle compound with a water buffalo tethered to the side of a conical grass hut. Every few seconds the animal groaned musically. Suddenly an Arab charged by on a white stallion. He shouted at the man, but got no answer. A little while later he saw a truck with a load of snow and several malamute dogs. He shouted again. The driver shouted something back, but didn't stop.

Throwing away his cigarette, he went through the swinging doors of the saloon. There was no back to the building and he found himself in a Paris street. He followed it to its end, coming out in a Romanesque courtyard. He heard voices a short distance away and went toward them. On a lawn of fiber, a group of men and women in riding costume were picnicking. They were eating cardboard food in front of a cellophane waterfall.

Faye Greener and her father, Harry, have maintained their theatrical poses of movie siren and vaudeville clown so long that, in the words of Comerchero, each "has been dispossessed of his personality—of his identity—through disuse."

West's obsession with flux is a central controlling force in *The Dream Life of Balso Snell*. In keeping with the protean nature of a dream, shapes are forever altering before Balso's eyes. His first sight of Miss McGeeney is of a slim young girl "standing naked before him . . . washing her hidden charms in a public fountain." She calls to him in the erotically charged language of the Romance.

> Throwing his arms around her, Balso interrupted her recitation sticking his tongue into her mouth. But when he closed his eyes to heighten the fun, he felt that he was embracing tweed. He opened them and saw that what he held in his arms was a middle-aged woman dressed in a mannish suit and wearing hornrimmed glasses.

Balso's orgasm at the end of the book, while dreaming of having sexual intercourse with Miss McGeeney (changed again, "alas! but with much of the old Mary left, particularly about the eyes,"), enacts not only the completion of his own desire but also the wish fulfillment of John Gilson's schoolboy dream of sleeping with her. Dreams figure in all the novels except *A Cool Million*—where the dream is conceived of as a nationwide and patriotic preoccupation with the getting and keeping of money. Critics have made much of the Freudian and Surrealistic impulse in West's frequent resort to dreams, and rightly so; but their significance for West is not restricted to the psychological and aesthetic. In their reflection of a volatile universe, they also have a strong metaphysical import.

Another instance of West's preoccupation with the metamorphosis of things is the recurrence in his novels of performers and of the blurring of distinction between performer and spectator. In one way or another almost all his characters pursue an occupation, usually as writer or actor or painter, which transforms one kind of reality into another kind. The poet Balso discovers to his dismay that the wooden horse "was inhabited solely by writers in search of an audience." Instead of writing he finds himself involuntarily reading the work of others. *Miss Lonelyhearts* is a story about a nameless man writing the daily "agony column" for a newspaper, answering letters, written under pseudonyms by the afflicted, for the entertainment of the majority of its readers. Here columnist and correspondent blur together in their dual categories of writer and reader. Even Lemuel Pitkin ends as a human prop at the Bijou Theater, dismantled nightly of his toupee, false teeth, glass eye, and wooden leg by the comedy team of Riley and Robbins. The complete symbiosis of performer and spectator occurs in *The Day of the Locust*, when the surrealistic actions of the mob become confused in Tod's mind with his painting of "The Burning of Los Angeles," which depicts such a mob savagely chasing the objects of their adulation. Here participant and observer (not to mention the actual and the fanciful) fuse indistinguishably into a macabre dance of death, celebrating the impermanence of all things.

The despair implicit in this obsession with change cannot be exaggerated. West's Jeremiahlike search for permanent values was forever overturning proof of the transiency of things. "West's brilliance" as a novelist, Comerchero observes, "proceeds from his ability to generalize frustration." West's vision of frustration stems from his metaphysical sense of the helplessness of man trapped in an unstable universe.

"If I could be Hamlet, or even a clown with a breaking heart 'neath this jester's motley," the writer of The Pamphlet exclaims, "the role [of being man] would be tolerable. But I must always find it necessary to burlesque the mystery of feeling at its source; I must laugh at myself, and if the laugh is 'bitter,' I must laugh at the laugh." These lines are often quoted as expressive of the strenuous effort of West to dissociate himself from the horrors of his age. In his novels he tried to realize distance by treating his fictional characters with extreme objectivity. But the cold malice with which he analyzes their faults, like the excessive scatology or sexual and bodily nausea found in all his writing, reveals the radical nature of his revulsion, and the extremity of his reaction, to the frustrated aspirations of his protagonists—which were also (with the exception of homosexuality) his own frustrations. The Westian man is an early species on the evolutionary scale of *genus victima*. Like the Neanderthal man, as compared to present-day *Homo sapiens*, he excites our morbid interest and disgust more than our sympathy or love. West's involvement with him is that of the prophet. He has the reformer's instinct. He wishes reality to be different from what it is and people from what they are. He hates what will not heed his jeremiads, unlike a Malamud or a Bellow, who can love their fictional *schlemiels* without feeling a strong urge to reform them. In this fact lies one of the fundamental differences between the idealistic naïveté of West and his generation and the radical sophistication of the Jewish-American writers of the fifties and sixties.

Strong overtones of antifascism and anticapitalism characterize West's novels as sincere expressions of their time. As Josephine Herbst remembers him, "The horror of this age was in West's nerves, in his blood." In his passionate search for something to believe in, West exhibits the desperate commitment of the thirties; but in his bitter sense of betrayal by ideas, he suffers the anguished disillusionment of the liberal of the thirties in the decades that followed. His need for detachment was intense; but the age and his background made that well nigh impossible for him to realize. At a time when most of his Jewish contemporaries were still writing realistically of the Jewish experience in America, West was attempting to define symbolistically the larger American experience. His vocabulary necessarily relied heavily on literary fashion. His vision of American life was inevitably narrow and limited. His insecure control of his material, despite his inventiveness and his expenditure of incredible labor on his stories, foredoomed the results to shakiness of form, uncertainty of tone, inconstancy and occasional vulgarity of language, and finickiness of output. His passionate involvement in ideas led to his quasi-identification with the search for values of his central characters. Unfortunately, such identification with his fictional creations also inhibited his judgment of their quest. His stories are more heated and polemical than is good for them. He too often lost what a later generation would call his cool. Yet in his exploration of the meaning of Hollywood and in his probe of the psychic blows suffered by being American, he courageously homesteaded forty acres on which Mailer, Bellow, Fiedler, and the other contemporary Jewish-American novelists are currently building a Levittown.

JAY MARTIN

# "*Abandon Everything!*"

*Abandon everything. Abandon Dada. Get rid of your wife. Give up your mistress. Give up your hopes and your fears. . . . Give up the substance for the shadow. Give up your easy way of life, and that which passes for a job with a future. Take to the roads. . . .*
—ANDRÉ BRETON, *Lâchez tout!* (1924)

B̲etween 1927 and the fall of 1930, when West was variously confronting his own artistic identity through association with Village and other intellectual groups, through his reading, and, perhaps most of all, by assessing and deciding on his future, he continued as assistant manager of the Kenmore Hall Hotel at 145 East 23 Street. West's Aunt Susan had married a well-known physician, whose brother, Morris Jarcho, was a plumbing sub-contractor, and it was through him that West was given this job when it appeared otherwise impossible for him to get one. In the collapse of the building trades, when a general contractor (like West's father) could no longer hold his assets, his sub-contractors for plumbing, bricklaying, and the other individual crafts frequently attached the completed building and together formed a corporation to administer it. This was true of both the Kenmore and the Sutton, a hotel where West was eventually to become manager. Ironically, the same economic circumstances which ruined his father also led to the jobs which were to have other effects on West's life.

The Kenmore Hall was uniquely suited among hotels built in the

From *Nathanael West: The Art of His Life*. Copyright © 1970 by Jay Martin. Farrar, Straus and Giroux.

late twenties to be successful during the Depression. Badly designed, with small rooms, no restaurant, and neither conference rooms nor a mezzanine, it was saved by its faults; in some ways, it had been planned as a kind of glorified rooming house, its small rooms renting at low rates, its lobby and drugstore, where all the guests necessarily congregated, becoming popular as unostentatious meeting places for young men and women.

Although most of the family recognized that hotel work was far from West's main interest, they were content to help him along. Moreover, he had the instincts of a good businessman: he was disciplined and well organized, with a love for moneyed life. His duties as night manager were not arduous—nor (for his tastes) was his salary of $35 a week a large one, even with extra benefits like his room, and meals at the drugstore. West did not hesitate to tell his friends that he "loathed" hotel work, although he sometimes concealed the fact that his family was partly running the hotel. But in obvious ways, the job was to be interesting: it gave him a certain position, and he could invite Sid Perelman, Max Bodenheim, Mike Gold, or Quent Reynolds up for lunch and a swim. It became known that Brown boys in town could stay free in rooms where the linen hadn't yet been changed. Perhaps, as night manager, he could humorously think of himself as another Stanley Sackett, night manager for the Madison Hotel, who wore only evening clothes and became a favorite of sophisticates and a model for a series of cartoons by Peter Arno. Certainly West too looked, as Arthur Kober remarks, "like someone out of Wall Street," "very formal indeed."

But most of all, the job at the Kenmore provided for West precisely what he had not had in New York before: a certain removal from his family and yet a fixed place—in short, the conditions for meditation. Infrequently in his room, more often sitting in the glassed-in hotel office—insulated from the people in the lobby, but still in visual contact with them—he was able to work on *The Dream Life of Balso Snell*. In the hotel, he developed his natural attitude of preoccupation into genuine meditation and night after night between 1927 and the last part of 1929 wrote and rewrote his book, first in pencil on yellow ruled paper, and eventually on typed sheets, correcting and retyping repeatedly. As late as 1930 he was calling it *The Journal of Balso Snell*. In some ways it was a journal of his own daily response to certain problems of attitude and definition, in art and life, then engaging him intensely. Only in minor details could *Balso Snell* be called directly autobiographical; but it is a book which does set down, boldly and directly, the character of West's imaginative life during the late twenties.

He made several attempts to have it published. At this time, of course, any avant-garde writer had real difficulty finding a publisher. Older, established firms—Houghton Mifflin or Harper, for instance—still retained certain commitments to the genteel past of New England respectability. Only a few commercial houses—notably B. W. Huebsch, Liveright, and Knopf—genuinely encouraged experimental writing, and even these leaned toward the writer who, if experimental, still had a certain position by virtue of earlier publications or frequent appearances in little magazines. A small press with a select audience was, therefore, West's only hope for publication. In one of the policy statements for Contact Editions, Robert McAlmon had summed up the credo of the small publisher: "Contact Editions are not concerned with what the 'public' wants. . . . There are commercial publishers who know the public and its tastes. If books seem to us to have something of individuality, intelligence, talent, and live sense of literature, and quality which has the odour and timbre of authenticity, we publish them. We admit that eccentricities exist." West therefore attempted to place his book with McAlmon's press. West, McAlmon wrote, "gave me a Ms. which was too Anatole France for me," and he refused it. Later, West appears to have hoped that David Moss, then manager of the Gotham Book Mart, the leading New York bookstore distributing avant-garde literature, would issue his book under the Gotham imprint, as Brentano's had done with many books earlier. In 1930, another small press, Brewer, Warren & Putnam, refused the completed manuscript, considering some sections obscene and blasphemous. That same year in a fascinating series of moves, David Moss and Martin Kamin founded a bookstore in the Barbizon-Plaza Hotel and proposed to McAlmon that "they would take on the publishing of books under the name of Contact Editions." They had collected a number of Contact Editions—books which McAlmon had difficulty getting into the United States and which he could find no way of distributing when he succeeded—and it seemed as if they might give him both an editorial and a distribution center. They suggested, in addition, that Contact, the magazine which McAlmon and William Carlos Williams had edited, be revived. Williams, practicing medicine in New Jersey and frequently visiting New York, was willing to become editor. McAlmon, though tempted, eventually allowing himself to be listed as associate editor of the magazine, and even taking part in one of its editorial conferences, nonetheless refused to continue editing either Contact Editions or Contact, and let both imprints pass into the hands of Moss and Kamin.

    In the meantime, West had followed Moss to his new bookstore and was purchasing fiction and art books there. There, too, he met slightly older writers like Williams, Nancy Cunard, and McAlmon, showing, Kamin recalls, both personal intensity, even a certain brashness, and a winning commitment to their common interest in artistic experiment. Early in the fall of 1930, West mentioned to Kamin that he had finished a manuscript, and Kamin, thinking of continuing the Contact series, offered to consider it. He asked William Carlos Williams to give an editorial opinion and soon he reported to Kamin that he was impressed. Perhaps this was predictable, since West, as Josephine Herbst has observed, "had something of . . . Williams' approach to language . . . that it be living and fresh." Williams, the first critic to give West the acceptance for which he yearned, never after wavered in his enthusiasm for West's work.

In consequence of Williams's report, *The Dream Life of Balso Snell* was accepted as the first Contact Edition to be published by Moss and Kamin. As it happened, it would also be the last. West's book would stand in 1931 as the conclusion of a list that epitomized—in Gertrude Stein, Hemingway, and Robert M. Coates's *Eater of Darkness*—the best experiment of the twenties. This was historically fitting, since West would carry out in the thirties the intentions and literary hopes of the twenties.

West reached an agreement with Moss and Kamin, not to subsidize the publication, but to guarantee the sale of 150 of the 500 copies printed. (As late as 1937 he still had a few copies remaining.) Dashiell Hammett read and criticized his final manuscript, and John Sanford helped him to correct proofs in an apartment on Bank Street which West rented for this purpose. At last, in the spring of 1931, handsomely bound in deluxe paper covers, 500 numbered copies ("300 for sale in America and 200 . . . for Great Britain and the Continent") of this octavo edition of *The Dream Life of Balso Snell* were offered to the public at $3 a copy.

When West had first submitted his manuscript to Kamin, he had as his epigraph a quotation from Kurt Schwitters that sums up his attitude toward the book: "Everything that the artist expectorates is art." However ugly the material, however mundane the substance—as in Duchamp's signing of a urinal—however offensive to ordinary or cultivated tastes, whatever the true artist produces constitutes art. This is the only way in the modern world, West was saying, that the integrity of art could be guaranteed. His art is his style, his way of behaving and taking and shaping reality, his way of telling truth. Like Schwitters's *Merzkunst* collage, West's book would be an act of defiance, not a gesture of despair. If he made a fictional collage out of scraps and fragments—the garbage of modern civilization—it was to deny that civilization ultimate power, since the artist, in his own power, could still make use of even the worst aspects of his culture. Like the "garbage monument" of a colleague of Schwitters's,

Johannes Baader, West's book would be implicitly dedicated to the "Greatness and Downfall" of his nation.

In his revisions he substituted for the Schwitters quotation a comic epigraph. His serious intentions, however, are expressed in an advertisement he wrote for the use of Moss and Kamin. Interesting because it states some attitudes only implied in the book, it is also a kind of manifesto. "English humor," it announces, "has always prided itself on being good-natured and in the best of taste. This fact makes it difficult to compare N. W. West with other comic writers, as he is vicious, mean, ugly, obscene and insane." However, the advertisement continues, West can be compared to French writers. "In his use of the violently disassociated, the dehumanized marvellous, the deliberately criminal and imbecilic, he is much like Guillaume Apollinaire, Jarry, Ribemont-Dessaignes, Raymond Roussel, and certain of the surréalistes." Balso Snell's journey, which may also, the ad explains, be compared to Lewis Carroll's famous work, consists of a series of "tales, [all of which] are elephantine close-ups of various literary positions and their technical method; close-ups that make Kurt Schwitters's definition, "Tout ce que l'artiste crache, c'est l'art!' seem like an understatement."

This advertisement makes plain that in 1931 West viewed himself as an artist whose comic vision has its closest parallels in the French tradition and nicely suggests the sense of literary internationalism which he shared at this period with his peers. Balso Snell resembles the short, tight kind of novel which he professed to admire—imaginative, highly witty, and inventive. Many of its themes and methods have close affiliations to Continental preoccupations. Breton, Picasso, Klee, Joyce, and others, of course, had experimented with the dream life of man, the night life of the soul. Scorning ordinary social values and emphasizing man's interior life, the main tendency of experimental literature between 1924 and 1930 had been to turn values inside out—to declare the primacy of dreams over acts, of violence over order, of the sexual gospel of the Marquis de Sade over that of the churches; of arbitrary overcalculated action; and of the criminal, insane man or clown over the bourgeois citizen. Reflecting these preoccupations, La Révolution Surréaliste, for instance, printed extracts from a collection of "beautiful crimes," as well as the depositions of crackpots and criminals, all collected in a mock-scientific way by a "Bureau Central de Recherches Surréalistes." Many of these same impulses West satirized in his Paris tale, "The Impostor."

"To be a writer, as such, was nothing, was passé," Matthew Josephson has summed up this impulse; "to be engaged in a variety of moral experiments was everything." In The Dream Life of Balso Snell, West conducts a moral experiment in the nature and principles of values by plunging into the underworld of the mind, where ordinary values are transformed, strangely twisted—in effect, transvalued—and alternative moralities are given painful birth. West, in America, had the same sense as his European contemporaries of this profound alteration of consciousness. He was hardly alone. The year 1931, when *Balso Snell* appeared, was the first year in American history when the number of people emigrating from the United States was larger than the number immigrating. In the same year, even so distinguished a spokesman of the establishment as Nicholas Murray Butler, president of Columbia University, described this time as one "like the fall of the Roman Empire, like the Renaissance, like the beginning of the political and social revolutions in England and in France in the seventeenth and eighteenth centuries." Now the American Dream seemed to be driving toward nightmare. West sends his "base" man, the material man, the man of smells, on a journey into this renaissance and revolution of the mind. He too emigrates, into a landscape of anguish and horror, by entering the bowels of the Trojan horse and there investigating the mental geography of the Western tradition.

The fiction of journey has built into it certain conventions or expectations, the chief of which, as in *Pilgrim's Progress* and *The Divine Comedy*, is that the journey may symbolize a moving upward, to illumination or purification; second, that it suggests a moving outward, a rebirth. In particular, the Trojan horse, whose body Balso enters, hints at epic triumphs, involvement with dangerous but successful adventuring. But in *Balso Snell*, movement is only vagrant wandering, as dream moves endlessly within dream, all equally grotesque. Instead of rebirth, the book ends merely in an unproductive orgasm, induced by the dream; what is revealed is not archetypal purity but the nightmarish corruption of the id, which West, like Freud, describes as a fetid swamp, "the swamps of my mind." The Trojan horse suggests not epic—West summarized his plans in 1924 as a "parody" of the Troy story—but deception, the deceitfulness of dreams, and thus of the life that these dreams symbolize. His favorite inscription for the book, calling attention to the universality but also to the individual applications of his satire, was: "From one horse's ass to another." All men are deceitful, base Trojan horses. If, in this context, "life," as the epigraph has it, "is a journey," then it is a journey through illusion, and the book which describes it constitutes, like France's *Penguin Island*, the anatomy of illusion, in which West uses as satiric material the ideals which his friends were sponsoring, and toward which he himself was to some extent inclined.

In this first novel West at once faced the problems which he was to take up in all his fiction: how to satirize illusions when they seem necessary in the modern world, when the future of all illusion seems only to be the proliferation of greater illusions; how to assign guilt in the post-Freudian age when even blame has been rendered difficult; and how to make these conditions tragic when both the need and the guilt for illusion lie in the very nature of man and his world. West understood only tentatively here, but with brilliant clarity in his later books, that he would need to invent new literary forms and attitudes whereby to express, for the modern sensibility, moral indignation without righteousness, and a tragic sense without a vision of redemption.

Balso Snell, the American Ulysses and successor to Cabell's Jurgen, is essentially a Babbitt of the imagination, "an ambassador from that ingenious people, the inventors and perfectors of the automatic water-closet," who gives aphoristic advice like: "Play games. Don't read so many books. Take cold showers. Eat more meat," and ". . . run about more. Read less and play baseball." Like any good American tourist, however strange the foreign customs in the bowels of the Trojan horse may be, he is not unduly impressed. He retains a calm demeanor in the face of chaos and, though declaring that "in his childhood things had been managed differently," he has ready both defenses of American life ("You call that dump grand and glorious, do you? Have you ever seen the Grand Central Station, or the Yale Bowl, or the Hollywood Tunnel, or the New Madison Square Garden?") and easy explanations for chaos ("the War, the invention of printing, nineteenth-century science, communism, the wearing of soft hats, the use of contraceptives, the large number of delicatessen stores . . ."). He is a direct descendant of Mark Twain's Innocents, and of other indigenous comic characters discussed by Constance Rourke in her *American Humor*, published the same year as *Balso*.

He comes not to Europe, of course, but to the dream world, in naïve search for principles of identity. One after another Balso encounters, and finds absurd, the major historic forms by which identity has been defined in Western civilization. A series of antagonists define themselves in terms of its major religions; in succession, here where the dream reveals the grotesque essence, Balso sees the absurdity of all—Greek, Jewish, Christian, and such modern religions as those of "Mother Eddy and Doctor Coué." All religions, he concludes, are but the human cry of the flesh against its own extinction: "I won't die! I am getting better and better. . . . The will is master o'er the flesh."

The religion of art, an alternate to these, he recognizes as similarly inadequate, a way of gaining fame, pleasure, admiration, or sexual success. John Raskolnikov Gilson, one of the fictive authors in the novel, writes a *Crime Journal* in which he describes a library as merely a vast charnel house of stinking corpses on which generation after generation feeds like parasites, and then themselves add to the steaming pile. Relying upon Otto Rank and Freud, West, in the consciousness of Balso, reduces art to its biological basis ("I need women and because I can't buy or force them, I have to make poems for them"). "Art," he concludes, "is a sublime excrement."

The central theme of *Balso Snell* is that in contemporary life art has become merely a way by which each man seeks to define his individual ego; his sense of the crisis in his identity has become both his religion and his art. One by one, West will satirize, in "elephantine close-ups," various literary positions. James Joyce had concluded his *Portrait of the Artist as a Young Man* by sending out his hero, an early Ulysses, to encounter his self in experience, and he had had him cry in conclusion: "Old father, old artificer, stand me now and ever in good stead." West's hero, mocking Joyce's epic quest, begins his odyssey with the ejaculation: "O Beer! O Meyerbeer! O Bach! O Offenbach! Stand me now as ever in good stead." On his journey he rejects—since he acts out their absurdity—the kinds of archetypal figures whereby West's artistic contemporaries were conducting the search for self: the criminal figure who discovers his self through his crimes (Dostoevsky's Raskolnikov, the Marquis de Sade); the insane hero, whose insanity is a way of reaching to the truths of self; the clown, the truth of whose self is in his absurdity (Rilke's *Duino Elegies*, Picasso); and the hero whose vision of self is of a streaming sequence of selves—what Ezra Pound called "a broken bundle of mirrors"—and whose identity is defined by the roles he can choose to play, the masks he can assume (Yeats, Conrad Aiken's *Blue Voyage*). Scrutinizing each, he finds all equally absurd. One of the titles by which Balso Snell names the character of his journey, "Anywhere Out of this World," is also the title of a poem by Baudelaire. Just as in that poem, all the attempts at self-definition are rejected; Balso too wants desperately to fly out of this world. He will do so—ending his dreams in an orgasm, as if his dreams and the identity he can find through them are worth no more than that. In this sense, West accurately told an interviewer that *Balso* was written "as a protest against writing books."

But he also told his cousin that *Balso Snell* was "a very professional book, a play on styles." In its stylistic exuberance lies the positive center of the book. West may have abandoned everything in the book by satirizing everything and even giving up the ordinary goal of fiction— representation of society, scene, and character—but his style remains brilliant and accomplished, the successful end of a literary journey. Regarded thus, the book is a boldly rhetorical work in which the author, along with his hero, explores the rhetoric or style of his contemporaries. Balso's journey is of the innocent abroad, but West's is the wise artist's journey in search of a style. The styles which he encounters—a kind of coming to grips with language "with the bare hands," as Williams would say of *Paterson*—are in search of authors. The wooden horse, Balso recognizes, "was inhabited solely by writers in search of an audience."

*Balso Snell* is, then, a language experiment in which West tests out various styles. In its claim for style as the medium of artistic truth—its separation of satire from moral intent—*The Dream Life of Balso Snell* reflects the literary faiths of the twenties in individual expression, in wit, and in defiance of convention. West at this stage was more eloquent in his revisions of his contemporaries than in his own visions but he was brilliant in his criticisms. Easily recognizable are his parodies of Rimbaud and Baudelaire (West plays on their theory of "correspondence"); J. K. Huysmans's *Là Bas* and *En Route*; Joyce and Proust (from whom the epigraph comes); any number of "objectivist" writers, including Williams and Pound; the Dada mode of surrendering language to chains of associa- tions in the subconscious mind, and the attempt to write prose from a poetic point of view, from Robert Desnos to Robert M. Coates; the fantastic comedy of S. J. Perelman's *Parlor, Bedlam and Bath* (originally called *Through the Fallopian Tubes on a Bicycle*); the style of the "tough" school of detective-fiction writers such as Dashiell Hammett; of realistic proletarian fiction like that of Gorky and his American followers in "socialist realism," who all, as was said of Gorky, "look at life from a basement . . . from which he sees only feet of men passing by rubbish pails that stand near his windows"; of *True Story*; of James Branch Cabell (from whom the original plot idea derived); of Rabelais and Voltaire; of dirty jokes (some of which West had told his friends earlier); and of Aldous Huxley and D. H. Lawrence. All are brilliantly etched, as West wrote on a sketch he drew of Beatrice Mathieu in 1930, "by the savage pencil of the master."

He is the master, and his book a masterful play on styles, by virtue of his ability to understand and thus to parody them all. Refusing to make an epic, a "Great American Novel," he made a lyric novel out of his violent American response to European materials. "Lyric novels," he wrote in 1933, "can be written according to Poe's definition of a lyric poem. The short novel is a distinct form especially fitted for use in this country." West, Kamin said, could have a "brashness arising out of his idealism" about art, and "he wanted to do something terribly distin- guished." His book reflects, obviously, intellectual arrogance; but, in his exploration of the styles of his contemporaries, he proves himself a distinguished stylist. For all of West's apparent disillusionment in the book, he, no less, romantically celebrates style. Gilbert Seldes complained in 1926 that American writing was lacking in satire and rebelliousness. West would uniquely fill this need. His satire and savagery, in *Balso Snell*, constituted positive claims for his ability to understand the absurdity of modern poses—role playing in artistic, mythical, or religious terms—and his stylistic dexterity was a declaration that he could see through his contemporaries' art.

In later novels West would make more refined use of his stylistic brilliance. *Balso Snell* shows his virtuosity; in *Miss Lonelyhearts* and *The Day of the Locust*, style is made to illuminate character. But this first novel is crucial to an understanding of West's development because in it he foreshadows in a rough way the attitudes and preoccupations of his later books. The phantom characters who people Balso's dreams—the sainted holy fool, the materialist, the cynic, the scapegoat, the cripple, the grotesque, the sterile modern woman, and the pervert—reappear transmuted. The Quester, Balso himself, will later become Miss Lonelyhearts, Lemuel Pitkin, and Tod Hackett. All are caught in their own or others' illusions. The paradoxical themes of the duality of body and soul, good and evil, of unfulfilling reality leading to unsatisfactory wishes, of violence and the futility of action, all first occur in *Balso*. The myths of success, redemption, innocence, and idealism West will examine again and again. In this first book West's hero enters the Trojan horse of illusion. In his last novel Tod Hackett finds among the "dream-dump" of old Hollywood sets "the wooden horse of Troy." Like Tod, West was to follow the path of Balso all along, through a world littered with the sad rubble of hopes and dreams.

# T. R. STEINER

# West's Lemuel and the American Dream

Nathanael West's A Cool Million remains the least appreciated of his works, to a large extent because it has not been read properly. Its mode of operation is only partially understood at best; hence readers' responses are at the same time not serious enough and too serious. Like the Horatio Alger novels, on which it is based (and in a way like Gulliver's Travels, from which it draws the name of its hero, Lemuel Pitkin), A Cool Million frequently purports to be a children's book. As such, although its literary mode may be parody or mock-heroic, West's novel is also fantasy, myth, dream-wish identification, imaginative "redemption," and pure play. Because of this important "latent content," the book much more resembles The Dream Life of Balso Snell and Miss Lonelyhearts (called a modern myth by Victor Comerchero) than one might first have suspected. Its great difference from these earlier works is that they are more arty—a quality toward which West manifested much ambivalence.

I do not deny that the book has "serious" social and political content, and clearly shows West's anxiety that a Hitlerian dictatorship might come to Depression-fragmented America. But this content is trite: demagoguery and the blind force of mass-man had been staples of cultural and political analysis since de Tocqueville, Burckhardt, and Nietzsche had outlined them as particular dangers of democracy. West seems not so much interested in the fact of these monstrosities as in the popular imagination which makes it easier for them to thrive. That, rather than Nathan

From The Southern Review 4, vol. 7 (October 1971). Copyright © 1971 by Louisiana State University.

"Shagpoke" Whipple, is the arch-villain of his book. As overt pulp-magazine fiction, A Cool Million is a mirror of the popular imagination—an early piece of pop art, like Rauschenberg or Lichtenstein, using American cultural materials to comment on them, chanting American themes in a skewed, that is to say, "true," fashion. Here, it insinuates, is the landscape of the American psyche, which needs and creates Horatio Alger, racial stereotypes, pulp pornography. If we required yet another foil to make the mode of A Cool Million clear, it would be the many commentators on mass culture from Freud to Robert Warshow and Susan Sontag, but most notably George Orwell in his examination of boys' weekly papers and lewd postcards to get at the common Englishman. For a comparable reason, West consciously wrote a pornographic penny dreadful.

It is, therefore, meaningless to talk of West's style in the book since his effort must have been to divest himself of style, to become a scarcely literate and dirty-minded adolescent. West "supplies" only the invisible frame—the skewing of speeches, the introduction of super-grotesqueries, the revelation of what happens after the jump-cut—in short, the consciousness which the reader perceives above and controlling the naïve materials, the consciousness revealed by the mere fact of West's recognizable name on the book. So, the Alger material becomes very sophisticated and the skeleton for, as well as merging with, a whole series of American motifs, fictions, and myths; American Dreams certainly, but also American Nightmares. The American Boy wants to succeed and honorably have the boss's daughter (or at least a clean "white" girl like Fiedler's Blonde Maiden) but he also wants to destroy (in fantasy roles like the gangster) and to brutally deflower. He wouldn't mind being Tom Baxter piggishly taking frail Betty; he lusts after the international, dark sex of Wung's House of All Nations, and like the American Girl, desires exotic experience (but preferably with fabricated authenticity). Alger's hero becomes the picaro (the myth tends readily toward this metamorphosis because of American cultural and geographic mobility), touching North and South, mine and corral, farm and frontier. Here are Davy Crockett, Abe Lincoln, and the martyr Patrick Henry; here, introduced in one of Whipple's speeches, the great military landmarks—"Remember the Alamo! Remember the Maine!" Here Chingachgook and the comity of American bloods like that in Cooper and Melville. In outline, sketchy, fragmented, jocose form, then, A Cool Million is the encyclopedia of mythic "America." And West realizes that the Dreams mask horrors and coexist with nightmares—American xenophobia, anxiety, fear of the culturally exotic. Hence the racial stereotypes: cops are always Irish and revel in brutality; Chinese are inscrutable "celestials"; Indians retain the redness of their savagery; Jews, in their craft and cunning, deceive and steal. American populism hates, fears, but also identifies with the foreign, which enables it to have its darker fantasies. It is like Hitler, who (according to Alan Ross and Norman Cohn) turned the Jew into both the dark father whom he strove to destroy and the dark actor who fulfilled his erotic wishes. Although the Deep South riot which West describes could happen, West is least concerned with describing present reality, or predicting the future; the riot is a "sign of the times," a symbolic probability (very much in the Aristotelian sense) given the real nature of the native American psyche. It is a pleasing fiction to that psyche, the inverse corollary to the "constructive" egoism of the Alger myth. West sees, indeed, that whatever their outward manifestation, however much self-control or sacrifice even our good myths demand, they are power-myths either in essence or application, violent by nature as is every page of A Cool Million.

The dreams of power are analyzed as to their archetypes; so is the dream of martyrdom. For the essential structure of the book is not the successful life of an Alger protagonist but the creation of a martyr-hero for Whipple's National Revolutionary Party—the life not of J. P. Morgan but a mock-Christ. Strangely, those critics who see West as a symbolist, his central fictions as quest and sacrifice, and Lonelyhearts as a modern Christ, have not recognized the underlying fable of A Cool Million. Like Christ but without His consciousness, Pitkin bears a Revealed New Life, suffers, and dies for his Dream, leaving his "message" to American youth. Lemuel (the name means, literally, "belonging to God") has no earthly father; we are asked to see him (through the name of his widowed mother Sarah) as Isaac, Christ's type as sacrificial victim in the Old Testament. Whipple is his spiritual father, sending him into the world with a blessing (and, ironically, like Judas "selling" him to that world with the loan of thirty dollars). Before the quest—an attempt quite literally to "save his house"—begins, Lem kills the "furious animal" which assails the innocent Betty, conquers the bestial, pig-eyed Tom Baxter, but is tricked by that fraudulent "butcher boy," in an incident prefiguring his future defeats. Still, Lem tries to live the destined life, is kind, charitable, self-sacrificing; experiences degradation and poverty for Whippleism (the avatar of the Dream); and is slowly destroyed by the world his message is trying to "save." (Modern America here is Sodom, the Cities of the Plain, Roman Judaea—or their modern manifestation, Eliot's Waste Land, which West clearly seems to call on.) At least once, Pitkin is explicitly likened to Christ. Having been arrested for trying to accuse the powerful brother-keeper Wu Fong, he protests: " 'But I'm innocent . . . I'm innocent,' repeated Lem, a little desperately. 'So was Christ,' said Mr. Barnes with a sigh, 'and they nailed him' " (Ch. 21). And they nail Pitkin, in the mock crucifixion of the music-hall scene. Standing between the two comics, Riley and Robbins (is it far-fetched to see this name as deliberately evoking the two thieves?), who use his destroyed body as a comic prop, Pitkin begins the revolutionary speech prepared for him by Whipple: " 'I am a clown . . . but there are times when even clowns must grow serious. This is such a time. I . . .' Lem got no further. A shot rang out and he fell dead, drilled through the heart by an assassin's bullet" (Ch. 31). Brilliantly, West prevents Lem from stepping out of his role. He must be interpreted by Whipple on the national holiday, Pitkin's Birthday, which combines in a socio-religious ceremony elements of Washington's and Lincoln's Birthdays, Armistice Day, and Christmas: "Simple was his pilgrimage and brief, yet a thousand years hence, no story, no tragedy, no epic poem will be filled with greater wonder, or be followed by mankind with deeper feeling, than that which tells of the life and death of Lemuel Pitkin. . . . Although dead, yet he speaks. . . . He did not live or die in vain. Through his martyrdom the National Revolutionary Party triumphed, and by that triumph this country was delivered. . . . America became again American." Pitkin the redeemer: although "dismantled," his mantle has fallen on other shoulders. The book ends with a striking triptych: on the reviewing stand, as thousands of American youth "March for Pitkin," are Pitkin's mother (his Mary), Betty Prail (surely in her prostitution the Magdalene) and Whipple, at once the God, Judas, and Pope of Pitkinism.

So, joco-seriously, West sees Christ the hero in Horatio Alger, and a large degree of the Alger quality in Christ. The Greatest Story Ever Told has become in this book pulp-magazine uplift, and West realizes that for the popular imagination, Christ (or the archetypal questing hero) can function either as victor or victim. The risen "Christ" is an identificatory model; the fallen, defenseless recipient of our yearning aggression. We worship the powerful, successful "Christ"; we prey on the meek, submissive, idealistic. Indeed, what West seems most responsive to in the Alger myth, and in some of the other American myths he parodies, is that they are exploitative. In the fallen world of modern America, the promises of the American Dream are used to harness the idealism, energy, and altruism of the young. The culture myth, in this novel transmitted by Whipple to Pitkin, implicitly says to the child, "The world is your oyster. Go out and succeed." But it does not prepare him for social and political realities; indeed, by its lie it disables him in the inevitable competition with knowing adults and boys who have wised up. Yet, the cultural ideal endures, virtually through the destruction of the idealistic child, betrayed promiscuously to sharper, con man, Indian, Southerner, WASP, Jew.

However sympathetic Whipple may be at times, however consciously idealistic, he is the exploiter (already in the first scene bilking the innocent Lem). And however much of a loony Pitkin is, he functions— like Candide or Parson Adams—as the ingenue in satire, establishing (obviously without force of validity) an unshakeable blind belief in the right, the good, the committed.

Through his belief in the Dream, Pitkin is not only like the shoddy, sentimental Alger, but also like Clyde Griffiths, Gatsby, and the host of ingenue martyr-heroes of American twentieth-century fiction. But in one very significant way, A Cool Million differs from the novels of West's later friend, Fitzgerald, and "Swedes" like Dreiser. Its difference lies in the fact that A Cool Million was written by a Jew, and West's Jewishness deepens as well as personalizes this seemingly abstract, shallow book. Although the two-dimensionality may be attributed to aesthetic distancing, I think that it resulted mainly from West's conscious attempt to use a "witty" symbolic mode and his desire, conscious or not, to mythicize his own cultural experience. By the "Jewish" element I do not mean something as simple as West's often cited "anti-Semitism," which we are told led to the unsympathetic portraits of Jews in this book and the others (where are there sympathetic portraits here of any ethnic type?), because I think that West was no more anti-Semitic than many assimilated Jews. (To call the low self-esteem or self-hatred of these people—often resulting from their acceptance of the American Dream—anti-Semitism is ludicrously inaccurate.) In A Cool Million, West's Jewishness begins to be seen in the intertwining of native American and Christian (and New Testament) with Jewish (and Old Testament) strains. The hero, his mother, his spiritual father, indeed almost every character in the book, has at least one Jewish (or Hebrew) name: Yankees like Nathan Whipple, Levi Underdown, Ephraim Pierce; Indians like Jake Raven and Israel Satinpenny; an Irish Moe Riley; and Jewish Patriarchs like Asa Goldstein, Ezra Silverblatt, Seth Abromovitz. There is a lot of incidental fooling with these names— Jake Raven is violent ("raving," "ravin"); Satinpenny's first name reminds us of the commonplace equation of Red Indians with the Lost Tribe; two characters "pierce" and "rile," two Jews, are associated with pelf—but I think that their main point is to posit modern America as a kind of conglomerate, ironic Chosen People, sharing not only names but characteristics and cultural "artifacts." Thus, Asa Goldstein sells "Colonial Exteriors and Interiors" and Ezra Silverblatt supplies coonskin caps and other accessories to Whipple's Party. (For their trading in Americana, even at their own expense, Jews are indeed satirized heavily.) But the Yankees and Indians also are characterized by their greed and financial rapacity, while the two lawyers who "get" Pitkin are Seth Abromovitz and Elisha Barnes. The characteristic which all share is their violence, whether overt like that of Irish cops, Southern lynch mobs, or Indians, or disguised like that of Warden Purdy, who has all of Pitkin's teeth knocked out "to prevent infection." By taking the melting-pot metaphor seriously, making it one constructive principle of his book, West suggests that the Hebrew, Christian, and American myths are interpenetrable, indeed, interchangeable for "explaining" life in these eclectic United States. All of them talk about one life, which is man's.

But I think that the cultural interpenetration points to an experience and a problem more personal for West. Where could young Nathan Weinstein (or his Jewish contemporaries) find identificatory cultural myths in a nation whose early heroes are Anglo-Saxon or Nordic, who bear "American" names like George Washington, Abe Lincoln, Ethan Allen, Nathanael Greene, Patrick Henry, Nathan Hale? If Jews had come to the United States in great numbers around the mid-nineteenth century, this might have proved a lesser problem because of the high esteem of Hebraism within the Boston-Concord circle. For two centuries Puritan and Quaker proper names had been consciously and happily chosen from Old Testament figures, and Melville's great diabolic hero is named after a King of Israel while the weaker—albeit less dangerous—men around him are called Starbuck, Stubb, and Flask. By the 1920s, with the anti-Semitism that attended mass immigration, there was little if any esteem: our culture heroes, "Black Jack" Pershing, George Herman "Babe" Ruth, Charles Lindbergh "the American Eagle" (Horatio Alger may well stand for all of these), were not Jews, and if they accidentally had Hebrew or "Jewish" names this stood in ironic counterpoint (as it does in A Cool Million) to their frequent anti-Semitism. Thus, in confronting American folk-heroes and culture myths, Jewish youth were at a farther remove than Hoosier farm-boys: the fictive distance of myth was there for everyone, but Horatio Alger did not even seem to be about Jews (this was also a problem for Poles, Italians, and Negroes, but West was none of these). Fiction after fiction said to them: "We're not about you." I am reminded of a fairly recent one, the Gillette Blade comic strip of the 1940s. Its obviously Anglo-Saxon heroes lived adventurous lives, saved archetypal American Beauties from horrible fates, and thus met their industrialist daddies. Then, metamorphosed by an obligatory shower and shave (the point of the ad), each hero would win both the Girl and the Job. But hath not the Jew a beard since it can be pulled? Mordecai Richler has spoken similarly of the dearth of Jewish identificatory models in sports, and thus can explain the almost hysterical ethnic responses to Sandy Koufax and Hank

Greenberg (*Commentary*, Nov. 1966). (I remember a different tactic: in the early forties identifying with football players whose first name was the same as mine; hence, sharp in memory is not only Tom Harmon but the forgotten Tom Kuzma.) *A Cool Million* is implicitly about this problem, and West, again joco-seriously, says that the American mythic landscape is about and for Jews if they attend to it closely enough. Another, a more decisive, way to get into "America" was to change one's name, and West also did that.

We must not forget that West, for all the protestations of his non-Jewishness, lived a life so typical culturally that as I read James Light's brief account of it I frequently lived over remembered scenes. The son of immigrant parents, he began early to drift away from what little ethnic heritage he had—I would guess, from Light's version, because of the religious indifference of his father and the nominalist conception of Judaism by his mother. After an undistinguished high school career, he divested all the trappings at Brown, becoming an aesthete and Brooks Brothers dandy, writing for the rather avant-garde college literary magazine and making many non-Jewish friends. Still, despite his friendship with members of the elite Christian fraternities, he was never pledged by one because of their exclusion clauses; and, later, despite his winning the Christian girl, he never wed her—perhaps in part, as Light suggests, because of "the religious difference." He changed his name in 1926, before leaving for France; moreover, he had been playing around with the persona "Nathan von Wallenstein Weinstein" for a long time. I would not do justice to the complexity of West's life, to his two-year Parisian sojourn and all of the other experiences which made him other than some pasteboard "fallen Jew," but the skeleton of that life is almost ludicrously exemplary, down to the pragmatic and possessive Jewish mother who moved in to serve "lavish meals" at his farm when he was a thirty-year-old practicing writer, and to his happy marriage of seven months—ended by double tragedy—to "My Sister Eileen," surely an archetypal American Girl.

So, *A Cool Million* is also symbolic spiritual autobiography—or for those who are wary of "biographical fallacy," an interplay of fictive positions which might have gone on in the head of West or some other second-generation "alien" boy. The novel records confrontation with the American myth. It certainly does not seem coincidental that Alice, the daughter of Levi Underdown, whom Lem saves by a bit of derring-do, echoes in name his sweetheart Alice Shephard; nor that this fictional "romantic" young lady, having "misunderstood the incident," at the same time protects and rejects Pitkin: "She smiled kindly at our hero, and led her irate parent from the scene" (Ch. 11). But this is at best windowdressing, an insider's joke, resembling others which seem directed at friends like S. J. Perelman. More importantly, much in the novel suggests that West identified with both his major characters. One, like Proust's Marcel and Kafka's "K.," carries the name of his creator—Nathan Whipple, Nathan Weinstein, Nathanael West. The other is the young hero, the Christ, the American quester. He belongs to God, and he is the Lamb of God, like Christ, like the symbolic "Isaac" sacrificed by Abraham, like the *lemmele* his name suggests. But like Christ, and as his role demonstrates, Lemuel is also the holy fool (in Yiddish, the *lemech*). His last name also provides a range of associations: "kin" of the everlasting "pit" as Comerchero suggests? A relative of the mass audience which sits in the pit? Like the flea Saint Puce of *Balso* who lives in the armpit of Our Lord? A little bit of damnation himself? Pitkin Avenue, the Fifth Avenue and Champs Elysees of Jewish Brownsville? The relationship of Whipple and Pitkin is complex: Whipple is adult, practical, experienced, platitudinous, but ultimately successful; Pitkin is child, innocent, without language, a failure, but idealistic. I have already shown Whipple to be the God-Judas-Pope of Pitkinism. The relationship of the two also resembles that between Abraham and Isaac—Whipple "silently communes" with the picture of Abe Lincoln (Ch. 3), obviously his model—but this mythic relation is ironically skewed like all the others as Abraham sacrifices his "son," not a symbol. All of the myths show division and ambivalence in West's imagination: an "adult" cultural voice presents images of success—known to be evil—to the aspiring adolescent, who is destroyed in their pursuit. And the adult self, Nathan, still strangely tied to West's former life, scourges the "American Boy" idealist, figuratively "whipping" him for temerity. It is the same kind of near-hysterical punishment of the questing innocent which underlies some of Swift's best satires: "Fool, how dare you aspire to a lot which is not man's? How dare you be other than a vile human." The author seems to be pointing to the probable cost of his having "gone West," in this book very nearly equated with having gone "Whipple," since that worthy allies himself with such American clichés and at one point leads a gold-mining expedition West. "Going West"—opting for a life that mirrors the national dream—may beckon to the adolescent as ideal personal fulfillment; for the adult it means taking the national lie with full comprehension, with little real to compensate for lost innocence, altruism, and the particulars of an individual past. The book ends with no resolution of its underlying conflict, no synthesis of impossible innocence and vile experience, no celebration of heroic loss in the face of insuperable odds. Nathan Whipple has only venal success; but Lem Pitkin has died meaninglessly, in fact, in support of Whipple's Know-Nothing American-ism. One cannot live either as Child or Adult. A *Cool Million* also seems to examine the author's artistic decisions and the meaning of going West as a novelist. Near the end of the book both Pitkin and Whipple are constantly before audiences and show two presentational styles: Pitkin is the straight man, boffoing audiences by his deformities (are there echoes of *Balso Snell* here?), witlessly feeding their destructive lust, but never in control of his own act; Whipple is in control, lulling or inciting them with flatulent pieties, but totally wrapped in an inhuman rhetoric. Lem is killed just as he is about to speak seriously in his own person; and Whipple gets the girl, Lem's proud mother (West's wanted him to go into a more successful line than writing), and power. To command the audience of a hundred thousand, however, he debases the materials of Lem's passion into the heroic inanities of Americanism. Might this not have seemed the danger if Nathanael were to go all the way West?

The reader may be sympathetic to my analysis of the book so far, but I could never convince him—nor would I try—that he was reading anything but a low burlesque, a piece of slapstick. The tone is little like that of other "serious" books, unlike that of *Balso*, which is self-consciously artistic and derivatively literary, unlike *Gulliver* or the learned wit of *Gargantua*; most, I suppose, like the black comedies of our time. How do we explain this crude tone? What is West saying by it? Apparently, that if our Dreams derive from the popular imagination, they inevitably embody and reflect the quality of that imagination. American life may be verifiably grotesque, incredibly destructive in its effects, but in the average mind it registers in a form banal, slightly titillating, clichéd, impossible to take seriously. The mass—for whatever reasons, not the least of which is the seduction of fantasy—is uncaring of, anesthetized to, real experience. In popular apprehension, rape, for example, is not the brutal and painful forcing of a real woman, but something histrionic, played out in an "ideal" world of fancy, somehow detached from rapist and rapee—therefore, potentially ludicrous: "In the half gloom of the cabin . . . the Pike man [was] busily tearing off Betty's sole remaining piece of underwear. She was struggling as best she could, but the ruffian from Missouri was too strong for her. . . . At the sight of poor Lem weltering in his own blood, Betty fainted. In no way disturbed, the Missourian went coolly about his nefari-ous business and soon accomplished his purpose" (Ch. 26). On the one hand, this event is made meaningless; on the other, it shows West can write better soft-core pornography than the professionals. The rape of Betty exemplifies two key effects of *A Cool Million*: while deliberately pandering to the American predilection for lust and violence, it drains, through the even-tempered mechanicalness of its language, all human significance from its events. West forces the reader to see the artificiality of this language, but seems in no way to comment on it. That is, he does not posit—even by indirection—a more humane or moral use of language, certainly not an "art" use. (Indeed, the pretension of art is one of the balloons he pricks repeatedly from *Balso Snell* on.) And once again, West uses the medium to comment pessimistically on his own writing. He seems to be saying, "Look how well I write in these trashy American forms." Another in the line of American apocalyptists, closer to loving pornography and violence than hating them, West seems to point to the degree to which American Dreams and the mass psyche have penetrated his own imagination.

*A Cool Million*, then, is about the American power-success-violence ethic and how much it has corrupted even its satirist. Surely West, with his knowledge of Spengler, recognized that by taking his new name he was identifying himself with the decline of a doomed civilization. In *Day of the Locust* he comes to the farthest American Abendland, California, where the refugees from the nation's great heart have come to die. "Going West" becomes synonymous with the death wish, and we have been told that of all humanity which West hated, he hated himself most. In this context, the epigraph of the book, "John D. Rockefeller would give a cool million to have a stomach like yours," is ambiguous and frightening. Clearly it points to the psychosomatic danger of following the American Dream in its real nature, since Rockefeller and Henry Ford are for Whipple and the book types of Horatio Alger. But who is the "you" to whom the epigraph is addressed? Is it the reader (the "cool million," the "hypocrite lecteur," West's *semblable* and *frère*) who can live in that world and read the fantasy-record of its degradation without flinching? Or is it the author himself, in one of his persons so inured to horror and filth that he can treat it lightly, so much of—or aloofly above—degraded mankind that he does not retch as he records?

It may be late in the day to speak of any important American writer, much less Nathanael West, as a Jewish writer, and to involve one's own experience of Jewishness in a discussion of him. To do so invites scorn and misunderstanding. To do so, now that the Jews have made it very nearly to the center of the White Establishment, and other groups are suffering even more intensely their traditional fate of exclusion, runs the risk of seeming dated. Yet Leslie Fiedler in a *Partisan* essay (Summer, 1967) called West, for *Balso Snell*, the first of the modern American Jewish writers, and he is right—at least as far as *Balso* and *A Cool Million* are concerned. It is valuable, even necessary, to approach West with some understanding of the Jewish cultural milieu, if only to counteract the effect of his near-convert's fascination with Christ in *Miss Lonelyhearts* and to open up the body of Jewish-Hebrew reference in his books. It may be helpful, although certainly not necessary, for the critic to be personally familiar with the particular cultural shocks which West seems to have been an heir to, however much he tried to avoid or deny them. For whatever degree of universality there is in West's fictions about the American scene, I am convinced that he was an intensely personal writer, with a Freudian's heightened awareness that an author by indirections talks of his own wishes and fears and that his symbols plot his own inner landscape.

MILES D. ORVELL

# The Messianic Sexuality of "Miss Lonelyhearts"

Nathanael West's *Miss Lonelyhearts* is a funny and a depressing book; it is also—because of its fragmented shape and imagistic logic—a difficult book. How, precisely, can we define the character's problem? And how are we to judge the crisis and resolution of the tale? What are its broad implications? These questions have been essayed before but not, I think, without making certain unwarranted assumptions about the psychology of the character. For example, some critics have felt the key to Miss Lonelyhearts lies in his putative homosexuality; yet Randall Reid's rebuttal of that view I take to be conclusive. Reid's own assumption is that there is a conflict within Miss Lonelyhearts, between his carnal urges and his impulse to imitate Christ; between Eros and Agape, to use the terms he prefers. Miss Lonelyhearts' tensions can be resolved, as Reid puts it, by "replacing Eros with Agape—only, that is, by transcending the human and invoking the divine." Yet is this view satisfactory?

The problem for the critic is an interesting one: he wants to understand the "psychology" of Miss Lonelyhearts but is wary—in the face of the fragmented evidence—of positing an etiology, particularly when he has read West's own comment, in "Some Notes on Miss L.," that "psychology has nothing to do with reality nor should it be used as motivation. The novelist is no longer a psychologist. Psychology can become something much more important." I am not sure how seriously we

---

From *Studies in Short Fiction* 2, vol. 10 (Spring 1973). Copyright © 1973 by Newberry College.

can take these cryptically tantalizing remarks, but it would not be inconsistent with their spirit—and the book supports us here—to say that West "used" psychology to elucidate the quality of a culture. (It was, after all, as a "priest of our time" that West thought of his protagonist.) And that is my own assumption: that Miss Lonelyhearts is not so much a case history as an example of one deeply felt response—perhaps the only one possible, West is saying—to the condition of the modern world.

We may locate most generally the source of Miss Lonelyhearts' malaise in the chapter "Miss Lonelyhearts on a Field Trip" when the columnist awaits the arrival of Fay Doyle in a little park whose decayed surface had earlier been described as "not the kind in which life generates" (p. 70. Page references are to *The Complete Works of Nathanael West*, ed. Alan Ross, New York: Farrar Straus, 1957). It is a perfect setting for Miss Lonelyhearts to ruminate on his own great exhaustion. Looking around him, he at last discovers in the encroaching skyscrapers—in their "tons of forced rock and tortured steel"—what he thinks is a clue: "Americans have dissipated their racial energy in an orgy of stone breaking. In their few years they have broken more stones than did centuries of Egyptians. And they have done their work hysterically, desperately, almost as if they knew that the stones would some day break them" (p. 100).

Earlier cultures like the Egyptian, West is saying, maintained themselves as balanced energy systems; our own dissipates its vital energy not only in the ceaseless construction, destruction, and reconstruction of its cities, but in the other evidences of orgiastic materialism—the pawnshop window's "paraphernalia of suffering" (p. 104)—that Miss Lonelyhearts is sensitive to. In a larger sense, the columnist's deadness seems almost a condition of material existence itself ("the physical world has a tropism for disorder, entropy" [*ibid.*]), and it is precisely this sense of a world run down, fragmented, chaotic, that pervades the urban imagery of *Miss Lonelyhearts*.

While enervation, then, defines the condition of the land, its people, and its would-be savior, that is not the whole story. At least with Miss Lonelyhearts there is also, and most significantly, a *fear* of the power of regeneration. West indicates this fear through certain highly charged dream-like scenes, and I might mention, as the first, an incident that precedes the columnist's evening with Mary Shrike. Miss Lonelyhearts has been out walking and has paused to rest in the little park that had earlier figured as an emblem of the earth's sterility. Now, slumped on a bench opposite the Mexican War obelisk, he fantasies in its shadow a monumental erection—and it frightens him: "The stone shaft cast a long, rigid shadow on the walk in front of him. He sat staring at it without knowing why until he noticed that it was lengthening in rapid jerks, not as shadows usually lengthen. He grew frightened and looked up quickly at the monument. It seemed red and swollen in the dying sun, as though it were about to spout a load of granite seed" (p. 89).

What went unnoticed before is that this fear of sexual power can be linked with Miss Lonelyhearts' fear of the power of Christ—that West has assumed a radical and unsuspected association of sexual and messianic energy. Early in the novella the columnist's long-standing obsession with Christ is revealed and the details of that obsession must be noted. Christ, for Miss Lonelyhearts, is not simply the all-embracing love that he reads of in *The Brothers Karamazov* and that Shrike mocks. The image of Christ stirs in him darker, more primitive powers that seem to give to the sterile world about him a primal vitality; and yet, again, fear prevents the flowering of this spiritual autoerotism:

> As a boy in his father's church, he had discovered that something stirred in him when he shouted the name of Christ, something secret and enormously powerful. He had played with this thing, but had never allowed it to come alive.
>
> He knew now what this thing was—hysteria, a snake whose scales are tiny mirrors in which the dead world takes on a semblance of life. And how dead the world is . . . a world of doorknobs.
>
> (p. 75)

Fulfilling his wish for potency, Miss Lonelyhearts then dreams that he is a magician "who did tricks with doorknobs. At his command they bled, flowered, spoke" (p. 76). But that is only the first part of his dream; for the reverse of the dream of desired potency is the dream of dreaded failure: "After his act was finished, he tried to lead his audience in prayer. But no matter how hard he struggled, his prayer was one Shrike had taught him and his voice was that of a conductor calling stations" (*ibid.*). Between excitement and fear, between potency and failure, Miss Lonelyhearts is ambivalently suspended.

This early chapter bears further scrutiny. It begins with a picture of Miss Lonelyhearts' monastic room, on a wall of which he has hung "an ivory Christ"—removed from the cross. The effect aimed at—a primitive intensity of feeling—is not immediately achieved: "Instead of writhing, the Christ remained calmly decorative" (p. 75). But when he fixes his eyes on the image and begins to chant his name orgiastically, the phallic figure (like the Mexican War obelisk later) frightens him: " 'Christ, Christ, Jesus Christ. Christ, Christ, Jesus Christ.' But the moment the snake started to uncoil in his brain, he became frightened and closed his eyes" (p. 76). A similar fear of the energy that is unleashed within him at the name of Christ is what inhibits the performance of the public, priestly role that Miss Lonelyhearts dreams of, in a scene he conjures up from college days: he has agreed, with some friends, to buy and roast a lamb in the woods, "on the condition that they sacrifice it to God before barbecuing it" (*ibid.*). At the moment of sacrifice, however, Miss Lonelyhearts orgiastically chants the name of Christ and this time his fear forces him to botch the killing. The dream ends a nightmare as the boys flee. But Miss Lonelyhearts, overcome with guilt at the misery of the mutilated lamb, goes back and crushes its head with a stone—thus foreshadowing his characteristic response to the suffering who appeal to him for help; or rather, his response to his inability to help them.

West has given us, then, a character for whom Christ is at once a sexual and a spiritual power—Eros *and* Agape—and yet who is himself, by virtue of his cynical culture, too "rational" to believe in him and too exhausted and fearful to accept irrationally that source of energy. The result is that Miss Lonelyhearts, as savior and as lover, is a failure; and as failure, capable of violent rage. Some such analysis may well lie behind West's observation, in "Some Notes on Violence," that "in America violence is idiomatic. . . . In America violence is daily." *Miss Lonelyhearts* is social criticism, but of a special sort, let it be noted. The sources of violence and frustration for West do not lie in any specific economic situation (he did not have, one might say, the optimism to be a Communist at this time and he shunned the polemic literature of the thirties) but rather in a more fundamental relationship of an individual to his culture, a Whitmanesque relationship that is felt in *Miss Lonelyhearts* chiefly as a need for manifold regeneration. It is as if Franklin's Poor Richard had awakened after some 200 years of fitful slumber to find an America neither healthy, wealthy, nor wise, and crying, in its depravity, for something like Jonathan Edwards' surprising conversion through the excellency of Christ. And for Miss Lonelyhearts, this excellency is sexual and spiritual.

I am not sure how West reached such a conception of Christ. He did read T. S. Eliot and Jessie Weston and may have come to it by route of the Fisher King. Conceivably it was the ironic flowering of his own dream of escape from what he considered the commercial commonplaceness of his Jewish background—for he had throughout college, it seems, a connoisseur's interest in church history and ritual, Christian mysticism and black magic.

What is more certain, however, is that there are, in the blend of satire and farce in West's first work, *The Dream Life of Balso Snell* (allowing for the admitted parody of J. K. Huysmans' carnal mysticism), certain adumbrations of the imagery and motifs of *Miss Lonelyhearts*. Thus, for example, early in the course of his intra-alimentary canal explorations, the adventuring Balso comes upon Maloney the Areopagite, a "catholic mystic," who is writing the biography of Saint Puce, "a flea who was born, lived, and died, beneath the arm of our Lord" (p. 11). What is interesting for the later *Miss Lonelyhearts* is Maloney's conception of the Godhead as a physical, procreative force (Maloney imagines the flea to have been fathered by the "Dove or Paraclete—the Sanctus Spiritus") and the emphasis on the manhood of the man-God Christ (Maloney envies the flea his physical as well as spiritual nourishment under the arm of Christ [see pp. 11–12]). A more direct anticipation of the messianic sexuality of Miss Lonelyhearts can be seen in the long, convoluted final episode of *Balso Snell*, where Balso dreams he loves a "beautiful hunchback" whom he rescues, by his passion, from a life of vicarious solaces and dreams (see p. 38). Balso's courtship seems a grotesque foreshadowing of Miss Lonelyhearts' own dreams of saving the deformed, the frustrated, and the victimized, by the force of his love. (That this was, indeed, an aspect of West's own imagined relationship toward the "masses" and toward the woman whom he eventually married, is suggested by Jay Martin in his biography of West.)

Returning now to *Miss Lonelyhearts*, we have an additional perspective from which to judge the culmination of the plot; for when Miss Lonelyhearts agrees to meet Fay Doyle (the weighty address of her letter somehow appeals to the columnist) it is clear that, in his own mind, the roles of savior and lover have become fused. This we can see in the image that occurs to him while he plays with the letter: "Like a pink tent, he set it over the desert [where, he imagines, his readership dwells]. Against the dark mahogany desk top, the cheap paper took on rich flesh tones. He thought of Mrs. Doyle as a tent, hair-covered and veined, and of himself as the skeleton in a water closet, the skull and cross-bones on a scholar's bookplate. When he made the skeleton enter the flesh tent, it flowered at every joint" (pp. 98–99). With brilliant economy, West uses the resources of surrealism to suggest a fusion of the sexual and the messianic obsessions: the inert skeleton flowering inside the flesh tent; the death's head regenerating inside the tabernacle in the desert.

In the event, however, Miss Lonelyhearts' vitality is not restored by that gross parody of the life-force, Mrs. Doyle. A few chapters later however, Peter Doyle, Fay's crippled husband, turns to Miss Lonelyhearts for help and the result, for the latter, is as close as he will come to feeling like a savior and acting like one. While reading Doyle's letter of appeal, Miss Lonelyhearts accidentally touches the cripple's hand underneath the speakeasy table: "He jerked away, but then drove his hand back and forced it to clasp the cripple's. After finishing the letter, he did not let go, but pressed it firmly with all the love he could manage. At first the cripple covered his embarrassment by disguising the meaning of the clasp with a handshake, but he soon gave in to it and they sat silently, hand in hand" (p. 126). Thus by accident Miss Lonelyhearts discovers a gesture—less than sexual yet more than spiritual—that not only expresses his own need to succor, but consoles the supplicant as well. The effect is intoxicating, and as they make their way back to Doyle's apartment, Miss Lonelyhearts calls on Christ in his joy.

But his triumph is short-lived. In the face of the Doyles' obvious amatory deprivations, Miss Lonelyhearts exhorts them to passion, and, realizing that the exhortation itself lacks passion, he calls forth his own familiar hysteria before the "natural excitement" of Christ: "Christ is love . . . Christ is the black fruit that hangs on the crosstree," he chants. "Man was lost by eating of the forbidden fruit. He shall be saved by eating of the bidden fruit. The black Christ-fruit, the love fruit . . ." (p. 129). (West likens the columnist's feeling at this point to "an empty bottle, shiny and sterile" [ibid.], an aptly hermaphroditic image of his unfruitful role vis-à-vis the Doyles. By the next page, with Mrs. Doyle making a mockery of his message and pressing her "big, strong body" against his own, that bottle is "slowly filled with warm, dirty water.") But the attempt to act out the priestly role is clearly a failure, and Miss Lonelyhearts' consequent frustration and feelings of impotence again induce rage which, completing the familiar pattern, in turn leads to violence. The columnist strikes out at Mrs. Doyle and flees from the house.

Following the climactic episode with the Doyles, Miss Lonelyhearts withdraws into a center of indifference, and, his feelings completely anaesthetized, he imagines his body to be a solid rock. It is a polysemous image, condensing economically several of his psychic needs: on one level, Miss Lonelyhearts' fear of the primitive power unleashed by Christ builds, after the horror of the Doyle episode (he had, it seems, only unleashed Mrs. Doyle's pent up aching waters upon himself), to a veritable petrifaction; certainly the rock is less vulnerable, less penetrable, than the open-ended bottle that preceded it. In addition, the rock carries the traditional Christian association of Peter as the rock upon which the church was built (thus anticipating the "religious experience" Miss Lonelyhearts is to have). In still another sense, Miss Lonelyhearts' dissipated energy seems, by a kind of homeopathic magic, to regather itself into the material likeness of the earlier, phallic Mexican War obelisk.

What is also achieved by the "solidification of his feeling, his conscience, his sense of reality, his self-knowledge" (p. 138) into the rock, is a temporary resolution of the crisis: his ambivalence toward his messianic-sexual identity is "settled" by a paralysis of will. At the same time, though, this paralysis sets free a secondary self—a sham of normality—to deal with the world. It is this latter factitious self that makes arrangements for a future happily married life with his perennial fiancée, Betty—without the usual agonies of conscience.

The price of such a rending of his identity is the fever that overtakes the columnist at the outset of the final chapter: "the rock became a furnace" (*ibid.*). But out of the suffering a "vision" does come; Miss Lonelyhearts does, as the chapter title ironically puts it, have "a religious experience." And there is—however briefly, however subjectively—a regeneration. As Miss Lonelyhearts lies in his bed, the Christ nailed treeless to the wall once more becomes the focus of his consciousness, and the surrounding "dead" furnishings of the room suddenly become a fish that rises to the bait of the fisher of men: " 'Christ! Christ!' This shout echoed through the innermost cells of his body" (p. 139). The old hysteria is released, only this time it is embraced. Miss Lonelyhearts' exhausted spirit is renewed in a moment that, recalling the earlier imagery of the skeleton and skull flowering in the tent, seems to suggest a diffusely sexual, diffusely spiritual regeneration: "His heart was a rose and in his skull another rose bloomed. The room was full of grace."

Whether or not the experience is "genuine" is, it seems to me, largely an irrelevant question. What matters is that Miss Lonelyhearts is himself, at this point, convinced that the experience is real: and in his ecstasy he goes to embrace the cripple Doyle (who has come to blow out the columnist's brains in retribution for what he believes was misconduct with his wife)—thus embracing all of his supplicants ("Desperate, Harold S., Catholic-mother" etc.) with messianic love and healing energies.

Earlier in the novella there is a scene in Delehanty's speakeasy where one of his associates remarks of Miss Lonelyhearts, "Even if he were to have a genuine religious experience, it would be personal and so meaningless, except to a psychologist." And someone else replies, "The trouble with him, the trouble with all of us, is that we have no outer life, only an inner one, and that by necessity" (*ibid.*). I would guess this is West talking here and it is a neat way of crystallizing the dilemma of Miss Lonelyhearts. As if to illustrate dramatically precisely what was meant, West shows us Miss Lonelyhearts, on the following page, dreamily recollecting a moment during his childhood when he had played a piece by Mozart on the piano and his sister had danced to it, "gravely and carefully, a simple dance yet formal" (p. 84). And he imagines the ordered geometry of the dance—"Square replacing oblong and being replaced by circle" (*ibid.*)—replacing the disorder of the world, until every child everywhere is dancing gravely, sweetly. But it is in the rhythm of West's world that this vision, this inner life, cannot remain intact long: the outside world, by its own necessity, collides with the inner one: "He stepped away from the bar and accidentally collided with a man holding a glass of beer. When he turned to beg the man's pardon, he received a punch in the mouth" (p. 85).

It is a scene that foreshadows the conclusion of the book—with this difference: having at last attained what he thought was a regeneration of his own vital energies, Miss Lonelyhearts tries, in one last desperate moment, magically to restore the exhausted and suffering world about him; to move, in other words, from the inner vision to the outer life. Walt Whitman had tried—in his own time, and with a precedent conception of the relatedness of the physical and the spiritual lives—to move from the inner vision to the world, and with a hard, underlying view of the speedy progress America was making toward a muscle-bound, impoverishing materialism; but for Whitman the move had been chiefly imaginative, a matter of poetry and prophecy, and so buoyed by a resurging optimism. West was heir to Whitman's insight that in our modern industrial society spiritual, sexual, and institutional energies are bound together; but it was West's twentieth-century view that regeneration is an agony and, it would seem, a deception. Redemption is impossible; collision—the punch in the mouth, the exploding gun—is inevitable. Miss Lonelyhearts' ascent to God ends with a dead fall "part of the way down the stairs" (p. 140).

MAX APPLE

# History and Case History in "Red Cavalry" and "The Day of the Locust"

There are many immediate comparisons between the works and careers of Isaac Babel and Nathanael West. Babel writing primarily in the 1920's, West in the '30's, both died without making a great impact on the literary world. Each was "promising" in his day, yet lived to be neglected, and each has been fully "resurrected" by the literary tastes of the 1970's. The "figure" of Isaac Babel, growing silent under the Stalinist regime he helped to create, is perhaps more familiar than Babel's stories, although a collection of his early works and other literary fragments is at this moment close to the top of the best seller lists. From the back cover of *The Lonely Years*, an earlier anthology of fragments, Babel's round, joyless face looks out of steel rimmed glasses in a thousand American bookstores. Babel, who finally could not "program" his genius to Soviet demands, is a kind of hero to contemporary Americans who select his works from the lists of their book clubs. Not really a "great," Babel has become in paperback America one to be reckoned with. The popularity of the resurrected West novels is more confined. *Miss Lonelyhearts* and *The Day of the Locust* are more likely to be found on freshman reading lists than on a *New York Times* chart.

The most immediately striking similarity between the Russian's short stories and the American's short novels is the precision of their

From *Nathanael West: The Cheaters and the Cheated, A Collection of Critical Essays*, edited by David Madden. Copyright © 1973 by David Madden. Everett/Edwards, Inc.

syntax and the imagistic speed of their sentences. "Forget the epic," West wrote. "In America fortunes do not accumulate, the soil does not grow, families have no history. Leave slow growth to the book reviewers, you have only time to explode." ("Some Notes on *Miss Lonelyhearts*," *Contempo*, May 15, 1933, p. 2.) Yet West's novels do not crash upon the senses to numb by sheer clatter of bombast. The "explosions" are not the "bombs of those realists" whom Nabokov characterizes as typing "powerful and stark" novels with their thumbs. West and Babel are masters of the power of "containment." Even in dispassionate understatement their events and images threaten sentence by sentence to burst into the wild rhetoric of a Dostoyevsky or a Faulkner. They do not. The effect is virtually the opposite of those grandiose periodic sentences of a Dr. Johnson which ramble gracefully, ironies in hand, toward a solemn conclusion. West and Babel drop periods like knives, using speed to avoid the "explosions" of sentiment. Yet these are not the kind of short sentences which everyone associates with Hemingway. West and Babel draw their "styles" not from the banality of the world as Hemingway does, but from the contrast between the physical awesomeness of events and the paltry resources of language. In a two and one half page story, "With Old Man Makhno," Babel presents a heroine who speaks three words, "Fetch some water." She is a peasant Jewess who has been raped the previous night by six of Makhno's Cossacks. She goes about her daily chores while a slow-witted boy, an aide-de-camp to the staff, reminisces upon what occurred the previous evening. The girl washes clothes. Her "legs, fat, brick red, swollen like globes, gave off a sickly sweet smell like fresh salted meat." (*Collected Stories of Isaac Babel*, World Publishing Co., 1955, p. 278. All page references are from this edition.) As he talks, the boy sticks "strips of gilt paper onto a German helmet" (278). This is not the "banality of evil," it is Babel's brutally understated prose assertion of an offense too awesome to become a story. A peasant girl ravished by diseased Cossacks, an idiot boy retelling her terror while posing before a mirror in a gilded helmet: Babel seems to carve these vignettes into the retina. The short, lyrical sentences are a kind of anesthetic, numbing one's perceptions with literary conventions. It is, after all, a "story." It ends quickly, and with no mess, one progresses to the next short description of life with the Revolution's Cossacks.

West's syntax is neither as brief nor as brutal as Babel's. The self-conscious playfulness of *The Dream Life of Balso Snell* never entirely disappears. West cannot resist the one-liner, the "Chief Kiss-My-Towkus," even in *The Day of the Locust*. Yet this playfulness hovers over the novels like a bird of prey. While Babel catalogues horrors which are the fruits of war, West presents the lives of people who have the leisure to "come to California to die." Suffering in wartime Russia may be no more justifiable than in peace-time Hollywood, yet there is at least some rhetorical satisfaction that underlying Babel's violence is an ideological stance. This posture is of course the belief that the crimes of the Revolution are justified by its glorious end, the very attitude which destroyed Trotsky and ultimately Babel himself. Although West's novels are less bloody than Babel's stories, the overall effect of West's violence is at least as pervasive, since it is always gratuitous violence. There is no revolution, no political or moral ideology, not even a flawed one, to give pseudo-justification to the suffering.

By presenting the exploits of soldiers, Babel implicitly utilizes the most ancient literary motif of men at war. His Cossacks, like Agamemnon's legions, draw ironic force from the contrast between their mean lives and ugly deaths and the abstract ideas of glory in battle or revolutionary equality. West ironically creates his own "Homer," but utilizes no such classical literary heritage. His "armies" await only the opening of a theatre. Without any literary heritage, West relies on internal structural devices for a "historical" sense in The Day of the Locust. He recapitulates violence he has already described. Thus Homer kills Adore Loomis in the same way that Juju kills the red cock. Like Juju, Homer jumps in the air and jabs Adore from above. He uses his heels as Juju used his gaffs. The murder is the only act that Homer commits without his hands. His personality, his very humanity, is encompassed in the few rituals he performs with his hands and fingers. Without these outward signs of order, he is loosed from civilization to kill as a bird in a staged battle.

Tod's role in the final mob scene also recapitulates the iconography of earlier violence committed upon birds. Attempting to escape, Tod performs upon a man what Earle does upon a quail. When Earle poached, he trapped the quail in a small wire basket. The birds "ran wildly along the inner edge and threw themselves at the wire. One of them, a cock, had a dainty plume on his head that curled forward almost to his beak. Earle caught the birds one at a time and pulled their heads off." (Complete Works of Nathanael West, Farrar, Straus, and Cudahy, 1957, pg. 330. All page references are to this edition.) Tod, trapped in the crowd, resembles the birds trapped in the cage. "He couldn't turn his body, but managed to get his head around. A very skinny boy, wearing a Western Union cap, had his back wedged against his shoulder" (416). The Western Union boy, like the cock with the "dainty plume," has his neck wrenched. Tod "finally got his left arm free and took the back of the boy's neck in his fingers. He twisted as hard as he could" (416).

Where Babel seemingly justifies the terror that precedes the dream of the Dictatorship of the Proletariat, West boldly mocks human affairs in the "dream capital." Hollywood is West's perfect symbol, for it offers not only "dreams" but sunshine and new hope. People slither into the California warmth for their last convulsive palpitations. They "writhe on the hard seats of their churches." At the "Tabernacle of the Third Coming," they listen to their messiahs shout "a crazy jumble of dietary rules, economics, and biblical threats." West's Hollywood is the dead end of the continent, the dream, and seemingly of sane personal relationships. It is on the edge not of revolution but of apocalypse. This is in sharp contrast to Babel's Russia of the 1920's where the "Messiah" has already arrived. Babel quotes Commissar Vinogradov as he tells the peasants of Berestechko, a recently plundered village, "You are in power. Everything is yours" (121). Babel's narrator walks through the little town "awaiting a new era and instead of human beings there go about mere faded schemata of frontier misfortunes." While the Cossack commissar speaks in a voice "fired with enthusiasm and the ringing of spurs," the peasants, Jews and tanners listen beneath "walls where nymphs with gouged-out eyes were leading a choral dance." Hollywood as much as Berestechko is the place of "faded schemata" where the visions of capitalism, Harry as salesman, Faye as actress, Abe as entrepreneur, even Tod as artist are the tantalizing manifestations of the American "new era," the revolution of the daydreams.

It is in *The Day of the Locust* that West, who utilizes the theme of dreams in each of his novels, confronts the rawest, least institutionalized dream, the personal fantasy. In his earlier novels, West chose the dreams of "art," "religion," and "success" as his satiric targets. In *The Day of the Locust*, the target is dream itself, the bit of fantasy and hope in the lives of the cheated and bored who have come to California to die. They are the "nymphs with gouged-out eyes" whose *danse macabre* is rhapsodic in Hollywood, stagnant in Wayneville, everywhere sustained by boredom and violence, and inevitably concluded in the chaos of its own empty movements. These are the people who order their lives by the everyday clichés "love" and "success" that are the heart of their mediocre fantasies.

West strikes first and hardest at love. Faye, the desired prize of virtually every man in the novel, is a classic bitch goddess. Tod knows that Faye's love is "an invitation to struggle hard and sharp . . . that if you threw yourself on her it would be like throwing yourself from the parapet of a skycraper . . . Your teeth would be driven into your skull like nails in a pine board . . . You wouldn't even have time to sweat or close your eyes" (271). Faye is "hollow"; she is all surface. "No matter how rough the sea got, she would go dancing over the same waves that sank iron ships and tore away piers of reinforced concrete" (406). Faye's youthful surface, "taut and vibrant . . . shiny as a new spoon," (304) is all there is. The dream of "love" is merely a combination of affectations.

After Faye, the love object, West's favorite target is "success." Only one character in *The Day of the Locust*, Claude Estee, is a Hollywood success. Stanley Edgar Hyman believes that Claude is "West's ideal vision of himself" (*Nathanael West*, University of Minnesota Press, Minneapolis, 1962, p. 44). If this is true, then West's image of himself is as grotesque as any of the characters he created. Claude is a member of another crowd, the bored rich, and this group is no less violent than the crowd of the poor and cheated. Claude lives in a house "that is an exact reproduction of the old Dupuy Mansion near Biloxi, Mississippi" (271). He is a dried up little man, but he dresses in flannels and tweeds. In his buttonhole is "a lemon flower" (272). "Here, you black rascal! A mint julep," he calls to a Chinese servant who comes running with a scotch and soda. Claude has the "success" that is the dream of the Greeners and the Mrs. Loomises, yet his act is as transparent as Faye's, without her "purity." He imagines a mythic past where the rich own the poor, and in his pool is a rubber model of a dead horse. Claude's crowd admires Mrs. Jenning, a madam "who runs her business as other women run lending libraries" (277). The only disapointing thing about Mrs. Jenning is her "refinement." The bored rich crave smut and obscenity as the bored poor crave the pretenses of taste and distinction. The causes of the two great scenes of violence in the novel are equally divided between rich and poor: Claude causes one, Homer and the "cheated" the other.

Babel's analogues to these American dreams of love and success are the Revolution's dreams of communal joy and glory in battle. The acts of Babel's soldiers are far less "decadent" than those of West's Californians. The Cossack cavalry is reduced by circumstance to testing itself through formal ritual. In one of Babel's most famous stories, "My First Goose," an intellectual gains his acceptance into the cavalry by killing a goose. "A severe-looking goose was waddling about the yard, inoffensively preening its feathers. I overtook it and pressed it to the ground. Its head cracked beneath my foot, cracked and emptied itself. The white neck lay stretched out in the dung, the wings twitched" (75). After demonstrating his brutality, the intellectual, a lawyer, is welcomed into the community. "Sit down and feed with us till your goose is done." After eating, he reads to his new comrades Lenin's speech to the Second Congress of the Comintern. He sleeps that night in the hay with his fellows. "We slept . . . warming one another, our legs intermingled. I dreamed and in my dreams saw women. But my heart stained with bloodshed grated and brimmed over"

(77). Brutality has led to acceptance. Beneath a moon that hangs above the yard "like a cheap earring," the lawyer reads Lenin triumphantly aloud, only to be answered by a commander's cliché, "Truth tickles everyone's nostrils" (77). The men sleep, but this single goose casts a pall on the Revolution.

Babel's use of the bird to foreshadow and parallel the slaughter of men is similar to West's. Babel's intellectual kills when his best instincts become shrouded by the "new values" of the Cossacks. The cockfight in *The Day of the Locust* takes place under far more bourgeois circumstances. Claude "just wants to see a fight" (379). His fifteen dollars is impetus enough to bring about the action. It is here that Abe Kusich finds himself most at home. Abe too is sub-human: he suffers and writhes with the cock in perhaps the most genuine "love" West portrays in the novel. Abe and the bird are equals. "The dwarf eyed the bird and the bird eyed him" (380). Abe begs Claude, "Please mister let me handle him" (379). The dwarf speaks of himself and the bird as "we," ministering to the cock as if it were his child. "The little man moaned over the bird . . . he spit into its gaping beak and took the comb between his lips and sucked the blood back into it . . . he inserted his little finger and scratched the bird's testicles" (382). When the red cock dies, only Abe groans with anguish. "Take off that stinking cannibal" (383), he screams to the laughing Miguel. In Babel's story it is the intellectual who has become the "stinking cannibal." The intellectual's justification for his behavior is Lenin's pronouncement that "there are shortages everywhere." Lenin meant only the material shortages, but West and Babel turn Lenin's truism into a brutal comment on the "new" men of Hollywood and of Russia. For the "shortages" that are apparent in *The Day of the Locust* and *Red Cavalry* are not the bodily needs but those "noumenal" necessities that define human behavior.

West and Babel, who resemble each other as highly self-conscious literary stylists, are even more closely aligned in their relationship to the past. Both writers are literally cut off from the traditional roots of fiction in time and place. Chaos is everywhere the Red Cavalry moves and in every facet of Tod's life in Hollywood. In Russia, men speak to each other in the sterile clichés of the Revolution; in Hollywood the characters banter the disembodied jargon of stale fantasies. No character has a "usable past": each is "boxed in" by the random violence of a particular moment. West speaks specifically of a "comic strip" technique in *Miss Lonelyhearts*. "The chapters to be squares in which many things happen through one action . . . I abandoned this idea but retained some of the comic strip technique: Each chapter instead of going forward in time, also goes backward, forward, up and down in space like a picture ("Some

Notes on *Miss Lonelyhearts*," p. 2). Both West and Babel achieve this "comic strip" technique in metaphysical as well as stylistic terms. Babel's "picture" of Russia is done in short, literally enclosed sentences. The continuity is in the narrative voice and in the ride of the Cavalry. Yet the ride is a random one and the narrator sees no particular order in the events he records. Whether a village is plundered sooner or later, the misery will always be there. This comic strip notion or independent experiences, pictures with a few words, depends upon easily recognizable figures who are not men.

The idea of the traditional novel and story has always been to create the illusion of a "real life." An eighteenth or nineteenth century novel is a "life and adventures"; even in a modern short story, the "epiphany" depends entirely upon the relation of the story's "illuminated moment" with the cumulative experiences of the people involved. The boxed comic strip technique denies all but spatial and chronological relationships. But most significantly, it denies the past. What happened to Dagwood Bumstead yesterday has no necessary relationship with what happens today. Comic strips have no past, only the raw materials of character and situation. This is almost precisely Babel's condition as a writer in the midst of the Revolution. How does one create the past of the "new man" when the revolution obliterates yesterday the way the morning paper changes the old comic strip? Yet men live by their accumulated memories, a man is his past. Babel, caught in the "present" of the revolution, is too honest to buy the easy Utopian dream, yet too much a "Red" to lapse into a lament for the old Russia. Beneath his hard cool eye and dispassionate posture, he allows a very subtle nostalgia that permeates his work and serves as an implicit judgement upon the revolution.

The narrator is most readily nostalgic when he encounters anything Jewish. In the story "Gedali," the narrator admits that on Sabbath eves he is "oppressed by the dense melancholy of memory" (69). In such a mood he roams through the Jewish quarter of Zhitomir, where he finds amid the ruin of Jewish shops only one survivor, old Gedali, a man who has said "yes" to the revolution. As the Jewish Cossack and the aged storekeeper await the Sabbath, Gedali asks the most telling questions about the revolution.

> The Poles, kind sir, shot because they were the Counter-Revolution. You shoot because you are the Revolution. But surely the Revolution means joy. And joy does not like orphans in the house. Good men do good deeds. The revolution is the good deed of good men. But good men do not kill. So it is bad people that are making the Revolution. But the Poles are bad people too. Then how is Gedali to tell which is Revolution? I used to study the Talmud, I love Rashi's Commentaries and the

books of Maimonides. And there are yet other understanding folk in Zhitomir. And here we are, all of us learned people falling on our faces and crying out in a loud voice: "Woe unto us, where is the joy-giving revolution?"

(71)

In Gedali's sentences lie all "shortages," the pressing questions: Who are the "good" and where is joy? What has the Talmud to do with the Revolution? Why must learned people fall on their faces? Gedali wants "an international of good people where every soul is given first class rations" (72). Gedali wants the utopia that coincides with his version of history, the "good" based upon "joy." The Jewish Cossack can only reply that the international "is eaten with gunpowder . . . and spiced with the best quality blood" (72). These two "new men" await the young Sabbath that comes to them out of the "blue gloom." The narrator's melancholy has led him to this confrontation with "the rotted Talmuds" of his youth. He knows that Gedali, Rashi, and the Sabbath are anachronisms, but if "joy" and "goodness" are also not part of the Revolution, what is to become of Zhitomir, the Cossacks, and the "faded schemata" who "own everything" while they await the new day? Babel does not answer this any more than he comments on other matters in *Red Cavalry*. Faced with the problem of men whose pasts have become immediately obsolete, Babel has created a spatial-temporal *Red Cavalry* that reads like *War and Peace* stuffed into *Winesburg, Ohio*. The peasants and townspeople of Russia reek with their "irrelevant" history in which there is no time to explore in "dense melancholy."

West has a far less formal concern than Babel with history. In Hollywood, "history" is as ill conceived and transparent as everything else. West devotes most of one chapter to "History" as Tod encounters it while searching for Faye on the set of "Waterloo." Tod walks past "a forty foot papier mâché sphinx . . . the Last Chance Saloon . . . a Paris street . . . Kamp Komfit . . . a Greek Temple dedicated to Eros . . . the wooden horse of Troy . . . the bones of a dinosaur . . . a corner of a Mayan temple" (353). Pausing to catch his breath, Tod realizes that the studio lot is a "history of civilization in the form of a dream dump. A Sargasso of the imagination!" (353). Yet Tod, who has such metaphysical reflections, can continue after this brief revery to search for Faye, his own hopeless two-dimensional dream.

Tod, like Babel's Jewish Cossack, brings with him the paraphernalia of judgement based on the past. Babel's narrator still feels "dense melancholy" on Sabbath Eve, but he is unable to do anything to relieve the misery around him. He is in fact and in deed one of the Cossacks. And Tod too is one of the Hollywood "grotesques." It is Tod's failure that raises West's novel above a Hollywood burlesque, for Tod, who cannot be reduced to a language of "Vas you dere, Sharley?" or a stereotype plot outline, is no more effective in the world than anyone else.

Tod's failure is like the failure of Miss Lonelyhearts, and, West would surely add, of Christ himself. Tod is not a dwarf or an actor. He has legitimate values and artistic insights. By showing Tod to be as incomplete as the grotesques surrounding him, West has returned to the objective of *The Dream Life of Balso Snell*. The "artist" in West's first novel writes to facilitate his seduction of "fat girls," and Tod is another version of twelve-year-old John Gilson. Easily missed in West's tricky syntax is the suggestion that Tod is perhaps not a very talented artist. " 'The Burning of Los Angeles,' a picture he was soon to paint, definitely proved he had talent" (261).

In spite of his "historical" insights, Tod is as dream-infected as the other Hollywood grotesques. Although a bit more articulate than the rest, he is also a "case study" as West uses personal history rather than the compressed historical panoramas of Babel. West said that "the great body of case histories can be used the way ancient writers use their myths" ("Some Notes on *Miss Lonelyhearts*," p. 2). This is on the surface not a very striking comment, since the modern novel has obviously specialized in psychology. But West puts his own idiosyncratic twist to the modern novel. For he means not generally that case histories can be the basis of fiction, but that they can be used specifically the way ancient writers "use their myths." Thus West uses case studies by stringing a whole series of them together rather than by performing a Jamesian or Lawrentian case analysis of a single character or even a single family. West "packs" Hollywood with case histories the way Babel "packs" the Revolution into *Red Cavalry*. Like a modern Euripides, West strings out his "case studies" —Homer, Harry, Faye, Abe, Claude—often teasing the reader by giving an alternate version of the expected case study. West does not dwell on personal history any more than Babel does on the military past. He picks his case studies in the middle of their misery and mixes them into the random violence that is the texture of their lives. The "whys" of the past are as obsolete as Babel's "rotted Talmuds." The future lies ahead for West's case studies in the form of more premieres and plane crashes.

In both *Red Cavalry* and *The Day of the Locust*, the disenchanted crowd with its ubiquitous collection of misery and vice replaces the historical background. There is no sense of time nor place, no leisurely descriptions of men or nature, not even any relief as in a "Big Two-Hearted River." Nature is as ominous as men in the literary landscapes of West and Babel. In *Miss Lonelyhearts* West quickly shatters the idea of pastoral retreat when Miss Lonelyhearts and Betty are told that "yids" have driven the deer away. When he looks about him, Miss Lonelyhearts sees that in the midst of spring "in the deep shade there was nothing but death—rotten leaves, gray and white fungi, and over everything a funereal hush" (114). Although he was the protege of Maxim Gorky, the great voice of "socialist realism," Babel resembles the Yiddish writers far more than the Russian in his treatment of nature. In the language of the ghetto there are not even words for the pastoral scenes that abound in all national literatures. Babel's Russian carries all the claustrophobic qualities of his life in the ghetto. Nature is only a series of images—words for literary effect. The only connection between men and the earth is that men are buried there.

In spite of the obvious terrors in both narratives, the effect of comparing *Red Cavalry* and *The Day of the Locust* is not as metaphysically debilitating as it would seem to be. In a society that has adopted "alienation," "violence," and "lack of communication" as intimate elements of a critical vocabulary it is not surprising that West and Babel have achieved such popular acclaim. Their fictions appeal to the sense of despair that the television news brings to our lives with regularity, often in color. Yet in our zeal for "brutal" and "apocalyptic" literature that seems to mirror our daily lives, West and Babel are no literary stand-ins for the one hour news special that tells us how bad the world is going to be because of air pollution, radiation, lack of birth control—whatever the topic and the sponsor of the day happen to be. West and Babel are not chroniclers of topical "issues" to be disregarded when the appropriate government agency takes charge. Whatever is wrong with Tod may be most clearly visible in Hollywood but is hardly confined to the dream capital. Similarly the milieu of Russian Civil War dramatically emphasizes the shadowy lives of the masses, but we knew they were shadows long before Lenin made them heirs of the earth. The pure and impenetrable Faye sitting in bed with her pack of cards, going through her daydreams with a formal and patterned dignity, is like a modern Helen taking a walk on the walls of a doomed city. We all know how the story ends, but the end is really the business of myth or science or religion. Even the knowledge of Troy's fall does not stem the momentary interest in Helen or the absolute judgement of her beauty. Because of their charged prose and their obvious appeal to the chaos of our times, West and Babel must not be mistaken for contemporary black humorists or chroniclers of the "absurd." They are literary formalists of impeccable stature who make out of human fragments and a surreal environment an ordered literary totality. Like Priam and the old men on the wall, they watch the movements of beauty which, at least in literature, can be isolated from the doom that echoes in her footsteps.

JAMES F. LIGHT

# Varieties of Satire in the Art of Nathanael West

Since the death of Nathanael West in 1940 his work has gone from relative obscurity to ever increasing interpretation and evaluation. Various of his works, under the impetus of increasing enthusiasm, have been praised as "superbly written," as "a minor classic [Miss Lonelyhearts]," as works [Miss Lonelyhearts and The Day of the Locust] "that deserve a place among the best twentieth century novels," and as "four novels" which are "permanent and true explorations into the Siberia of the human spirit." The major sources for West's art, such as James Joyce and the French surrealists, have been analyzed in detail, and even the most minute influences, such as Lynd Ward and Gilbert Seldes, have been tracked down with sedulous care. Victor Comerchero, in Nathanael West: The Ironic Prophet, has theorized that West used a "mythic lens through which to view his age," so that Miss Lonelyhearts "is a moving modernization of the Grail legend," and the totality of West's work is one vast, oblique revelation of West—or "Westian man"—himself: "Individually, each of West's characters remains a carica- ture; cumulatively, they create an engrossing picture of a 'type,' of a 'collective man' who has been created in West's own image." Stanley Hyman, in his monograph Nathanael West, finds Miss Lonelyhearts one of the three greatest novels of the twentieth century and claims that West converted the "sickness and fears" of modern existence into "convincing present-day forms of the great myths: The Quest, The Scapegoat, The

From Studies in American Humor 1, vol. 2 (April 1975). Copyright © 1975 by Jack Meathenia.

Holy Fool, The Dance of Death." Jay Martin, in his enthusiasm, finds that West, in his work as a whole, completed "a series of anti-novels in which is summarized the history of the twentieth century poetic imagination, from symbolism through surrealism and super-realism."

Nathanael West is obviously well on the way to becoming canonized—even the literary anthologies are now including his work— and as if to place the ultimate seal of approval upon his art, the movies *Lonelyhearts* (1959) and *The Day of the Locust* (1975) have insisted even more reverently than have the academic critics upon the fact that West's art is both profound and prophetic. The movie *The Day of the Locust*, for instance, captures, with considerable fidelity, a number of the more memorable images of the novel, and then depicts, with lengthy and pretentious fire, thunder, and brimstone, the apocalyptic vision on which the novel ends. In an epilogue, the movie adds another scene and another image, neither of which West had the foresight to include in the novel, in which Faye Greener returns to Tod Hackett's apartment to gaze sentimentally upon a rose which she had earlier seen blooming from a crack in one of the apartment walls. The pretentiousness of that symbolic rose, with its implications of beauty, fertility, and religion so totally in contrast to West's vision, suggests another falsification. That is that West's art itself is being distorted by the pretentiousness with which it is being treated by some of his admirers. Before it is too late, perhaps it is justifiable to suggest that even though West is both a serious and a profound artist, he is first and foremost a satirist who felt in his bones "the necessity for laughing at everything—love, death, ambition, etc." What West thought of as "my particular kind of joking"—in which "there is nothing to root for . . . and what is even worse, no rooters"—is the joking with which West had the greatest success, but it should not be forgotten that West attempted a variety of satire in his work. That diversity expressed itself in individual works, as well as in the body of West's work, and it ranged from folk humor, most especially in the tall tale tradition, to the dominant surrealistic humor in *The Dream Life of Balso Snell*, to the prevailing black humor in *Miss Lonelyhearts*, to the essential parody and burlesque in *A Cool Million*, to the dominant apocalyptic humor in *The Day of the Locust*, to the allusive humor which runs as a recurring strain throughout West's work.

West's interest in folk humor is apparent in his first published work. Called *A Barefaced Lie*, it appeared in 1929 in *Overland Monthly* and was obviously indebted to such tall tales as Mark Twain's "Jim Baker's Bluejay Yarn" and T. B. Thorpe's "The Big Bear of Arkansas." In West's

tale, the narrator seeks out a stagecoach driver named Boulder Bill because, as he notes in a passage reminiscent of the opening of Twain's "The
Celebrated Jumping Frog of Calaveras County," "I had been advised by
my friend, Red Patterson, the gum booter, to ride only with Boulder
Bill—and to listen politely to all he had to say." When the narrator finds
Boulder Bill, he turns out to be a huge man with a voice that even in a
"whisper . . . was audible a block away." Boulder Bill invites the narrator
to sit in front with him on the stagecoach ride, but insists that another
passenger ride in the rear. The reason for this, Boulder Bill explains, is
that the second passenger is a "low-down ornery skunk . . . the most
bare-faced, mean, siwash liar that ever hit the country, and I can prove it
to you." To make his point, Boulder Bill tells of how a few days earlier, he
had been visiting with his friends in a saloon and had told them of an
experience he had had while putting packsaddles in the dark on a number
of mules. Among the mules, according to Boulder Bill, was a bear, and
Bill had cinched a packsaddle on him without knowing that he was a
bear. Boulder Bill's friends "listened decently" to the story and "then
talked it over," but in the midst of the discussion a "big-mouthed Yahoo"
—the passenger whom Boulder Bill had earlier insisted sit in the rear of
the stagecoach—"started on a regular hyena laugh" and said "That explains it." When invited to elaborate, the "Yahoo" tells of how, on the
same day that Boulder Bill had cinched the bear and only a few hours
later, he had seen

> an old bear standing on a stump grunting and jabbering away like he was
> the boss of things, and there was two more bears down on the bar
> a-packing a load of salmon on another bear what had a packsaddle on,
> and two more bears still was catching salmon and carrying them up to
> the packyard. . . .

This tale sets everyone in the saloon to laughing, pounding each other on
the back, and then to looking at Boulder Bill and snickering. For that
reason Boulder Bill no longer feels free to show his face in the saloon, all
because of that "Yahoo" who had told nothing but "bare-faced bear lies,
pardner—bare-faced bear lies. . . ."

   Hardly a masterpiece, *A Barefaced Lie* proclaims the theme with
which West's entire art is obsessed—lies and their exposure—and is a
progenitor of the use of tall talk and tall tales in West's later work. An
example of West's later use of tall talk occurs in *A Cool Million* in the
character of the "rip-tail roarer" from Pike County who claims, "I kin whip
my weight in wildcats, am a match for a dozen Injins to oncet, and can
tackle a lion without flinchin'." Typical of West's exotic variations of the

tall tale is the howler told by Miss McGeeney in *The Dream Life of Balso Snell*. Miss McGeeney is writing a biography, entitled *Samuel Perkins: Smeller*, of the man who wrote the biography of E. F. Fitzgerald, who wrote the biography of D. H. Hobson, who wrote the biography of James Boswell, who wrote the biography of Samuel Johnson; and it is Miss McGeeney's fond hope that in time someone "must surely take the hint" and write her own biography, so that "we will all go rattling down the halls of time . . . a tin can on the tail of Dr. Johnson." In her research, Miss McGeeney has been most especially impressed with the fact that all the veins and wrinkles of Perkins' body flowed directly toward his nose, and that fact implied the marvelous quality of his nose. Almost blind, totally deaf, and practically devoid of other sensory apparatus, Perkins had compensated for these defects by developing the capacities of his nose until he "could smell a chord in D Minor. . . . It has been said of him that he could smell an isosceles triangle. . . ." As an artist, dedicated to fullness of experience, Perkins had married, and from the variety of the odors of his wife's body "he had built . . . an architecture and an aesthetic, a music and a mathematic. . . . He had even discovered a politic, a hierarchy of odors: self-government direct. . . ." In Miss McGeeney's tale, West is undeniably satirizing the preciousness of some artists and the folly of some academic critics, but it is clear that the method of his satire is exaggeration, and the inspiration, at least in part, is the tall tale.

A second artistic form which West used for satiric effects is surrealism. Like satire itself, surrealism depends for its effects upon distortion (though the aim of surrealism—as, for instance, in Kafka's *The Metamorphosis*—is not necessarily humorous), and the purpose of the sincere surrealist is, through multiple kinds of distortion, to mock "rational" perceptions and to intimate the higher reality—the surréel—of the subconscious, illogical inward world of man. What West did in *The Dream Life of Balso Snell* was to use the forms of surrealism to satirize the spiritual pretensions of the surrealist—a fact which helps to explain West's irritation at Clifton Fadiman's claim that he was "The ablest of our surrealist authors." In fulfilling this aim, West constructed a novel which dramatizes the chaotic ramblings of a wet dream. The dream-like illogic of the novel, less eerie than absurd, begins when the dream-hero, Balso Snell, while wandering around the ancient city of Troy, comes upon the famous Trojan Horse and enters it through the "Anus Mirabilis." The removal from reality is intensified in such episodes as that in which the hero, Balso Snell, reads a pair of letters within a dream within a dream, while the letters themselves narrate the speculations of a character named Beagle Hamlet Darwin over what might have happened if he had taken his mistress, Janey Davenport, to Paris with him. Throughout the novel West also uses shocking conceits to mock "rational" ideas and attitudes. The artistic creations of the male artist become comparable to the house of flowers built by the Amblyornis Inornata, a homely bird, in an effort to compare with the brilliant feathers of the Bird of Paradise, and the attempt "to exteriorize internal feathers" for both the Inornato and the human artist is the same: to attract the female. In another conceit the sexual urge becomes a chauffeur, dressed in ugly clothing and wearing a derby hat, that drives the automobile called man. In yet another conceit, man's dreams of eternal life become comparable to a race of men, the Phoenix Excrementi, who "eat themselves, digest themselves, and give birth to themselves by evacuating their bowels."

The characters of the novel, united only in the fact that they are all frustrated writers in search of an audience, are absurdly distorted creatures who force their opinions and their manuscripts upon Balso. Among them are a naked man, wearing only a derby hat with thorns protruding from it, who is "Attempting to crucify himself with thumb-tacks" and who tells the tale of the martyrdom of a flea, St. Puce, upon the body of Christ; a boy in short pants who writes a Dostoevskyan journal about the murder of an idiot; a nude girl bathing her charms in an outdoor fountain who miraculously is transformed, when Balso kisses her, into a middle-aged woman in mannish tweeds; and a beautiful hunchback with one-hundred and forty-four teeth in rows of four who asks Balso to prove his love for her by murdering Beagle Hamlet Darwin, the man who has seduced and then abandoned her.

The narrative, the conceits, and the characters of *The Dream Life* are obviously inspired by the distortions of surrealism, but the implications of the pretentiousness of each of the tales that Balso hears is that art is not the "divine excrement" romanticized by George Moore but is instead closer to the balls, the physical reality, of Snell. When he enters the "Anus Mirabilis" of the Trojan Horse, Balso does so by reciting an invocation inspired by James Joyce, and seeking, like Joyce's Stephen Dedalus at the conclusion of *The Portrait of the Artist*, "To encounter for the millionth time the reality of experience," Balso finds that reality in sex. For West, however, the reality which is the animal sexual instinct must be preceded in man by the falsity which is the romantic sexual game. In the last chapter of *The Dream Life*, therefore, Balso Snell argues the case for sexual intercourse to his indifferent beloved. In hilarious parody, Balso asserts the political argument (intercourse is an expression of free-dom), the philosophical argument (pleasure is desirable), the argument from art (the artist "must know what all the shooting is about"), and the argument from time ("The seconds, how they fly"). On her back, with her knees spread invitingly apart, Miss McGeeney listens patiently until Balso throws himself down beside her, at which point she coyly resists and then ultimately yields: "Moooompitcher yaaaah. . . . Drag me down into the mire, drag. Yes! And with your hair the lust from my eyes brush. Yes . . . Yes . . . Oph! Ah!" In such intercourse is the real "Yes" to the universe, the "Yes" that Joyce's Molly Blüm recognized in her soliloquy at the end of *Ulysses* and which West parodies through Miss McGeeney's "Yes." In this union comes the release of the little death, and in it is "the mystic doctrine, the purification, the syllable 'Om'. . . ." This is the truth revealed by the climax of Balso's wet dream, and the surrealistic conception that through dreams and fantasies one might transcend the physical and find some supreme union with the universe is nonsense. West's advice to surrealists who believe such foolishness—or to anyone deluded by the pretensions of art, religion, or thought—is implied in his creature John Raskolnikov Gilson, who tries to retain his hold on reality by writing in his *Journal* "*while smelling the moistened forefinger of my left hand.*" For fakers who would not heed such advice, West, like his creator Gilson, would have "the ceiling of the theatre . . . open and cover the occupants with tons of loose excrement."

A third kind of humor in West's work is the prevailing black humor of *Miss Lonelyhearts*. Such humor, or at least "grotesque black humor" rather than "absurd black humor," is rooted in total despair, sees the universe as absurd, and often uses violent and shocking images or surrealistic images yoking disparate concepts to destroy the complacency of its audience. Of such humor one critic writes:

> Black humor often reveals life's shabbiness and criticizes in the manner of satire. But unlike satire, it does not assume a set of norms, implicit or explicit, against which one may contrast the mad world depicted by the author. It relies neither on "common sense" as a guide to proposition and decorum, nor on social, religious, or moral convention. This is not to say that the reader of black humor is without norms. He has them, and the writer of black humor exploits them. The reader's sense of decency allows the writer to shock, the reader's humanity allows him to horrify, the reader's sense of verisimilitude enables him to outrage, and the reader's familiarity with dramatic and fictional conventions allows him to parody. . . . Moreover, black humor challenges not only the standards of judgment on which the satirist relies, but also the very faculties of judgment.

The plot structure of *Miss Lonelyhearts,* yoking the concept of the martyrdom of Christ to the agony of an advice-to-the-lovelorn columnist, and implying a parallel between the myth of Christ's journey to the cross and the pilgrimage of Miss Lonelyhearts to his death, is not only a far fetched conceit but also a narrative calculated to shock conventionally religious minds. In an earlier time this kind of humor, or humour, would have been attributed to the black bile produced by the brain and responsible for human melancholy, but the ironic contrast implied in the central conceit of the novel brings, or is intended to bring, a thin and bitter smile to the modern reader. That vein of humor is apparent on the first page of the novel when the feature editor of the newspaper on which Miss Lonelyhearts works parodies the "Anima Christi":

> Soul of Miss L, glorify me.
> Body of Miss L, nourish me.
> Blood of Miss L, intoxicate me.

And it is evident in the countless letters of the helpless of the universe—Sick-of-it-all, Desperate, Broad Shoulders—that recount what life is like if one has, for instance, been born without a nose and must "sit and look at myself all day and cry. . . . My mother loves me but she crys terrible when she looks at me." The humor of the letters, however, turns inward upon Miss Lonelyhearts and, as he explains to his fiancée, "shows him that he is the victim of the joke and not its perpetrator." The consequent examination of the values on which his life is based leads to an even blacker joke: Miss Lonelyhearts desires to succor with love the helpless cripples of the universe, and his attempt to do so leads to his sickness, his hallucinations, and ultimately his death at the hands of one of those whom he would save. His "martyrdom" parodies that of Christ and by implication mocks the meaningfulness of either.

The universe in which West's indictment of Christian mythology takes place is typical of the creations of the writers of black humor. Violence is everywhere, especially exemplified in the sexual violence so common in the letters Miss Lonelyhearts receives, and order is non-existent. At one time in his quest for order in an irrational world, Miss Lonelyhearts remembers his sister dancing gravely and precisely to the patterned music of Mozart. So musing, he turns from the bar, accidentally jostles another man, and before he can beg pardon, receives a punch in the mouth. In this disordered wasteland, water, love, and fertility are missing; none of the flowers of spring are in the park, and even the year before, as Miss Lonelyhearts remembers it, "It had taken all the brutality of July to torture a few green spikes through the exhausted earth."

One character especially embodies the tone of black literary humor in *Miss Lonelyhearts*. He is the feature editor of the newspaper for which

Miss Lonelyhearts works, and is named Shrike, after the bird which impales its prey upon a cross of thorns. A complete nihilist, he is a joke machine capable of such blasphemy as "I am a great saint. . . . I can walk on my own water. Haven't you heard of Shrike's Passion in the Luncheonette, or the Agony in the Soda Fountain?" Like all black humorists, Shrike is the foe of sentimentality, so that he can parody the most moving of the letters to Miss Lonelyhearts, as, for instance, when he creates a situation in which a young boy wants a violin but unfortunately is paralyzed and must be doomed only to clutch a toy violin to his chest while he makes the sounds of his music with his mouth. But, ends Shrike, "one can learn much from this parable. Label the boy Labor, the violin Capital, and so on. . . ." For Shrike, the dreams of man, in all their infinite variety, are material for ridicule. In the chapter "Miss Lonelyhearts in the Dismal Swamp," a perfect example of the fusion of wit and despair in black humor, Shrike parodies such escapes as the sail, the South Seas, hedonism, and religion. The escape to Art he ridicules to Miss Lonelyhearts:

> When you are cold, warm yourself before the flaming tints of Titian, when you are hungry, nourish yourself with great spiritual food . . . smoke a 3 B pipe, and remember these immortal lines: *When to the suddenness of melody the echo parting falls the failing day.* What a rhythm! Tell them to keep their society whores and pressed duck with oranges. For you *l'art vivant*, the living art, as you call it. Tell them that you know that your shoes are broken and that there are pimples on your face, yes, and that you have buck teeth and a club foot, but that you don't care, for tomorrow they are playing Beethoven's last quartets . . . and at home you have Shakespeare's plays in one volume.

Of all the dreams, the one that for Shrike is most absurd is the myth of Christ, the Miss Lonelyhearts of Miss Lonelyhearts, and Shrike's sharpest gibes are directed at that Fantasy. Mocking the aspirations of Miss Lonelyhearts, Shrike composes a biography—"The gospel according to Shrike"—in which Miss Lonelyhearts "wends his weary way" from the "University of Hard Knocks" to the "bed of his first whore," always "struggling valiantly to realize a high ideal," always climbing ever upward, "rung by weary rung . . . breathless with hallowed fire." What Shrike omits is the most bitter joke of all: Miss Lonelyhearts' accidental, meaningless death.

Yet another form of satire that West used in his art is the dominant parody and farce of *A Cool Million*. Indebted to the exaggerations of the tall tale and anticipating the pursuit of logic to insane conclusions exemplified in such novelists of the absurd as Joseph Heller, *A Cool Million* or *The Dismantling of Lemuel Pitkin* takes its narrative inspiration primarily from Voltaire—West thought of his novel as a twentieth-century *Candide*—so that the innocent hero of West's novel, like Voltaire's hero, sets out from home to seek his fortune. The adventures of both Lemuel Pitkin and Candide reveal a world of violence and greed—all of it dramatized farcically—and in it Lemuel loses his teeth, his eye, a thumb, a leg, his scalp, and ultimately his life. Where Candide ultimately learns something—and thus rejects the optimism of his tutor, Dr. Pangloss, that all is for the best in this best of all possible worlds—the ever gullible Lemuel remains faithful to the simplicities of the American dream preached by Lemuel's tutor Nathan "Shagpoke" Whipple. Like Abe Lincoln, whose life exemplifies for "Shagpoke" Whipple the fulfillment of the American dream, Lemuel dies in a theatre by an assassin's bullet, and his birthday is commemorated as a national holiday. Both holidays, West implies, have identical purposes: to preach the virtues of the American dream, by which every American boy can go into the world and by hard work, honesty, and probity make his fortune and win The Girl, and in so doing to delude and exploit the gullibles of America. Through the manipulation of such fools, dictators come to power, and Lincoln's faith that you can't fool all of the people all of the time is irrelevant, for West, to that truth.

In his mockery of optimistic faith in both the American dream and the American people, West's most obvious parody is that of such novels of Horatio Alger as *Onward and Upward, Bound to Rise,* and *Sink or Swim.* Such Alger novels as these told, in plodding prose directed to the "dear reader," the story of "our hero" as he rose from low estate, most often as a newsboy or shoeshine boy, to wealth and fame. West not only parodied the language of Alger, but at times lifted phrases and sentences directly, so that *A Cool Million,* most especially in the first half of the novel, is laden with such clichés as "a veil of tears"; such archaisms as "our hero was loth to lie"; such heavy or unnaturally colloquial dialogue as "In these effete times, it is rare indeed for one to witness a hero in action," or "Me lad, the jig is up"; such moral asides as "justice will out"; and such authorial intrusions as "As it will only delay my narrative . . . I will skip to his last sentence." Like Alger, West ends numerous chapters with melodramatic cliffhangers, and then shifts to another thread of his narrative; at the end of chapter three, for instance, Tom Baxter is left admiring the prostrate form of Lemuel's girl friend Betty Prail—"His little pig-like eyes shone with bestiality"—while the author begins the ensuing chapter, in Algerian prudery, with, "It is with reluctance that I leave Miss Prail . . . but I cannot with propriety continue my narrative beyond the point at which the bully undressed this unfortunate young lady."

In addition to the parody of Alger's prose, West mocks the rise of

Alger's heroes by the dismantling of his own, and he does so in the typical coincidences and situations of the Algerian Novel. Such a coincidence occurs when Lemuel visits New York's Chinatown, and Betty Prail, who is being held by Chinese White-slavers, throws a bottle with a note at his feet; but instead of rescuing Betty, Lemuel himself is captured by the white slavers and dressed in a sailor suit to appease the sexual appetite of the Maharajah of Kanurani. Such an Algerian situation arises when Lemuel rescues a rich man and his pretty daughter from the path of frightened, onrushing horses; but West's world is not Alger's, so that Lemuel, instead of receiving the just rewards he deserves in an equitable world, loses his false teeth, is reprimanded as a careless groom by the rich man he has saved, cannot respond because his teeth are gone, and is injured by a flying stone so that ultimately he loses his eye.

A second object of parody is the leader, the beliefs, the forms, and the human materials of German fascism. The clown named Adolf Hitler, who was in the mid-thirties often conceived of as a ridiculous house painter with an absurd mustache, West molded into the native American type that West felt was embodied in the former American President Calvin Coolidge. To that dangerous clown, West gave the name Nathan "Shagpoke" Whipple. Out of his nationalist beliefs, his faith in the supremacy of white, Protestant Americans, and his memories of the German National Socialist Party, Whipple creates the platform for the National Revolutionary Party, popularly known as the Leather Shirts, and from his soapbox he preaches: "We must drive the Jewish international bankers out of Wall Street! We must destroy the Bolshevik labor unions! We must purge our country of all the alien elements and ideas that now interest her!" For his "storm troops" Whipple creates a native uniform—a coonskin cap, a deerskin shirt, and mocassins—and in the Southern heartland of America, where Whipple's rhetoric functions most effectively, he so arouses his supporters that

> They ran up the Confederate flag on the courthouse pole, and prepared to die in its defense.
>    Other, more practical-minded citizens proceeded to rob the bank and loot the principal stores, and to free all their relatives who had the misfortune to be in jail.
>    As time went on, the riot grew more general in character. . . . The heads of Negroes were paraded on poles. A Jewish drummer was nailed to the door of his hotel room. The housekeeper of the local Catholic priest was raped.

Beyond these major stylistic and thematic parodies, two others deserve mention. One is West's derision of radical writers and the propagandistic art they create. The author of such nonsense in A Cool Million is the poet Sylvanus Snodgrasse, who turns to communism because the American public does not buy his work. The same lack of talent that impedes his popular success, however, pervades his propaganda, so that his playlet about a "sleek salesman" who deceives widows and orphans into buying worthless bonds is filled with the sentiment and images— three children who cry "Goo, goo," two millionaires who laugh as they step over the dead bodies of those they've defrauded—reminiscent of such proletarian literature of the thirties as Clifford Odets's Waiting for Lefty. Finally, one must note West's parody of the "Buy American" campaign inspired by the Hearst chain of newspapers and for a while in the thirties a significant force in the market place. In A Cool Million a Chinese businessman whose trade is white slavery adopts, for commercial reasons, the Hearst credo, and transforms his bordello from a "House of All Nations" to a hundred percent American establishment. In his enthusiasm Wu Fong insists on artistic consistency, so that the food, the furnishings, and the costumes of his establishment are appropriate to the milieu of each of the girls. For instance, the room of Princess Roan Fawn is "papered with birch bark to make it look like a wigwam"; she does her "business on the floor"; her native costume is total nudity save for a wolf's tooth necklace and a bull's eye blanket; and her customers are served "baked dog and firewater" for dinner. This artistic attention to detail is so great that West observes, in a moral, Algerian parenthesis, that Wu Fong might have used his talents honestly, and "made even more money without having to carry the stigma of being a brothel-keeper. Alas!".

Yet another aspect of the humor of A Cool Million seems less inspired by Voltaire, Alger, and German fascism than it does by the pure farce of Punch and Judy and the Keystone Kops. One example of this kind of burlesque occurs when Lemuel is duped into participating in a confidence game by pretending to lose his glass eye in a jewelry store and then to offer a thousand dollar reward for its return. Even more of a travesty is the job he takes in which, as a member of a comedy team, he is beaten violently so that his teeth, eye, wig, and leg are clubbed from his body. The extremes of this kind of humor, and of the humor of A Cool Million, generally are more appropriate to the talent of S. J. Perelman, to whom A Cool Million is dedicated, than to the genius of Nathanael West, and perhaps for this reason A Cool Million is less successful artistically than any of West's other novels.

Nathanael West's last novel, The Day of the Locust, is not very funny, and West knew it well. Thinking of The Day, and apparently forgetting such works as The Dream Life and A Cool Million, West could write, "I do consider myself a comic writer, perhaps in an older and a much different tradition than Benchley or Sullivan. Humor is another thing. I am not a humorous writer I must admit and have no desire to be one." Even the reason for the lack of laughter in *The Day*, West expressed in his comment in the novel, "It is hard to laugh at the need for beauty and romance, no matter how tasteless, even horrible, the results of that need are. But it is easy to sigh. Few things are sadder than the truly monstrous."

In dramatizing *The Day*, West emphasized the experiences of two newcomers, Tod Hackett and Homer Simpson, in the promised land—one character claims "it's a paradise on earth"—of the Angelenos. Los Angeles, however, is an ironic paradise, and its citizens are more grotesque than angelic. Violence, corruption, and perversity infest the city, from bloody and illegal cockfights, to pornographic movies in brothels which are triumphs "of industrial design," where the refined madame "makes vice attractive by skillful packaging," to children singing blues songs with sexual groans and suggestive gestures. Eros, the God of love, lies face downward on a forgotten movie set overrun with bottles and newspapers, and love itself is mocked by comic rhetoric: "Love is like a vending machine, eh? . . . You insert a coin and press down the lever. There's some mechanical activity inside the bowels of the device. You receive a small sweet . . . and walk away, trying to look as though nothing had happened. It's good, but it's not for pictures." Dissolution and death are omnipresent, from the concern of one character with the formal arrangements of funerals to the obsession of Tod Hackett with such painters of decay as Salvator Rosa and Francesco Guardi. The meaning of death is continually mocked by such images as that of the clown, Harry Greener, in his coffin ("He looked like the interlocutor in a minstrel show,") to the conversation piece that one couple puts in their swimming pool (a rubber imitation of a dead horse, with an "enormous distended belly" and a mouth, from which a black tongue hangs, set in an "agonized grin,") to a movie scene of the Battle of Waterloo (which diminishes the heroism and the agony of the actual battle to the trivial farce of a movie set that collapses and leaves the producer with the problem of resolving the insurance claims of the wounded). In this angelic world, deceit, more than anything else, is the fundamental reality: houses are made of "plaster, lath, and paper" and have no architectural stability or human dignity; the natural colors of food are intensified by artificial lighting that makes oranges red, lemons yellow, and steaks rose; the dress of people bears no relation to their occupation or their nature; and above all, the movies made in the land of the angels bear no more relation to reality than do the props—picknickers on a fibre lawn, for instance, eat "cardboard food in front of a cellophane waterfall"—that are created to give the illusion of truth.

Save for Tod Hackett, the artist-observer, the people that inhabit this city are grotesques, some of them deceivers who are, for the most part, peripherally associated with the world of dreams called Hollywood, others of them the deceived who have slaved all their lives and then, in search of Paradise, have come to Los Angeles to die. In the latter there exists an inarticulate frustration and rage, stemming from their inward sterility of spirit, that nothing, not even violence, can permanently appease. It is these pathetic and frightening creatures, whom Homer Simpson embodies, that attend the services of such bizarre churches as the "Tabernacle of the Third Coming," where Tod hears one angry parishioner bring the message that he had "seen the Tiger of Wrath stalking the walls of the citadel and the Jackal of Lust skulking in the shrubbery," and it is out of the rage of these that there arises the inspiration for Tod Hackett's painting "The Burning of Los Angeles" and the apocalyptic violence on which the novel ends.

The central, bitter apocalyptic humor of the novel lies in the contrast between the Biblical revelation of St. John the divine and the revelation of Tod Hacket expressed in his painting of "The Burning of Los Angeles." Where St. John foresaw God's destruction of Rome, the Whore of Babylon, because of the materialism of the city and its violations of God's laws, Tod sees only a meaningless destruction of the city of the angels by a mass of human locusts. Possibly inspired by a messiah similar to the "super Dr. Know-All Pierce-All" who had come to power in Germany, these creatures must soon become uncontrollable because they have found, in their search for the promised land, that "the sun is a joke. Oranges can't titillate their jaded palates. Nothing can ever be violent enough to make taut their slack minds and bodies. They have been cheated and betrayed." For such as these, life itself is a small-minded joke played by an ignorant child like the monster Adore, who tries to lure Homer Simpson to pick up a purse tied to a string and then, when Homer won't play, flings a stone in his face. For such as these, life itself is a stone in the face, full only of boredom and bitterness that can never be resolved, just as Homer's sobs have neither accent nor progress and "would never reach a climax." For such as these, the only solution to their lives is death. It is that which they seek in the darkened churches where they worship the celluloid stars of the silver screen. It is that which Homer subconsciously seeks in his pursuit of the movie extra, Faye Greener, a creature whose invitation, even in the movies in which she appears as a seductive temptress, is "closer to murder than to love. If you threw yourself on her, it would be like throwing yourself from the parapet of a skyscraper." In his rampaging violence at the end of the novel, Homer invites his own death, and in it he achieves the only victory of his life. In the same way, the violence of the mob at the movie premiere has as its aim not only the conscious destruction of those who have cheated and betrayed them but also the subconscious destruction of self. In violence is momentary joy and in death is final victory—that assertion is West's answer to St. John's vision of the New Jerusalem and his invitation (Revelation 22,17) to "Come, let him who desires take the water of life without price." In the irony of that answer lies the essence of West's apocalyptic humor in *The Day*.

In his first novel, West conceived a character named Beagle Hamlet Darwin who commented in a letter to his mistress: "You once said to me that I talk like a man in a book. I not only talk but think and feel like one. I have spent my life in books; literature has deeply dyed my brain its own color." What Darwin says about himself is true also of Darwin's creator, and the evidence of this is in the innumerable allusions in West's novels. These range from the purely private, such as West's veiled allusion in *A Cool Million* to Alice Shepard, a former girl friend, as the Southern whore, Alice Sweethorne; to the very obvious, such as the Algerian language and situations in *A Cool Million*; to the extremely complicated, such as the echoes of Eliot's *Waste Land* and Christian mythology in *Miss Lonelyhearts*, which inspired Victor Comerchero to assert that "The world of *Miss Lonelyhearts* is the fallen world of myth"; to the allusive pastiches, such as the parodies on the philosophic and poetic arguments justifying sexual intercourse on which *The Dream Life of Balso Snell* ends. Perhaps no allusion in West's work, however, is more meaningful to his art as a whole, more frightening in its implications, or more witty in its expression than Beagle Hamlet Darwin's references in *The Dream Life* to Christ, Dionysius, and Gargantua. Calling on Dionysius to assist him in explaining "The tragedy of all of us," Darwin asserts the concept of spiritual Darwinism. Beagle Hamlet Darwin's theory states that each of us, from birth onward, is doomed to dream of being more than animal and thus to compete with the likes of Dionysius, born three times, or Christ, born of a virgin. The conception of common men, however, is more humorous than remarkable, for the human lover does not approach his beloved "in the shape of a swan, a bull, or a shower of gold" but rather he comes "with his pants unsupported by braces . . . from the bath-room." Similar is the reality of normal birth, where there are no kings, no doves, no stars of Bethlehem, but "only old Doctor Haasenchweitz who wore rubber gloves and carried a towel over his arm like a waiter." Thinking of this contrast, Darwin realizes the tragedy of the competition in which men must spend their lives, "a competition that demanded their being more than animals." Because of this inward need, men must forever dream, and to support their dreams they pathetically juggle the paraphernalia that they have created to justify their foolishness: "an Ivory Tower, a Still White Bird, The Holy Grail, The Nails, The Scourge, The Thorns, and a piece of The True Cross." Throughout his art West mocked this folly by satirizing, in a variety of forms, the dreams of man, but since he also comprehended that to live without dreams was worse than to exist with no dreams at all, he had no answer to this dilemma, and his art expresses none. Because of this lack of any ultimate answer, West's satire seems most successful when it is most irreverent, most scatological, most despairing, and most complex, but these qualities should never obscure the fact that it is laughter that is at the center of West's art.

JEFFREY L. DUNCAN

# The Problem of Language in "Miss Lonelyhearts"

Almost halfway through his story Miss Lonelyhearts gets sick. His sickness is essentially spiritual—he is, the chapter title says, "in the Dismal Swamp"—and it has been brought on by his job. His girl friend, Betty, brings him some hot soup and advice: quit, try another line of work. He tells her that quitting would not help much because he would still remember the letters. She does not understand, so he offers her an explanation of unusual length and formality:

> Perhaps I can make you understand. Let's start from the beginning. A man is hired to give advice to the readers of a newspaper. The job is a circulation stunt and the whole staff considers it a joke. He welcomes the job, for it might lead to a gossip column, and anyway he's tired of being a leg man. He too considers the job a joke, but after several months at it, the joke begins to escape him. He sees that the majority of the letters are profoundly humble pleas for moral and spiritual advice, that they are inarticulate expressions of genuine suffering. He also discovers that his correspondents take him seriously. For the first time in his life, he is forced to examine the values by which he lives. This examination shows him that he is the victim of the joke and not its perpetrator.
>
> (*Miss Lonelyhearts* and *The Day of the Locust*, 1933, rpt. New York: New Directions, 1962, p. 211. Hereafter cited in parentheses within the text.)

Here he stops, satisfied it seems that there is no more to say. Betty still does not understand, to no one's surprise, but we do: Miss Lonelyhearts cannot answer the letters because he has found that his values do not,

From *Iowa Review* 1, vol. 8 (Winter 1977). Copyright © 1977 by University of Iowa.

cannot, justify genuine suffering, including his own. (For he is suffering too, languishing in the dismal swamp.) Hence he is the victim of the joke: the advice-giver is himself sick-of-it-all, in desperate need of advice.

He does not say what his values are (or were), but he does not really need to. He has found them, he implies, not just wanting, but false. His crisis then is intensely personal, because *he* has been false, and still is. He no longer claims a proper name, and he wears at all times his workaday nom de plume, a woman's at that. But not only is he no lady, he cannot fulfill the requirements, as he construes them, that his pseud-onym entails. He has become a misnomer. In one sense, though, the name suits him: he is as lonely a heart as any of his correspondents. Accordingly, the only identity he feels entitled to is the same one they assume, the victim. Better any identity than none, we might say, but not so. For he has come to doubt all values and therefore the value of suffering itself. If it has no value, neither does the role of victim. One simply suffers, that's all, without upshot or significance, the butt of a joke.

What makes the joke *bad* is the fact, as Miss Lonelyhearts sees it, that the suffering his correspondents express is genuine. Others have agreed. In his review of the novel, for instance, William Carlos Williams protested, "The letters which West uses freely and at length must be authentic. I can't believe anything else. The unsuspected world they reveal is beyond ordinary thought." Thirty some years later Randall Reid said the same thing: "They [the letters] have the vividness and the unarguable reality of a revelation." Both statements, cueing off Miss Lonelyhearts, couple authenticity and revelation. The letters reveal a reality that is unarguable. They are, like revelation, their own evidence. Upon seeing them one believes them, if not instantaneously, like Wil-liams, then slowly, gradually like Miss Lonelyhearts. Their truth, in other words, is not a matter of fact, but an article of faith, and no one has questioned it. I think we should, just as I think that, deep down, Miss Lonelyhearts himself does. At issue is a central concern, the nature of language, both as a theme and as the medium of West's novel.

Miss Lonelyhearts deals primarily not with people, but with letters, with various orders and disorders of words. In his personal relations he is not engaged in dialogue, the language of spontaneous give and take, nearly so much as he is confronted with speeches, with words as deliber-ately composed as those of the letters, if not more so. Notably, in the two days (and chapters) before he beds himself in the dismal swamp, he hears two speeches, one by Mary Shrike, then one by Fay Doyle, that amount to letters in the flesh. "People like Mary were unable to do without such tales. They told them because they wanted to talk about something besides clothing or business or the movies, because they wanted to talk about something poetic" (p. 199). Like Mary like Fay: they simply have different poetics. Understandably Miss Lonelyhearts listens to neither. They reveal a reality, unarguably, but it is hardly one of genuine suffering, much less of profound humility. Instead they betray mere attitudes struck, postures assumed, poses wantonly displayed, a comic pornography of suffering and trouble. If they express anything authentic—though it is doubtful that these women give a fig about authenticity—it is a desire for suffering, for indisputable reality, personal significance. And if they are to be pitied, it is because they do not, perhaps cannot, suffer.

That is, they have nothing really to speak of, Mary and Fay. Their words merely fill in their blanks. And what is true of them may also— since West's characters are consistently thin—be true of the others, of Betty, of Desperate, of Broad Shoulders, of Shrike, of Miss Lonelyhearts himself. For that reason, if no other, Shrike can burlesque the letters, the expressions of undeserved, unmitigated suffering, just as effectively as he can parody the conventional formulae of value, of the life worth living:

> This one is a jim-dandy. A young boy wants a violin. It looks simple; all you have to do is get the kid one. But then you discover that he has dictated the letter to his little sister. He is paralyzed and can't even feed himself. He has a toy violin and hugs it to his chest, imitating the sound of playing with his mouth. How pathetic! However, one can learn much from this parable. Label the boy Labor, the violin Capital, and so on . . .
>
> (p. 240)

> So you buy a farm and walk behind your horse's moist behind, no collar or tie, plowing your broad swift acres. As you turn up the rich black soil, the wind carries the smell of pine and dung across the fields and the rhythm of an old, old work enters your soul. To this rhythm, you sow and weep and chivy your kine, not kin or kind, between the pregnant rows of corn and taters.
>
> (p. 212)

Shrike can handle them with equal facility because he insists that they bear the same message, and that it is their only message: the human race is a poet that writes the eccentric propositions of its fate, and propositions, fate, the race itself amount only to so much noisy breath, hot air, flatulence.

Miss Lonelyhearts reluctantly suspects as much. That is why he can find no sincere answers, why he can take nothing he says or thinks seriously, why he lacks the courage of his clichés, why he converts even an original formulation immediately into a cliché. "Man has a tropism for order," he thinks to himself; "The physical world has a tropism for disorder, entropy. Man against Nature . . . the battle of the centuries." A capital "N" no less. Four sentences later he dismisses it for good: "All order is doomed, yet the battle is worthwhile" (p. 209). No wonder then that only a little while later he casts his explanation to Betty in the third person—it accommodates exactly his ironic self-consciousness, the distance between what he wants to believe and what he suspects. No wonder as well that his explanation sounds like another speech, one that he has often rehearsed to himself; it is so pat, so articulate, the cool, collected rhetoric of desperation, of futile resolves, private last-stands. For if he can only bring himself to believe what he says, that the suffering is genuine, he may yet hope to believe that it can be justified. That is, faith, once succumbed to, may wax and multiply like irony succumbed to. But the "if" is difficult; it requires breaking the force of irony, which is considerable. Not only can it move mountains, it can annihilate them. And people, too.

Irony is not always humorous, but humor is always ironic. And the letters in the book are humorous.

> I am in such pain I dont know what to do sometimes I think I will kill myself my kidneys hurt so much. . . . I was operatored on twice and my husband promised no more children on the doctors advice as he said I might die but when I got back from the hospital he broke his promise and now I am going to have a baby and I don't think I can stand it my kidneys hurt so much.
>
> (p. 170)

The writers have had nothing to do with the terrible turns their fates have taken—they are innocent—and neither they nor anyone else can do a thing about their difficulties. Their problems are, by their own terms, insoluble; they themselves are, by their own accounts, schlemiels with Weltschmerz; "I don't know what to do," concludes Sick-of-it-all (p. 170). "Ought I commit suicide?" queries Desperate (p. 171). "What is the whole stinking business for?" muses Peter Doyle (p. 232). They are actually seeking confirmation, not advice; they want someone else to see them as they see themselves. Also, the letters are all graced by the common touch, illiteracy. The writers seem sublimely unaware that their words, like double agents, constantly betray them. "But he [Broad Shoulders' boarder] tries to make me bad and as there is nobody in the house when he comes home drunk on Saturday night I dont know what to do but so far I didnt let him" (p. 226). Betrayal is revelation, but of a fundamentally ambiguous sort: we cannot say whether the words of the letters misrepresent or faithfully execute their authors as they really are. Either way, though, they are funny. The slip of the tongue, Freudian or otherwise, reliably gets a laugh.

Miss Lonelyhearts, however, no longer finds the letters funny because he assumes they are authentic. Genuine suffering, he tells Betty, is no joke. This difference between his response and ours gets us at last into the troubled heart of the novel. Suffering is not funny, certainly, but it has been since Eden, no less than vanity and folly, the very stuff of humor. Pathos, too, of course, and tragedy, but we pay for the loss of Paradise with laughter as well as tears, and comedy is one of the more common forms of man's inhumanity to man. But nothing is more human, for we are considering one application of our capacity for abstraction, our ability to translate instances of suffering and pain into symbol systems that go absurdly awry. Humor is a function of symbolic consciousness. It involves the displacement if not the annihilation of persons, their particular reality, by words, a particular scheme of concepts. The unnamed perpetrator of the joke is language, like West's, for example, when he describes the letters as all alike, "stamped from the dough of suffering with a heart-shaped cookie knife" (p. 169). Just as West's words undercut the letters, so the letters' words displace their writers: "it dont pay to be inocent and is only a big disapointment" (p. 170). Miss Lonelyhearts no longer finds the letters funny because he refuses to consent to this displacement, to bless this annihilation with a laugh. He looks over or through their words to their writers, as he imagines them: profoundly humble, genuinely suffering, terribly real.

But Shrike recognizes a laugh when he sees one, and Miss Lonelyhearts knows it. That is why he has to insist that the letters are not funny: they are not because in truth they are, and that, in his opinion, is wrong, all wrong. For it is not just the letters—he doesn't find anything funny. He will not be a party to humor per se, and therefore, consistently enough, he tries to leave the premises of language altogether, in violence, in women's flesh, in a rural retreat, and in a hand-holding soul-session in a speakeasy.

His expeditions fail, hardly to his surprise, because in them he only finds himself engaged face-to-face with more words on the loose. Sometimes they are spoken, sometimes they are enacted, but they are always there, inescapable. "With the return of self-consciousness, he knew that only violence could make him supple" (p. 183). Spiritually speaking, I take it. His violence serves a metaphysical cause self-consciously conceived. Instead of delivering him from language into whatever—say reality—it necessarily forces him into obeisance to language. For language is its maker. He works over the clean old man for his story, the dubious words of his life—"Yes, I know, your tale is a sad one. Tell it, damn you, tell it" (p. 191)—and sees him at last as the embodiment of his correspondents, his letters. Mary gives him a little of her body to tell him all of her tale; Fay uses her story as a pretext for sex, but she also uses sex as a pretext for her story. Betty believes in a *Sunset* version of *Walden*, and for a while Miss Lonelyhearts is able to relax in her belief, but when they get back to the city he realizes that "he had begun to think himself a faker and a fool" (p. 220). So he is back in language again, and not at all sure that he ever really left it. Like violence, his session of silence with Doyle serves a metaphysical purpose self-consciously forced to its crisis: "He . . . drove his hand back and forced it to clasp the cripple's . . . pressed it firmly with all the love he could manage" (p. 232). This may be a flight of the alone to the alone, but the wings are words, words like "love" and "communion," like "together" and "alone." His only real hope, then, as he has seen it all along, is Christ, appropriately enough.

Let us go back to the dismal swamp. "He was thinking of how Shrike had accelerated his sickness by teaching him to handle his one escape, Christ, with a thick glove of words" (p. 212). Shrike does not get his entire due: he has taught Miss Lonelyhearts to handle everything with a thick glove of words, to suspect that there may be nothing really for the glove to handle, nothing for it to do but make figures of itself, or that the glove, like a magician's white one, renders whatever reality it handles null and void. Genuine magic, though, not legerdemain. Destructive force. The word "escape," in this context, usually means a flight from reality to some more tenable opposite. In Miss Lonelyhearts' case, however, it seems to mean a flight from words in and of themselves to that only (as he sees it) which can redeem them, put them in their proper place—a flight from the terrible logic of Shrike to the Logos itself, Christ, the Word made flesh. The Word informs flesh, flesh substantiates the Word: reality then carries a life-time guarantee, its value insured by language. Then tropes can become unironic Truth, victims can become martyrs, and Paradise, that place of complete integration, can be regained.

Or so a Christian might have it: not an escape, like Tahiti, the soil, hedonism, or art, but a redemption. West's script, however, follows the Christian's with a thumb on its nose and its fingers sadly crossed. Peter Doyle's letter moves Miss Lonelyhearts to holding hands. Later, though, Doyle's hearthside demeanor bankrupts the credibility of his prose, so much that Miss Lonelyhearts takes himself to bed. This time, however, instead of languishing in despair, he becomes the rock. In that metaphor of the Church he has finally, he solipsistically thinks, found himself. "The rock was a solidification of his feeling, his conscience, his sense of reality, his self-knowledge" (p. 245). Thus solidified, though, he feels nothing, and nothing (except the rock) seems real. Betty is a party dress to whom he can say anything without deliberately lying because there is no one to lie to and nothing to lie about. "He could have planned anything. A castle in Spain and love on a balcony or a pirate trip and love on a tropical island" (p. 245). He has changed the game from show-and-tell to play-pretend. As a preliminary to his union with Christ he seems to have gained himself by renouncing words and the world, as he had apparently hoped. But he has actually done nothing of the sort: Miss Lonelyhearts, a pseudonym, has merely become a metaphor, the rock, in a world that was never his.

Up to this point he has always been afraid of Christ. "As a boy in his father's church, he had discovered that something stirred in him when he shouted the name of Christ, something secret and enormously powerful" (p. 179). Later he construes this thing in clinical terms, as hysteria, though he wishes he could believe that it is more than that, that it is actual divinity. Whatever it actually is, his fear is the traditional one of self-relinquishment, of letting go. But now that he has such a definitive sense of self—a rock is definite, if nothing else—he is ironically no longer afraid, and silently shouting the name Christ to himself, he gives himself up and over and has his union. "Christ is life and light" (p. 245). He is also love and Miss Lonelyhearts' new feature editor (p. 246).

He is, in other words, yet another metaphor, a whole string of them—not the Word, but a word, signifying neither more nor less than any other. Nothing is redeemed, least of all language. Doyle arrives, bad poetry on a field rampant. He has come in the name of secular romantic love to avenge Miss Lonelyhearts' alleged insult to his wife's honor. The allegation is hers, of course, and it is as false as her honor, as her husband's love, as his mission's motive. Miss Lonelyhearts sees him as a sign and, mistaking his warning for a humble plea, goes in the name of divine love to perform a literal miracle, to save Doyle, to save all his correspondents in Doyle's figure, just as he had sought to hurt them all in the figure of the clean old man. Doyle loses heart, so to speak, and tries to flee. Betty, the idle figure of Miss Lonelyhearts' secular fancy, blunders in. Doyle's gun accidentally goes off, and Miss Lonelyhearts meets his end at last, not as martyr, but as unwitting victim, and not as victim of "reality" but of a symbol system gone absurdly awry—of a joke, if you will—because there is no other way for it to go. There is no truth for Miss Lonelyhearts, only words.

It may seem then that Shrike has the last word. All we really have, all we really are, says Shrike, is words, but he does not stop there. There is no cause for grief, he consistently implies, only occasion for jokes. Jokes are his form of prophecy, and they are self-fulfilling. Their form is their content, for their only point is the perfect pointlessness of it all. Nothing is wrong because nothing ever was or could be right. Nothing really matters, not even the fact that nothing really matters. This second step, though, Shrike follows by choice, not of logical necessity. He pronounces "truth" only in order to evade it, to protect himself from pain. Between nothing and grief he will take nothing, not because it is true, finally, but because it is easier.

But while Shrike may take this second step for the sake of comfort, one could argue that the novel takes it of necessity. In open concord with Shrike, it depicts language as radically false, a fundamentally misleading order of being, or nonbeing, as the case may be. Yet the novel is itself a form of language. It would seem then that either the theme must render the form futile, a design of dumb noise, or the form must render the theme gratuitous. But if the theme is gratuitous, the form is perforce futile: it is predicated on counterfeit, a phony issue. Either way (or both ways?) the novel would amount to a display in negation, like the self-dismantling sculpture of Tinguely, like the jokes of Shrike. But Shrike is good only for a laugh, whereas the last elaborate joke of the novel occasions dismay. That is, we respond as if both the statement and the structure were ontologically sound. Now it could be that West has misled us to the very end, that we, to the extent that we care about the outcome, are the unwitting butts of his joke and he is snickering up his sleeve. If so, then West's novel would seem to give us the void as a stripper, taking it all off. On the other hand, our response may be warranted. Curiously enough, we have the same problem with the book that Miss Lonelyhearts has with the letters: whatever we finally deem it, we are necessarily engaged in an act of faith. But we need not, as a consequence, simply toss the book up for grabs.

For the sake of his faith, Miss Lonelyhearts must ignore the bad language of the letters. We enjoy the same language because it is so good: "I bought a new sowing machine as I do some sowing for other people to make both ends meet . . ." (p. 225). The paradox is simple yet profound. All of the demonstrations of bad language—the letters, Miss Lonelyhearts' awful answers, Shrike's parodies—all involve not only an exhibition of West's skill, but of the adequacy of language to his skill. In order to make humorous "nonsense" (as in the quote just cited), language must be able to make common sense. Further, it must make both kinds at once, since it is precisely the play of the one off the other that is funny. A joke reveals the meaningfulness of language. And like revelation, it constitutes its own evidence: the simple fact that it is funny, that *we* laugh, makes the case.

Now we can understand why Shrike is such a desperate character, insistent, shrill. He cannot make his point—the meaninglessness of it *all*—without contradicting himself. Jokes are his form of prophecy, and they betray him every time. He is the victim of his own success. He grieves, in his fashion, that he cannot have nothing.

But the fact that language is meaningful does not necessarily mean that it is significant, any more than a correct sentence is necessarily true. A philosophical idealist might disagree, of course, but West's characters are not idealists. They want some words that signify something beyond their own sound and sense, something, preferably a redemptive Absolute, that can be empirically ascertained. Miss Lonelyhearts, for example, has no quarrel with the coherence of Betty's "world view," but with its significance. Her order, as far as he is concerned, does not match reality—they are an odd pair—whereas his own disorder does (p. 183). His experience tells him so, or so he thinks. However, we cannot say whether his confusion results from or produces the confusion he perceives, nor whether the world he perceives is in fact a disorder. For it is not the relation between words and reality that West depicts, it is the disjunction: his characters cannot find out what, if anything, lies on the other side of their words. As a bridge, language breaks; as a window, it shuts out, like stained glass, and keeps his characters in. But it does not become genuinely false, actually misleading, until West's characters believe the bridge is sound, the window perfectly transparent, their words reliably significant, true. As, for instance, when Shrike insists there is nought beyond, and when Miss Lonelyhearts insists there is confusion, or Christ, the Word intact. They do not know, literally, what they are talking about.

Words in the novel fail to do the job West's characters assign them—to reveal a reality beyond themselves. But at the same time the words of the novel, West's words, manage quite successfully to do their job, to reveal all they need to, the patterns their sound and sense make: "the gray sky looked as if it had been rubbed with a soiled eraser. It held no angels, flaming crosses, olive-bearing doves, wheels within wheels. Only a newspaper struggled in the air like a kite with a broken spine" (pp. 174–75). These words do not match reality, fit any empirical facts. Neither do they distort any facts or displace reality. They are not *about* something beyond themselves, an actual person's experience, a historical event. They constitute, rather, their own reality, and their only job is to be true to the structure of which they are a part, that is, to be right, self-consistent, aesthetically correct. Were it some other character than

Miss Lonelyhearts sitting there, the sky might very properly contain angels, crosses, doves, wheels, a cloud that speaks, a breeze that inspires, a pulse that beats. In art, language is free of obligation to referents; it is free to be strictly itself, and it stands or falls entirely on its own. And when it stands, it satisfies the idealist and the empiricist alike, for it is simultaneously as conceptual as any law and as phenomenal as an apple falling. It is completely sensible. The poet, as Emerson happily put it, "adorns nature with a new thing."

Our relationship with the novel, then, is not exactly analogous to Miss Lonelyhearts' with the letters. The language of each (even when it is the same) draws different duty. For that reason, the demonstrable error of his and his companions' ways does not necessarily compromise the validity of ours. We place our bets on a different thing, and we have demonstrably good grounds for our wager, namely, the novel's coherence. Being or nonbeing, it is an *order* of experience. Thus the novel's theme does not necessarily undermine its form. Still, we must recognize that the center of the analogy holds: the novel's coherence depends upon our faith. The world seems able to survive capricious gods, but a work of fiction cannot survive an unreliable third-person narrator. (First-person narrators are a different story, of course, but their implied third-person narrators are not.) Try to imagine, for instance, the last passage I quoted as misleading, false, the sky as actually blue, bearing crosses, wheels, and so forth. The whole show stops; all bets are off. But we in fact read on because we trust the narrator. In order to read on, we must. And in reading on we find constant justification of our faith: the novel elaborates its problem without sentimental dodges or cheap solutions. True to itself, it is true to us. As for those novels that self-consciously make even their third-person reliability suspect, our willing suspension of belief amounts to a working agreement based on the same trust, that they will prove to be meaningful orders of experience. But by meaningful I do not want to suggest comfortable or reassuring. On the contrary, almost all art worth the name repays our faith by raising hell within us, with our cherished assumptions and secret illusions, with our workaday values and beliefs. For it takes us as far as words can go, and thus brings us face-to-face, finally, with silence, mystery. "Emotion" comes from *emovere*, "to move out of," "disturb." Let us momentarily suppose that West has conned us at the end. Now that we are on to it, we can easily dismiss the book, for he has given us the void *merely* as a stripper, a tease, not a real threat but a pretense of one. "Ah," we can say in relief, "he didn't mean it after all."

But West's novel does disturb us, threaten, because its form makes its theme intensely meaningful, utterly real. Here we witness words falling short of reality, and here, and here, and we watch their continual shortcomings compose an actual pattern of doom. We are unsettled because most of us are, like Dr. Johnson, rock-kickers—we ordinarily assume that our words signify something beyond themselves—and reading this story forces us to face the possibility that they do not. The story defines the issue that has become major in certain circles, "the problem of language." But West simultaneously solves the problem *in* the form, every word of the way. For unlike his characters, malpracticing empiricists all, and unlike most of us, West was, as an artist, a practicing idealist. We know that he got the idea for his novel from seeing actual letters to an advice columnist. Had he been concerned with historical-empirical fidelity, he could have used them more-or-less intact. But we also know that he changed them radically, that he in truth wrote his own letters, to make them right, aesthetically correct. All artists, of course, change things to suit their purposes, but their purposes have a single premise, that the work of art must be absolutely true to itself, self-integral, one. Then it can stand and unfold itself, an articulated body of ideas, an avatar of Being.

The novel is an order of being, finally, because in it West shows us that words realize our possibilities as well as define our limits. Miss Lonelyhearts looks at a gray sky and, empiricist that he is, sees only a dirty *tabula rasa*. Against that he sees the most referential and hence ephemeral of all literature, a newspaper, failing (naturally) to soar. But West's words lift nicely, bearing for the space of our imagination all the significance Miss Lonelyhearts misses in his, not in the form of crosses and doves, to be sure, but in the form of figures, of ideas, of words touched with life and touching us with the same.

West's other three stories suffer to varying degrees in comparison with *Miss Lonelyhearts*. They demonstrate a precise but simplistic satire, a sentimental obsession with easy pickings: in *The Dream Life of Balso Snell*, the contrived labyrinths of literary journeys, in *A Cool Million*, the Horatio Alger myth, in *The Day of the Locust*, the Hollywood motif. The unreality of West's marks is patent, their exposure therefore, funny or not, perfunctory: "The fat lady in the yachting cap was going shopping, not boating; the man in the Norfolk jacket and Tyrolean hat was returning, not from a mountain, but an insurance office . . ." (p. 2). They expose bills of fraudulent goods that we, his readers, declined to buy in the first place; hence they do not disturb, they merely confirm our glib assumptions. *Miss Lonelyhearts*, on the other hand, makes us reconsider.

Here is the difference I mean:

It is hard to laugh at the need for beauty and romance, no matter how tasteless, even horrible, the results of that need are. But it is easy to sigh. Few things are sadder than the truly monstrous.

(*The Day of the Locust*, p. 4)

. . . I would like to have boy friends like the other girls and go out on Saturday nites, but no boy will take me because I was born without a nose—although I am a good dancer and have a nice shape and my father buys me pretty clothes.

(*Miss Lonelyhearts*, p. 171)

A girl without a nose is monstrous, truly, yet it is hard not to laugh, particularly when she expresses her need for beauty and romance. A nice shape does not compensate for a noseless face. Perhaps it should, but it does not. Perhaps we should not laugh, either, but we do. Perhaps words should not take precedence over persons, but here (pretending for the moment the girl is real) they do. On the other hand, West does not permit us to indulge in cant. The letter's words spell out a troublesome truth, that this girl, however unfortunate, has tacky values. She would give a great deal to be Homecoming Queen. Victims can be insufferably vain, no less than Presidents, and pity can be primarily self-gratifying. My point is that in the first passage West is keeping certain suppositions intact—the value, for instance, of pity—while in the second he orders his words so that we have to recognize ourselves as we truly are, not as we might prefer to suppose we are. It is recognizing this difference that makes us laugh, and our laughter implies a major admission: that the idealist's absolute may finally be more significant, more real, than we mere mortals are.

We regard West loosely as a writer ahead of his time. I would say that it is specifically *Miss Lonelyhearts* that warrants his reputation, and that it anticipates in particular the work of Barth, Barthelme, Coover, Elkin, Gardner, Pynchon, of all those writers loosely bunched as comic whose humor, by trying its own limts, examines how language does and undoes us, what it gives and what it takes, what it may mean and what it may not, and if we are at last full of fear and wonder, we should be: Being is finally awful, no matter how we look at it.

DEBORAH WYRICK

# Dadaist Collage Structure and Nathanael West's "Dream Life of Balso Snell"

Most critics admire the structural mastery of Nathanael West's short novels, and many of them base their analyses upon the works' relationships with the visual arts. *Miss Lonelyhearts*, for instance, has been found to have a comic strip structure; *The Day of the Locust* can be seen as a combination of Eisensteinian film technique, ritual drama, and verbal "quotations" from old master paintings. Even the imploded Horatio Alger narrative of *A Cool Million* has been scripted into a Grade B double feature filler. Surprisingly, the question of structure in West's first novel, *The Dream Life of Balso Snell*, has been largely ignored. Instead, critics agree that it is formless, chaotic, a juvenile pastiche of bathroom jokes, college magazine parody, and borrowings from contemporary avant-garde authors. This consensus is not difficult to understand, for the sixty-two-page novella—which chronicles the journey of an everyman artist through the entrails of the Trojan horse, records his encounters with crazed representatives of Western culture, and climaxes with an unsatisfying nocturnal emission—twists and turns like the intestines which serve as its setting. If one remembers, however, that architectural principles of West's other novels are drawn from the visual arts, one perhaps is justified in looking for a similar structural matrix for *Balso Snell*.

West's interest in the visual arts dates back at least as far as his high

From *Studies in the English Novel* 3, vol. 11 (Fall 1979). Copyright © 1979 by North Texas State University.

school years, when he drew cartoons for his summer camp newspaper. In college, he not only enrolled in art history courses, he also illustrated the Brown literary magazine, began a lifelong friendship with artist and author S. J. Perelman, and planned a series of books on great artists—a project on which he worked desultorily during his postgraduate trip to Paris in 1926. In Paris, he met Max Ernst, Louis Aragon, and Philippe Soupault, and he attached himself to the Dada/Surrealist bohemian circle. Although *Balso Snell* was not published until 1931, it was written between 1922 and 1929, the years West spent at Brown and in Paris, a time in which West was preoccupied with modern art. Consequently, one would not be surprised to find evidence of this interest in *Balso Snell*.

The evidentiary key lies in West's original epigraph for the book, a pronouncement by the German Dadaist artist Kurt Schwitters: "Everything that the artist expectorates is art." This sentiment was retained in the final version of the book through the statement of George Moore, "art is a sublime excrement." (*The Dream Life of Balso Snell*, in *The Complete Works of Nathanael West*, New York: Farrar, Straus & Giroux, 1975, p. 8. All further references to this novella will be to this edition.) In one sense, the Schwitters motto is a commentary on the philosophy behind the novella—that art is literally a wasteland, that Western culture is composed of the excretions and eliminations of humanity. In another sense, the motto and its companion epigram by Moore give a gloss on the controlling excremental joke which provides design for the novella. People buried in cloaca, throats which sound like flushing toilets, actions occurring in bathrooms, and ceilings which release fecal matter upon playgoers are just a few of West's scatological variations (e.g., pp. 8, 18, 24, 31, 55). Finally, however, the Schwitters reference implies not only an aesthetic but also a technique. Schwitters, an influential practicing artist as well as a Dadaist spokesman, was known for his *Merzbilder* (junk constructions), collages composed of contents of his wastebasket or of detritus discovered on the streets. Inheriting the art of collage from Picasso and Braque who, in the years after 1912, began pasting paper and material on to canvas rather than imitating their textures in paint, Schwitters radicalized this technique by building it from junk in order to express the Dadaist view of art as refuse. In *Balso Snell*, West translates visual collage into literary collage. Like Schwitters, his choice and arrangement of materials make a strong Dadaist statement.

The most striking features of visual collage are the use of borrowed or found materials rejuvenated by their placement in an unexpected context, the technique of superimposition, and the aesthetically pleasurable surprise afforded by the exercise of artistic control on an assemblage of seemingly unrelated items. *The Dream Life of Balso Snell* exhibits all three features. First, West filches freely from a plethora of other authors. His literary borrowings can be garbled into burlesque, like his mangling of Stephen Dedalus's invocation into, " 'O Beer! O Meyerbeer! O Bach! O Offenbach! Stand me now as ever in good stead' " (p. 4). They can be exact, like the Euripidean prayer which becomes ludicrous when it is used as an expatriate cad's acknowledgement of the death of his mistress (p. 53). They can be imitations, like the serious-toned Dostoevskian murder which dislocates surrealistically when West makes a twelve-year-old boy, John Gilson, the perpetrator (pp. 18–21). Usually, these snippets of other authors are close enough to the originals to give the impression that West is, like visual collagists, creating out of preexisting substances. When West warps them humorously, the effect is rather like Picasso's dissected bicycle antelope or Max Ernst's placement of anatomy manual cut-outs upon painted tightropes and trapezes; the pleasure arises from the mental comparison of the original object and its function to the transformed object and its new function.

The second structural collage technique is superimposition. In a Schwitters construction, for example, a paint-mixing stick can traverse a scrap of chicken wire which, in turn, is affixed to a torn newspaper glued to the canvas. This technique explodes the rigid two-dimensionality of traditional painting. Similarly, *The Dream Life of Balso Snell* breaks through the temporal confines of the novella by layering different literary units within single episodes, units stacked like upended nesting boxes shuttling back and forth in time in order to give a collagelike spatial texture and a Jungian temporal simultaneity.

For example, the sixth of the seven divisions which make up *Balso Snell* contains at least eight discrete formal entities piled one atop the other (pp. 37–56). The first level finds Balso Snell drinking in a café built into the horse's intestinal wall. He falls asleep and proceeds to the second level, in which he meets a gorgeous hunchback named Janey Davenport. In order to send Balso on a mock-chivalric quest, she presents him with a letter which becomes the third level of the section. At first, the letter to Janey from her lover, Beagle Darwin, explains his refusal to take her with him to Paris; but the letter also contains the fourth formal level of this episode—a fictionalized scenario about Janey's reactions to pregnancy which ends in her suicide. Returning to the second level, Janey shows Balso another letter, this one becoming the fifth separate element of the section. The new letter, also from Beagle to Janey, contains a sixth element—a third-person account of Beagle's projected reaction to Janey's projected death. Within this account resides the seventh level, a first-person soliloquy in which Beagle, now a hybrid Hamlet/Pagliacci, fulminates upon the tragedy of man. From this platform, he jumps onto the eighth level of the section, a play within a play complete with characters, dialogue, a chorus, and its own superimpositional flourishes of allusions to Greek playwrights, the Bible, Alexander Pope, and François Villon. This portion of *Balso Snell* ends as Beagle goes into his juggling act. Through the device of superimposition, man the actor—like Picasso's tragic clowns—can be painted from a cubistic perspective which changes sequential observation into simultaneous perception. Abruptly, the next section begins when the protagonist wakes up in the café, the elaborate multistoried Janey Davenport episode having collapsed like Alice's house of cards. West uses this superimpositional structure with varying degrees of complexity throughout the book.

The third aspect of collage, the exercise of artistic control to unite apparently disparate elements, is at once the most elusive and the most fascinating as it applies to *The Dream Life of Balso Snell*. Just as the creator of a visual collage amalgamates his materials with repeated motifs of line, color, and spatial harmonies, West consolidates his literary collage with repeated motifs of style, symbol, and theme. West has packed his novella so densely that it would be impractical to unravel all these strands in a short analysis; nevertheless, an examination of some of his unifying threads can reveal the intricate texture of his work.

Allied to the stylistic technique of literary parody which laces the book from start to finish is West's habit of cultural name-dropping. For instance, his characters sprinkle their dialogue with roll calls of the famous, ranging from artists to religious figures to mythological personages. West also uses other stylistic unifying devices. Balso Snell, nominally a poet, can be counted upon to speak in clichés, emblems of bourgeois obtuseness and Dadaist ciphers of the modern breakdown in communcation. Reassuring a Semitic guide, he states, " 'I admire the Jews; they are a thrifty race. Some of my best friends are Jews' " (p. 8). He advises a morbid ascetic to " '[p]lay games. Don't read so many books. Take cold showers. Eat more meat' " (p. 13) and suggests that the psychotic Gilson ought to " 'run about more. Read less and play baseball' " (p. 23). Here the protagonist responds to a series of confessions, another device which knits together the novella. Just as the grotesques of *Winesburg, Ohio*, reveal their secrets to George Willard, the grotesques of the Trojan horse confess their hidden natures to Balso Snell. The guide confesses his Jewishness, the ascetic his religio-erotic obsession; John Gilson's Journal forms a criminal and moral confession (pp. 16–22) as do the dream letters of Beagle Darwin. A confession is an emptying out of unwanted aspects of self; as such, it is parallel to the Schwitters and Moore conceptions of art as expectoration and excrement. Akin to the confession is the ejaculatory lament. Most of the characters at one time or another erupt into Othello-esque series of "O! O! O!s," interjections which, as will be shown, also have thematic significance.

Other recurring stylistic devices are literalization and mock dialectic. For example, Maloney the Areopagite's account of St. Puce, the flea who lived in Christ's armpit, presents a literalization of Christ as the eucharistic meal and the temple of believers. Later, John Gilson literalizes his vulnerability by saying, "I wore my heart and genitals around my neck" (p. 26); he literalizes his driving sexual desire as "the chauffeur within me" (p. 29). These sorts of literalizations create absurd images with a visual power similar to paintings by Ernst and Magritte. In addition, mock dialectic is set up throughout the book. However, when Christianity confronts Judaism, when actors confront their audiences, when—in general—the illusions of the mind confront the realities of the body, the result is not a synthesis. It may be nihilistic denial of both alternating poles of reference, or it may be a call similar to the one which rises from Jonathan Swift—whose ridiculously rational Houyhnhnms and filthily libidinous Yahoos must be among Balso Snell's dark muses—for readers to find the positive ground between the negative poles of reference. One cannot be sure whether West is urging readers to plunge into the gulf with Baudelaire or to bridge it with Swift.

Finally, throughout the book, West manipulates the symbolist technique of synaesthesia. St. Puce revels in sensual ecstasy with " '[t]he music of Our Lord's skin sliding over his flesh. . . . The odors of His Body—more fragrant than the Temple of Solomon . . .' " (p. 12). John Gilson describes a reader's communion at a library in which books which "smelt like the breaths of their authors" seemed "to turn into flesh" (p. 17). The most extended instance of synaesthesia attaches to Gilson's teacher, Miss McGeeney's, biographical subject Samuel Perkins—the ultimate synaesthetic man who could " 'smell a chord in D minor . . . [or] the caress of velvet' " (p. 35). Synaesthesia not only blends the individual senses, it also magnifies sensual perception as a whole into a guiding force of existence, a force propelled by Freudian physical compulsion and by Swiftian physical revulsion.

In *The Dream Life of Balso Snell*, one cannot separate symbol from theme, for West repeats and embellishes symbols throughout the book in order to create thematic unity. His symbol clusters and their resulting thematic patterns are circular rather than linear; in fact, they resemble interlocking radial webs of meaning. As has been noted earlier, the most memorable symbols are excremental and anal. Like Père Ubu's constantly reiterated scatological interjections, the fecal and rectal references in *Balso Snell* provide both shock value and thematic amplification. Not only is art excrement, so are love and sex. Balso's "Phoenix Excrementi," who devour themselves and give themselves rebirth through evacuation, show an "infantile cloacal conception of birth." As Gilson beats his mistress, he screams, " 'O constipation of desire! O diarrhoea of love' " (p. 27). Beagle Darwin defines the tragedy of life as when "[c]oming from the bathroom, you discover that you have gonorrhoea, or you get a telegram that your mother is dead . . ." (p. 51). Balso's passion for Miss McGeeney is recorded as " 'Oh!' His mouth formed an O with lips torn angry in laying duck's eggs from a chicken's rectum" (p. 57). These examples illustrate a constellation of images of sex and the life cycle, waste material, and death or violence. Actually, all sex is violent in *Balso Snell*. Gilson's murder of the idiot dishwasher is a ritual castration ending in a mock-Elizabethan "little death" (p. 22); seduction becomes the breaking down of the walls of womanhood (p. 23); Balso is driven to hit Miss McGeeney "in the gut"—a blow against the feminine principle (p. 36); Janey's love for Beagle will end in suicide for her and artistic death for him; Balso's final wet dream is couched in violent military metaphors (pp. 61–62).

Again using the collage technique of superimposition, West erects smaller symbolic superstructures upon this larger thematic framework. There are images of impotence and autoeroticism: Gilson "climbed into [himself] like a bear into a hollow tree" (p. 17); Perkins's penile nose reminds Miss McGeeney of the Brobdingnagian phallus of a self-abuser she had known (p. 34). These images couple with fears of androgynous sexual identity. For example, after the murder, Gilson—rather like Eliot's Tiresias—feels "like a happy girl" and trolls for sailors, subsequently inducing orgasm and vomiting (pp. 21–22); Balso's sexual assault on Miss McGeeney transforms her into "a middle aged woman dressed in a mannish suit" (p. 32). Animal symbolism of horses, birds, and dogs reinforces the theme of violence, excrement, and the physical self.

Similarly, the theme of violence, excrement, and the mental self is conveyed through West's use of theatrical symbolism. The novella begins with a reference to the "actor-emperor" Nero (p. 4); it contains, as mentioned earlier, parodies of Shakespeare, of opera, and of Greek tragedies. At the book's midpoint, Gilson plans an art theater production at the end of which "the ceiling of the theater will be made to open and cover the occupants with tons of loose excrement" (p. 31), thereby creating a *deus ex entrailia* which condemns art, artists, and patrons alike. The characters in *Balso Snell*, frequently criticized as flat, are in fact a series of tragic and comic masks for the disintegrated psyche, a function clarified by the description of the idiot dishwasher. "[A] fat, pink and grey pig of a man . . . [h]is neck . . . smooth, white, fat, and covered all over with tiny blue veins like a piece of cheap marble," he symbolizes man in his grossest physicality, the supremacy of body over mind; consequently, "[h]e did not have a skull on the top of his neck, only a face . . . a face without side, back or top, like a mask" (p. 18). The ultimate reduction of art to a manifestation of sexual instinct is made by Gilson, when he states that "[a]ll my acting has but one purpose, the attraction of the female" (p. 26), and is echoed by Beagle Darwin's " '[l]ife is but the span from womb to tomb . . . a spasm of volupty: then . . . the comedy is over . . . ring down the curtain . . .' " (p. 50). Other arts are subjected to the same sort of physical reduction: Balso calls " 'a beautiful Doric prostate gland' " a piece of " 'exposed plumbing' " (p. 6); he learns that " 'the virtue of some sixteen year old maiden was the price paid for Ingres' La Source' " (p. 8); he promises to " 'replace music in your affections' " when he tries to seduce Janey (p. 38); he drags Miss McGeeney off to the bushes with *carpe diem* poetry (p. 59).

Acting both as nucleus and circumference to this thematic and imagistic web is West's most subtle symbol—the circle. As noted above, characters in *Balso Snell* expel circles as the caterpillar did in *Alice in Wonderland*. These "O's" not only express bafflement or longing, they visually represent a problem central to individual creative existence. Although life is circular and finally hollow, its final scene may involve a surrender to romantic monism. Balso's guide explains the situation at the beginning of the book: " 'If the world is one (everything part of the same thing—called by Picasso nature) then nothing either begins or ends . . . nature is a circle' " (p. 9). This philosophy frightens Balso so much that he tears loose and flees from the agglutinant Singular. Nevertheless, he cannot escape. The paean to roundness (pp. 4–5) with which he initiates his quest for individuality foreshadows his defeat. Each episode brings Balso in contact with characters who reaffirm the relentless circularity of life and the plurality-annihilating monism which it generates. In the middle of the book, Miss McGeeney calls " 'the senses a circle' " which moves from birth to romance to excremental decay and back to birth (pp. 35–36), rather like the life processes of the "Phoenix Excrementi" and of Janey Davenport. At last, Balso capitulates to his sexual urges and is swallowed by a physical union which metamorphoses into a facetious philosophical reconciliation of opposites. "The Two become One. The One that is all things . . . the sacrificial egg, the altar, the ego and the alter ego . . . the syllable 'Om' . . ." (p. 61). This absorption into universal unity produces the death of the individual—certainly the death of the artist. "His body broke free of the bard. It took on a life of its own; a life that knew nothing of the poet Balso. Only to death can this . . . be likened" (p. 61).

No more profoundly antimonistic or antitraditional statement could be made. The artist's quest for individuality ends in a black hole which sucks him into oblivion and sends art, sex, love, culture, and religion rushing in after him. This nihilistic message, then, helps identify *The Dream Life of Balso Snell* as a Dadaist work in intent as well as in structure. Acts of negative creation characterized by self-destruction, despair, shock value, spoof, nonsense, theatricality, spontaneity, and anticlassicism, Dadaist artworks—by their strident outrageousness—both exalt the personality of their creators and eulogize the "negative gesture which was to be the opposite of art, the violent language which was to be the execution of existing poetry." Like all varieties of Expressionist art, they appear in times of tension as revolts against the tyranny of mathematical thought, technical progress, and cultural dehumanization. Nevertheless, an attack on art through art, no matter how self-denigrating the artistic vehicle, always leads to a reaffirmation of art itself. Just as Balso could not escape the enclosing circles of being, the artist cannot escape his own creations. As the Dadaist author Tristan Tzara wrote in 1917, "DADA remains in the European framework of weaknesses; still it is a bunch of excrement, but we want to shit in different colors to ornament the zoo of art. . . ." Similarly, the intricate Dada collage structure employed by Nathanael West brands *The Dream Life of Balso Snell* as a genuine, if off-color, artistic creation. Like Schwitters—and, perhaps, in spite of his own intentions— West's aesthetic sensibilities transform ugly material into a beautiful composition. He ends up with a Dadaist collage that, by its very artistry, celebrates that which it wishes to destroy.

JOHN KEYES

# Personality in the Land of Wish: Popular Motifs in Nathanael West's "The Day of the Locust"

It is by now a critical commonplace that the fiction of Nathanael West is rooted in and a comment on, the popular culture of his time: the newspaper, the comic strip, the detective fiction in *Miss Lonelyhearts*; the Horatio Alger myth in *A Cool Million*; the cinema in *The Day of the Locust*. But there is another species of the popular, integral to the structure and substance of his final novel, that has never been acknowledged or perceived, much less examined in detail. The subject of *The Day of the Locust* is fulfillment, the prerogative not only of cinema, but, in its different ways, of fairy tale as well; it is an ironic fulfillment, however, one exposing the limitations of wish, for behind the assumed role or mask of the Hollywood character we find neither a self nor a void but another and complementary role, perhaps identity, with its roots in this very different sort of popular culture. Hence, it is somewhat astonishing that the novel has not been typified before through that most elementary of critical devices, the simple cataloguing of its cast: platinum-haired heroine; moralizing hero; two "ruling" figures of socio-economic substance; helpful dwarf; servant giant; cowboy "earl"; primitive (a surrogate for the beast); sinister or defunct parental figures (wicked mother and

From *The University of Windsor Review* 1 and 2, vol. 15 (1979–80). Copyright © 1980 by *The University of Windsor Review*.

derelict father who is also a professional clown)—all set in a silvery never-never land whose business is to make dreams come true. A trifle motley perhaps, but certainly a generic blend: one species of traditional folktale, the fairy tale or Märchen, with the folklore of industrial man.

The novel is West's *Blonde Beauty*, the quest of the girl with the golden hair, who is several Märchen heroines in one: Cinderella, Snow White, Beauty, Goldilocks. Faye Greener's handling of the Cinderella theme, the chorus girl's big chance, gave a realistic turn to miraculous events; she, like the artists of the Middle Ages, "seemed to think that fantasy could be made plausible by a hum-drum technique." Since West's plausibility factor depends upon inversion, Faye, as we shall see, becomes Blonde Beauty as angel child as well as castrating bitch. Hence, the evident childlike references in her description: although seventeen, she is "as shiny as a new spoon . . . . dressed like a child of twelve in a white cotton dress with a blue sailor collar"; she is associated with children's food, with candy, ice cream, sodas, gingersnaps; and she eats like a child—she puts butter on her bread, covers it with sugar and takes a "big bite." Hence, too, her relation to children's literature, to fairy tale or nursery motifs.

Cinderella, as the others, is a type of the rejected child, in flux from the extreme of gratuitous deprivation or persecution to that of somewhat gratuitous reward. The motherless Faye, later orphaned, is also an outcast waif, a Hollywood extra as fervently imbued with the clichés of the business which rejects her, as her prototypes were with their own simple faiths. Perrault's Cinderella, however cloying to the adult, with a sweet-nurtured child with good taste; West's rude, quick-tempered Faye seems more appreciative of the Tarzan archetype. The relationship between the two can be examined in the "Cinderella Bar" episode, a parody of the royal ball where the transformed hearth-child enraptures the king's son. The bar is "a little stucco building in the shape of a lady's slipper," an echo of Grimm's golden slipper stuck on the staircase. Its "floor show consisted of female impersonators." The transformation motif thus becomes a sexual transvestism so extreme it is what it would imitate; it is the imitation of the man which is obscene. Perhaps the peasant as princess, whether Cinderella or Faye, should be first that which she is, before she aspires to be more. As Perrault's young prince was taken, so enchanted with Cinderella he could eat nothing, so Homer will not drink (it makes him sick). Faye, however, "in a nasty mood," forces champagne cocktails and brandy down her provider's throat, because his superiority is driving her crazy. The persecuted heroine thus turns persecutive—a response to boredom, at first unconscious, later malicious. But there is more: West realizes, as Perrault and Grimm do not, that perfection irritates, that the unrelieved example of constant virtue is a psychological as well as a moral affront to those of us, who, like the stepsisters, have no hope of maintaining the standard. Hence, Homer's "generosity was still more irritating. It was so helpless and unselfish that it made her feel mean and cruel, no matter how hard she tried to be kind." There are further reductions at the child's expense; the prince would dance with no one but Cinderella; "This is my partner," said Grimm's, permitting no cut-ins. Faye is really less in demand, dancing with an unidentified pickup and with Tod, who begs her to sleep with him. Even the compliment on her beauty—"I said you were the most beautiful girl in the place"—is reductive, a trade-last. And Homer's identification of fairies as "Momo," reflects more than the homosexual's mother-centred propensities; it reminds us, remotely, of the absent Fairy Godmother. It is understandable, then, that Faye, as anti-Cinderella, should hate them: what have they ever done for her?

The motif of supernatural assistance is, of course, fulfilled in the novel, although it is undercut. It need not be a Fairy Godmother; friendly, domesticated beasts and maternal old women are also found. As Grimm's Cinderella is aided by pigeons and turtle-doves, his Two-Eyes by a "wise woman," so Faye, destitute upon the death of Harry, is aided by a Dove called Mary; both the appelative and the behaviour—she takes Faye into her arms—suggest she fulfills both human and animal functions. She is only ironically successful. In the Grimm variant, "One Eye, Two-Eyes, and Three-Eyes," the destitute Two-Eyes, upon the helpful wise woman's advice, buries the entrails of an enchanted goat, slaughtered by her envious mother, which had been her sole source of provision; up comes a tree with silver leaves and golden apples. Mary Dove tries too, in a series of unconscious puns: "Show some guts, kid. Come on now, show some guts." But no enchanted apples appear; instead, there is merely an attempt to escape: as Grimm's Cinderella escaped into a pigeon-house, so Faye escapes into a coo. It is the officious Mrs. Johnson, the janitress, more hearth-linked, with a "face like a baked apple, soft and blotched"—she has no doubt been too near the fire—who sets the scene straight with an authoritative and businesslike manner, appropriate responses for this business landscape; but she offers only short-term assistance. For the longer period, Mary suffices, providing the requisite solution, although she forfeits the maternal pose to do it; both girls become very tough: "They laughed shrilly and went into the bathroom with their arms around each other." The standard of socio-economic gratification for prior deprivation—the royal marriage—is thus represented by the Dove's employer, Audrey Jenning, the woman embodying those traits our society esteems: culture and refinement, sound business sense, skillful packaging of the industrial product—and who has Mrs. Prince to tea. Will Cinderella, call girl in her chauffeured coach, someday call on Mr. Prince? The magic city's rewards are ironic; the hearth-child is back "on the turf."

But only, she claims, to pay for the funeral of her father. For Faye, true fulfillment is found in stardom, cinematic success, failing that, in being successfully cinematic with her public, her collection of men. If not in this episode, at least in others, she is, like Cinderella, a creature of entrances; perhaps the royal ball is the cock fight as well, where she peacocks for them all. She also acquires her rich garments and coach, although she momentarily steps out of the Cinderella mold to do it, moving, like Goldilocks, the nursery set freeloader, into the bear-like Homer's thatch-roofed "Irish" cottage; she exploits him for a "coat of summer ermine and a light blue Buick runabout." She gets her six attendants too: they are more likely lizards from the water-butt transformed to liveried footmen (West's Hollywood is a cactus garden), than mice transformed to horses (the horses can in any case be found, transformed again, under the hood of her Buick). Certainly Faye treats them as her footmen: she pats Abe, the dwarf, on his head and tweaks his nose; Miguel calls her "mum" and both he and Earle are welcomed with "stilted condescension"; "Mamma spank" she has told both Tod and Homer; even Claude has a "begging note in his voice." This American child-heroine instinctively understands the sexual power latent in the mother. Finally, like Cinderella, she disappears into the night, not in rags and a pumpkin, but, we must assume, with all she can, including both Buick and ermine, leaving behind, as clue to identity if not whereabouts, not a glass slipper, but a broken flask of gardenia perfume, a reminder, in the shattered receptacle, both of the anti-virginal capacity and the synthetic nature of this garden princess. The only compensation for the male, it seems, is the transvestite's lullaby: "Little man, you're crying, / I know why you're blue, / Someone took your kiddycar away." Better to go to sleep now: which, at the end of this children's matinee, is just what Homer does.

The other roles receive lesser stress. If, in some versions, though not in all, Goldilocks takes from the bears out of necessity, with Faye it is sheer aggrandizement masquerading as a business deal; if Goldilocks represents a sort of selfless socialism, Faye, then, is aggressive capitalism. In Grimm's "Little Snow White," moreover, the outcast child, in dire hunger, takes food from the absent dwarfs, but only a little from each "for she did not wish to take all from one only." Allowed to stay as a domestic, to cook, sew, wash, knit, she is treated as a sister; West's dwarf is more appreciative: "What a quiff! What a quiff!" he cries, "as though hypnotized"; and it is Homer who does the housework so his Goldilocks-Snow White will stay. Tod, however, fulfills the magic mirror motif of the Snow White analogue, unable to take his eyes from the fairest one of all, the photograph in the upper corner of his mirror frame: a still from a two-reel farce with Faye in harem costume, occasion less of envy than of masochistic fantasy. Nor do enchanted objects pose a threat for the anti-Snow-White type; she understands too well the economics of survival. Faye may gulp her food, but poisoned apples could never lodge in her throat; she "gobbled up" Homer's salad, but ate the "large red apple . . . more slowly, nibbling daintily, her smallest finger curled away from the rest of her hand." The poisoned comb West handles with a pun: the bloody comb of the "dirty black hen" which Faye does not mind because "it's only natural." Nor is lace a danger; does she not dance on the crest (the comb) of the waves, only caught for the moment in its net of lace?

As Beauty, her preference for the primitive, the "gorilla," Miguel, to the earl, Shoop, is evident; the motif echoes both fairy tale and cinema as the heroine willingly seeks the embraces of the "monster" to those of the figure, however, ludicrous, signifying rescue. Beauty, of course, was rewarded for learning to discount appearance; accepting the Beast for what he is, not for what he seems to be, she sees him become a Prince, both figures in one, a literal dream come true, an apotheosis which is also sublimation. Miguel's gorilla nature only seems apparent (he merely wears a sweater called a "gorilla"); but in actual fact he is the novel's primitive, Faye's Tarzan: he sat "full in the light of the fire. His skin glowed and the oil in his black curls sparkled." Faye's unsublimated desire for him stands in ironic counterpoint to her cinematic aspirations which are forms of sublimation. The net effect is complicated: the reader reacts not only to West's text, but to his own conceptions of, and prior reactions to, the function and intrinsic worth of both cinema and fairy tale. Thus cynicism toward either can render Faye's response more genuine: an expression of uncomplicated id. But both, especially the simplicity of fairy tale, can comment upon our cynicism.

Since so many figures circle around Faye or what she represents, the novel seems a redaction of the type, the *Quest of the Princess with the Golden Hair*. Motifs common to this type are: a hero in quest of the princess; assistance of a magic horse, or, less commonly, a ship; loathesome animals which defile a prince's food (often represented as Harpies, winged female creatures); tasks imposed upon the hero (taming fierce animals or ploughing a field); happy ending with marriage of hero and princess. The princess may have solar connections: "in at least two fairy stories [she] is . . . named the Virgin of the Sun." Faye, too, is near to this: she seems linked to vegetation or Creation Myth. In her "new flower print dress . . . she was much more than pretty. . . . She looked just born, everything moist and fresh, volatile and perfumed"; not a Culture Hero, but an anti-Culture Heroine for a microcosmic society of male effetism, she stimulates not birth but the events which terminate the novel. In West, at least, the quest seems an ironic wasteland variant: parodic heroes seeking a mock sun or vegetative goddess in what is really a cultural desert. The winged loathesome animal motif is fulfilled by the titular and symbolic "Locust," which destroys not vegetation but the princely city itself.

My concerns, however, are with the hero. One obvious nominee is the rejected cowboy, Earle Shoop, linked to both horse and ship: "Let him ride a horse," says Mary Dove to Faye, "he's a cowboy, ain't he?"; and Earle Shoop = earlship (plus an echo of sloop from G. "Schlup"?). But even if in parodic form he fulfills the "tasks," taming fierce animals by caging and beheading quail, ploughing fields with his "crude hoedown," he is too obviously mechanical and cartoon-like to be of much concern. The real hero is Tod, related not only to the tasks of quest encapsulated on the studio back lot, but also to those of watch or wooing adventures. Deprived by nature and circumstance, he cannot fulfill the tests of woo: "He had nothing to offer [Faye], neither money nor looks, and she could only love a handsome man and would only let a wealthy man love her." Nor, despite his observations and moral commentary, does he fulfill the functions of watch: like Prufrock, he is too much a part of the society he judges to presume to watch or warn; his Jeremiah instinct is a response to frustration, sublimated lust; and his art is less restorative than corrosive. Of course, he needs assistance, and he gets it, from another fairy-tale type, the helpful dwarf, Abe Kusich. But helpfulness becomes pugnacious interference, the magic horse a tip on the fifth at Caliente, Tragopan, the pheasant (etymologically, Gk. trágo(s), goat + Pān, Pan), an introduction to the phallic principle, which may, as well, be a reference to the cuckold; the tragopan has two fleshy, erectile horns on its head, and Tod is really the stuff of which cuckolds are made. "You could learn from him" (from Abe), Tod tells Homer. Indeed, both dwarf and giant are linked and counterpoised through head imagery, the latter's "small," the former's "slightly hydrocephalic." But the large, sloppy, "almost doltish" Tod, might learn from him too. Is Abe's tip, then, a "bum steer"? Perhaps for Tod it is, since it leads him indirectly to the castrating Faye, the mock sun goddess. We remember the bum steers of Hemingway, where the potentialities of sunrise were linked to the metaphor of phallicism. Better, I suppose, in a world as harsh as this one, to do your own horse riding, or to be the bull, not the hack or jade. Abe may be smashed on the wall like a rabbit, but he gleefully feels he "fixed that buckeroo." He at least can drive away, consigning them all to hell: Tod Hackett is driven.

Homer embodies all the archetypal traits of the giants of folklore. Despite his automatonic nature, he is human; he is also ironically related to the dragon concept: his "feelings were so intense that his head bobbed stiffly on his neck like that of a toy Chinese dragon." He is productive of changes in the landscape; he initiates the apocalyptic riot. He participates in the double nature of the archetype; at once benevolent, kindly, stupid and servile, he is metamorphosed finally, by provocation, into the ogre, a type of the man- or child-eating giant. His relationships throughout are with children; the Romola Martin episode, despite its metallic and homosexual associations, contains precise childlike references, and is the type of the other two, those with Faye and Adore Loomis. Homer's sexual contacts are basically childlike; those with children are basically sexual. Thus Adore's purse-on-a-string routine (recalling his sailboat on a string, which recalls Faye's blue sailor collar) is a sexual lure, both umbilical and uterine, which the sleepwalking giant, already in Uterine Flight, ignores. It is the stone hurled by Adore which brings him to life, a motif echoing and inverting David's struggle with the Biblical Goliath. Homer, the philistine giant from a philistine midwest, through murder of the "beloved" David figure, Adore, symbolically destroys Hollywood's quasi-culture. He is last seen, appropriately, in a harsh Goya image, the giant slaying episode at the hands of the mob; he is shoved against the sky, his jaw hanging open to scream: "A hand reached up and caught him by his open mouth and pulled him forward and down."

The remaining figures fall into the appropriate slots. Thus, Claude Estee, American aristocrat as Civil War colonel, represents the male side of the Hollywood reward, the embodiment of the questing hero's aspirations, not the heroine's (ostensibly, you should get the golden-haired figure if you can become the prince). Despite his marriage to Alice (Gmc.: of noble rank), it is the Claude-Audrey Jenning association which completes the royal marriage motif: the connecting link is prostitution, whether metaphoric or literal. This structural alignment is paralleled by another system of value, the family unit, perverted through continuance of the business ethic and weakened through the absence of a necessary member. West counterpoints the fatherless son with the motherless daughter, showing both mother-son and father-daughter relationships to be exploitative and rejecting. Maybelle Loomis is an ironic inversion of the wicked mother figure; rejecting her child through over- not under-attention, she exploits him for economic gain. Parental wish is here imposed upon the child. Harry Greener, though his prime function is as clown, is the masculine complement to Maybelle: less concerned with his daughter's professional or personal aspirations than with the bitter memories of the rejections of his past. The child's wish is here ignored by the parent. Both relationships deteriorate to mechanistic reflexes, to the artifices and mannerisms of the acting profession, to spurious forms of playing a role rather than the authenticity of Being. Not just the individual then, but the family, the microcosmic social unit supposed to substructure a meaningful community, is also fragmented. Synthesis of these fragments to one unit, to family completion, seems no more rewarding than their separation; metaphorically speaking, new fragments could splinter off, father-son and mother-daughter, Maybelle-Faye and Harry-Adore, all of which may be reflected in the opposed consequences of the fate of the children. Tod fears Faye would break his back; Homer, Tod's alter ego, frustrated by Faye, breaks the back of Adore, the child who stands in counterpoint to her. Thus, by the novel's end, both Harry and Adore are gone, while Maybelle and Faye remain, a new synthesis reflecting the greater resilience of the aggressive female principle. But it is hardly a reproductive synthesis.

The Day of the Locust, then, is a novel rooted in the popular in a double sense: in what has developed from, or been created by, the people (the fairy tale); and in what is created for the people, i.e., for popular consumption (the Hollywood culture, the cinema). Only the latter has been recorded in the prior criticism. But the novel is only partially comprehensible if we fail to perceive the relationship between its two species of the popular, a relationship with numerous artistic functions and effects. Certainly it tempers allegations of West's grotesquerie. And psychologically, West's treatment of the literature of wish should at least have been a therapeutic exercise, an attempt to free his projected or implied self from one symptom of that "Disease" from which, according to W. H. Auden, not only his characters but his historical self reputedly suffered. More significantly, it is also an instrument in the analysis of that disease, especially in its initial symptom, the incapacity to convert wish into desire. West's attitude to the fairy tale is not ironic; the objective relationship of fairy tale to Hollywood is. The wish, the refusal to be oneself, as Auden puts it, may be "innocent and frivolous . . . or a serious expression of guilt and despair"; the former condition applies to the Märchen (where wishes are fulfilled in the subconscious and there is no need of desire), the latter to the cinematic landscape (where wishes are frustrated in the conscious world of action and there is no ability to form a true desire); and it is, of course, this negative sort of private wish which is the true species of the national. The novel is thus a form of reciprocal comment, of each side upon the other, fairy tale upon Hollywood cinema, and West can make his points without recourse to propaganda. This being so, it becomes successful proletarian literature in the wider sense of the term, a working class literature which can afford to obviate the propagandistic and the revolutionary; as William Empson says:

> The wider sense of the term includes such folk-literature as is by the people, for the people, and about the people. But most fairy stories and ballads, though "by" and "for," are not "about"; whereas pastoral though "about" is not "by" or "for."

Since pastoral, to Empson, is exemplified today by a more narrow view of proletarian, by a literature of workers, West's ironic variant is an attempt to be all three: its background fairy tale, with its roots in folk tradition, is essentially by the people (and for them as well), the foreground narrative, with its source in Hollywood, is about them, and the reciprocal dialogue between the two offers a corrective, especially upon the foreground. His proletarian book thus becomes an incisive political and humanistic instrument, constituting through its form, a successful and convincing argument for a more organic and natural, far less mechanistic society.

# Chronology

| | |
|---|---|
| 1903 | Born Nathan Weinstein, in New York City on October 17, son of Anna Wallenstein Weinstein, and Max Weinstein, a building contractor, both born in Russia. |
| 1920 | After three poor academic years, leaves DeWitt Clinton High School without graduating. |
| 1921 | Enters Tufts College in September, but leaves after two months. |
| 1922 | Transfers to Brown University in February. |
| 1924 | Graduates from Brown University in June. |
| 1926–27 | Lives in Paris. |
| 1931 | *The Dream Life of Balso Snell.* |
| 1932 | Edits little magazine, *Contact*, with William Carlos Williams. |
| 1933 | *Miss Lonelyhearts.* Works as scriptwriter for Columbia Studios. |
| 1934 | *A Cool Million.* |
| 1936 | Scriptwriter for Republic Studios, later for R.K.O. and Universal. |
| 1939 | *The Day of the Locust.* |
| 1940 | Marries Eileen McKenney on April 19 in Beverly Hills, California. Killed, with his wife, in an automobile accident on December 22 near El Centro, California. |

# Contributors

HAROLD BLOOM, Sterling Professor of the Humanities at Yale University, is the author of *The Anxiety of Influence, Poetry and Repression* and many other volumes of literary criticism. His forthcoming study, *Freud: Transference and Authority*, attempts a full-scale reading of all of Freud's major writings. He is the general editor of *The Chelsea House Library of Literary Criticism*.

STANLEY EDGAR HYMAN was Professor of Literature at Bennington College. His books include *The Tangled Bank* and *The Armed Vision*.

W. H. AUDEN was widely considered to be the leading British poet of his generation. Besides his collected poems, his major work is to be found in *The Early Auden* and *The Dyer's Hand*.

ALVIN B. KERNAN, Kenan Professor of the Humanities at Princeton University, is the author of *The Cankered Muse, The Plot of Satire* and *The Imaginary Library*, among other works.

DANIEL AARON is Professor Emeritus of English at Harvard. His books include *Writers on the Left* and *The Unwritten War: American Writers in the Civil War*.

R. W. B. LEWIS, Gray Professor of Rhetoric at Yale University, has written *The American Adam, The Picaresque Saint, Trials of the Word* and studies of Edith Wharton and Hart Crane.

MAX F. SCHULZ is Chairman of the Department of English Literature at the University of Southern California.

JAY MARTIN, Professor of English at the University of Southern California, is the author of critical biographies of Nathanael West and Conrad Aiken.

T. R. STEINER teaches English at the University of California at Santa Barbara. He has written books on neoclassical translation and on the rise of the city in neoclassical literature.

MILES D. ORVELL teaches at Temple University and is the author of *Invisible Parade: Fiction of Flannery O'Connor*.

MAX APPLE teaches creative writing at Rice University. He is the author of *The Oranging of America* and *Zip!*

JAMES F. LIGHT, Professor of English and Dean of the College of Liberal Arts at Southern Illinois University, is the author of *Nathanael West: An Interpretative Study*.

JEFFREY L. DUNCAN teaches at Eastern Michigan University. He has written on Emerson and Thoreau, and is the author of *The Metaphor of the Word in Nineteenth-Century American Literature*.

DEBORAH WYRICK is a graduate student in English at Duke University.

JOHN KEYES is Professor of English at Ryerson.

# Bibliography

Abrahams, Roger D. "Androgynes Bound: Nathanael West's *Miss Lonelyhearts*." In *Seven Contemporary Authors*. Edited by Thomas B. Whitbread. Austin: University of Texas Press, 1966.

Andreach, Robert J. "Nathanael West's *Miss Lonelyhearts*: Between the Dead Pan and the Unborn Christ." *Modern Fiction Studies* 2, vol. 12 (1966): 251–60.

Baxter, Charles. "Nathanael West: Dead Letters and the Martyred Novelist." *West Coast Review* 2, vol. 9 (1974): 3–11.

Brown, Daniel R. "The War Within Nathanael West: Naturalism and Existentialism." *Modern Fiction Studies* 2, vol. 2 (1974): 181–202.

Conroy, Mark. "Letters and Spirit in *Miss Lonelyhearts*." *The University of Windsor Review* 1, vol. 17 (1982): 5–20.

Duncan, Jeffrey L. "The Problem of Language in *Miss Lonelyhearts*." *Iowa Review* 1, vol. 8: 116–28.

Flavin, Robert J. "Animal Imagery in the Works of Nathanael West." *Thoth* 5, (1964): 25–30.

Geha, Richard, Jr. "*Miss Lonelyhearts*: A Dual Division of Mercy." *Hartford Studies in Literature* 3 (1971): 116–31.

Gilmore, Thomas B., Jr. "The Dark Night of the Cave: A Rejoinder to Kernan on *The Day of the Locust*." *Satire Newsletter* 2 (1965): 95–100.

Hanlon, Robert M., S.J. "The Parody of the Sacred in Nathanael West's *Miss Lonelyhearts*." *The International Fiction Review* 2, vol. 4 (1977): 190–93.

Hollis, C. Carroll. "Nathanael West and Surrealist Violence." *Fresco* 7 (Fall 1957): 5–21.

Light, James F. *Nathanael West: An Interpretive Study*. Evanston: Northwestern University Press, 1961.

Madden, David, ed. *Nathanael West: The Cheater and the Cheated*. Deland, Fla.: Everett/Edwards, 1973.

Mankin, Paul A. "The Fight Against Institutions in the Parodic Discourse of Nathanael West and Boris Vian." In *Proceedings of the 7th Congress of the International Comparative Literature Association*, vol. 1. Edited by Milan V. Dimîó and Juan Ferraté. Stuttgart: Kunst und Wissen, Erich Beiber, 1979.

Martin, Jay. *Nathanael West: The Art of His Life*. New York: Farrar, Straus and Giroux, 1970.

———, ed. *Nathanael West: A Collection of Critical Essays*. Englewood Cliffs, N.J.: Prentice-Hall, Inc., 1971.

Reid, Randall. *The Fiction of Nathanael West: No Redeemer, No Promised Land*. Chicago and London: The University of Chicago Press, 1967.

Schoenewolf, Carroll. "Jamesian Psychology and Nathanael West's *Miss Lonelyhearts*." *San Jose Studies* 3, vol. 3 (1981): 80–86.

Shepard, Douglas. "Nathanael West Rewrites Horatio Alger, Jr." *Satire Newsletter* 3 (1965): 13–28.

Trachtenberg, Stanley. "West's Locusts: Laughing at the Laugh." *Michigan Quarterly Review* 2, vol. 14 (1975): 187–98.

Tropp, Martin. "Nathanael West and the Persistence of Hope." *Renascence* 4, vol. 31 (1979): 205–14.

Tuch, Ronald. "The Dismantled Self in the Fiction of Nathanael West." *Psychocultural Review* 1 (1977): 43–48.

Walsh, Joy. "*Miss Lonelyhearts*: The Problem of Touching and the Primary Need of Fictions." *Notes on Modern American Literature* 1, vol. 6 (1982).

Ward, J. A. "The Hollywood Metaphor: The Marx Brothers, S. J. Perelman, and Nathanael West." *Southern Review* 3, vol. 12 (1975): 659–72.

Wells, Walter. "Shriek of the Locusts." In *Tycoons and Locusts*. Carbondale: Southern Illinois University Press, 1973.

White, William. *Nathanael West: A Comprehensive Bibliography*. Kent, Ohio: Kent State University Press, 1975.

Widmer, Kingsley. *Nathanael West*. Boston: Twayne Publishers, 1982.

———. "The Sweet, Savage Prophecies of Nathanael West." In *The Thirties*. Edited by Warren French. Deland, Fla.: Everett / Edwards, 1967.

Zlotnick, Joan. "The Medium is the Message, Or is it?: A Study of Nathanael West's Comic Strip Novel." *Journal of Popular Culture* 1, vol. 5 (1971): 236–40.

# Acknowledgments

"Nathanael West" by Stanley Edgar Hyman from *University of Minnesota Pamphlets on American Writers* 21 by Stanley Edgar Hyman, copyright © 1962 by University of Minnesota. Reprinted by permission.

"Interlude: West's Disease" by W. H. Auden from *The Dyer's Hand and Other Essays* by W. H. Auden, copyright © 1957 by W. H. Auden. Reprinted by permission.

"The Mob Tendency: *The Day of the Locust*" by Alvin B. Kernan from *The Plot of Satire* by Alvin B. Kernan, copyright © 1965 by Yale University. Reprinted by permission.

"Late Thoughts on Nathanael West" by Daniel Aaron from *The Massachusetts Review* 6 (Winter-Spring 1965), copyright © 1965 by *The Massachusetts Review*, Inc. Reprinted by permission.

"Days of Wrath and Laughter: West" by R. W. B. Lewis from *Trials of the Word* by R. W. B. Lewis, copyright © 1965 by R. W. B. Lewis. Reprinted by permission.

"Nathanael West's 'Desperate Detachment' " by Max F. Schulz from *Radical Sophistication: Studies in Contemporary Jewish-American Novelists* by Max F. Schulz, copyright © 1969 by Max F. Schulz. Reprinted by permission.

" 'Abandon Everything!' " by Jay Martin from *Nathanael West: The Art of His Life* by Jay Martin, copyright © 1970 by Jay Martin. Reprinted by permission.

"West's Lemuel and the American Dream" by T. R. Steiner from *The Southern Review* 4, vol. 7 (October 1971), copyright © 1971 by Louisiana State University. Reprinted by permission.

"The Messianic Sexuality of *Miss Lonelyhearts*" by Miles D. Orvell from *Studies in Short Fiction* 2, vol. 10 (Spring 1973), copyright © 1973 by Newberry College. Reprinted by permission.

"History and Case History in *Red Cavalry* and *The Day of the Locust*" by Max Apple from *Nathanael West: The Cheaters and the Cheated, A Collection of*

# Index

**A**

aesthetic stoicism, 5
Agee, James, 62
Aiken, Conrad, 96
Alger, Horatio, 81–2, 99, 137, 155, 157,
    165
    myth, 101
    novels, 99
*American Humor* (Rourke), 95
American Writers Congress, 15
*Americana*, 14
anti-Semitism, 1, 13, 67, 103–04
Apollinaire, Guillaume, 93
Aragon, Louis, 158
Arno, Peter, 90
Atkinson, Brooks, 15
Auden, W. H., 172

**B**

Babel, Isaac
    West and, 119–28
*Barefaced Lie, A*, 130–31
Baudelaire, Charles, 12, 96–97, 161
beauty, 166
Bellow, Saul, 1, 87
Benchley, Robert, 66
Bible, the, 160
"Big Bear of Arkansas, The" (Thorpe),
    130
*Blonde Beauty*, 166
*Blue Voyage* (Aiken), 96
Bodenheim, Max, 90
Bosch, Hieronymus, 66
Botticelli, Sandro, 53
*Bottom Dogs*, (Dahlberg), 62
*Bound to Rise* (Alger), 137
Brentano's, 91
Brewer, Warren & Putnam, 91
Brodkey, Harold, 2
*Brothers Karamazov, The* (Dostoevski), 79,
    113
Bunyan, John, 63, 65
Burckhardt, Jacob, 99

Burke, Kenneth, 67
    definition of humor of, 67
"Business Deal," 14
Butler, Nicholas Murray, 94
Byron, George Gordon, Lord, 78

**C**

Cabell, James Branch, 97
Caldwell, Erskine, 13
*Candide* (Voltaire), 137
capitalism, American, 81
Carroll, Lewis, 93
*Casements*, 13
"Celebrated Jumping Frog of Calaveras
    County, The," (Twain), 131
Cerf, Bennett, 15
*Cheated, The*, 34
    *see also Day of the Locust*
Christianity, 16
Cinderella, 166–68
Coates, Robert, M.
    West and, 29
Columbia Pictures, 15
Comerchero, Victor, 86, 99, 106, 129
*Commentary*, 105
communication, 36, 128
communism, 68
Communist criticism, 62–63, 66
Communist Party, 15, 62, 66
Contact Editions, 91–92
*Contact*, 14, 36, 92
*Contempo*, 13–15, 120
*Cool Million, A*, 1, 8, 14–15, 27, 43, 45,
    65, 69–71, 75, 81, 85, 99–107,
    130, 136, 139, 142, 155, 157, 165
    *Candide* and, 137
    comic tone, 66, 69, 81–83
    critics and, 66
    *Day of the Locust* and, 31, 72
    dedication, 66, 139
    form, lack of, 28
    Horatio Alger and, 65, 82
    indictment of America, in, 29

*Cool Million, A (continued)*
　　*Justine* and, 45–46
　　*Miss Lonelyhearts* and, 27–30
　　parody, 27, 82, 137
　　plot, 27–28
　　satire and, 71
　　screen treatment, 15
　　sex and, 30
　　totalitarianism and, 29
　　writing of, 14
Coolidge, Calvin, 8
creation myth, 170
Crichton, Kyle, 66–67
*Crying of Lot 49, The*, 1
Cummings, E. E., 62

**D**
Dadaism, 158–64
Dahlberg, Edward, 62
Daumier, Honoré, 49–50
"Dawn Ginsburg's Revenge" (Perelman),
　　66
*Day of the Locust, The* 1, 15, 29–40,
　　49–60, 72–75, 81, 83–84, 90,
　　98–99, 120–24, 130, 139, 142,
　　155, 165–73
　　action, 37
　　central character, 49
　　communication, 36
　　conclusion, 32, 34, 57, 59
　　death and, 37, 53–54
　　dreams and, 56–58
　　failure, 39
　　form of, 59
　　*Gulliver's Travels* (Swift), and, 83–84
　　humor in, 38, 52–53
　　illusion, 58–69
　　imagery, 33, 37, 39
　　language, 38
　　literary technique, 1, 37–38
　　Marxism and, 34
　　*Miss Lonelyhearts* and, 31, 39
　　nature and, 32
　　plot, 30, 57
　　popular, 119
　　sales, 15
　　title, 31
　　violence, 59
　　West's novels and, 73
"Death," 13
depression, 62, 65, 90, 99

disease, 54–55, 65
"Dismantling of Lemuel Pitkin, The,"
　　136
　　*see also Cool Million, A*
*Divine Comedy, The* (Dante), 94
*Don Juan* (Byron), 78
Dostoevski, Feodor, 11, 43, 63, 76,
　　120
dreams, 42, 63
　　convention, 41
　　*see also Day of the Locust,*
*Dream Life of Balso Snell, The*, 1, 13–14,
　　16–17, 75–81, 85, 92–94, 99,
　　106, 114–15, 120, 127, 131–33,
　　142, 155, 157–64
　　autobiography and, 90
　　comic imagination, 17
　　complexity, 18
　　Contact Edition, 92
　　*Cool Million A*, and, 27
　　Dadaism, 158–64
　　dedication, 14
　　form, 18
　　later work and, 18
　　love and, 78
　　*Miss Lonelyhearts* and, 19
　　publication, 92
　　review, 13
　　sales, 92
　　satire, 76
　　scatology, 18
　　weakness, 18
Dryden, John, 75
*Duino Elegies* (Rilke), 96
*Dunciad, The* (Pope), 51, 59

**E**
Edison, Thomas, 82
Eliot, T. S., 114
Emerson, Ralph Waldo, 154
Empson, William, 173
*En Route* (Huysmans), 97
*Endymion* (Keats), 76
Ernst, Max, 158, 161
esotericism, Jewish, 1
"Euripides—A Playwright," 13
Exodus, 31

**F**
Farrell, James T., 13
fascism, 35, 66

Faulkner, William, 1, 69
   *A Cool Million* and, 65
   West and, 1
Fearing, Kenneth, 62
Fielder, Leslie, 108
*fin de siecle*, 63
Firbank, Ronald, 5
Fitzgerald, F. Scott, 5, 14, 27, 61, 63
*Five Came Back*, 14
Flores, Angel, 61, 63
Ford, Henry, 82
Forsythe, Robert, *see* Kyle Crichton
Frank, Jacob, 7
Frankists, 2
French literature, influence on West, 15, 93
Freud, Sigmund, 2, 4, 64
   humor, essay on, 4
*From Flushing to Calvary* (Dahlberg), 62

**G**

*Gargantua* (Rabelais), 107
Gauguin, Paul, 4
"Gedali" (Babel), 125
gnosticism, 4, 7
   Jewish, 1, 2, 8
Gold, Mike, 90
Goldilocks, 166, 168–69
Gorky, Maxim, 128
Gotham Book Mart, 91
Goya, Francisco, 49
*Gravity's Rainbow* (Pynchon), 1
*Great Gatsby, The* (Fitzgerald), 1, 27
   *Miss Lonelyhearts* and, 27
Greeley, Horace, 13
Greene, Graham, 80
Grimm, Jakob, 166
Guggenheim Foundation, 14
*Gulliver's Travels* (Swift), 83, 99, 107
   *Day of the Locust* and, 83

**H**

*Hamlet, The* (Faulkner), 69
Hammett, Dashiell, 13, 92
Hearst, William Randolph, 66
Heller, Joseph, 136
Hemingway, Ernest, 5, 27, 120
Herbst, Josephine, 63, 78, 87, 92
Hitler, Adolf, 29, 101
Hofstadter, Richard, 71
Hollywood, 14, 15, 72, 75, 83, 121, 124, 128, 172–73

Homer, Winslow, 49
homosexuality, 23–24, 80, 87, 111
Horace, 51
Houghton Mifflin, 91
humor, 4, 52–53, 139
Huxley, Aldous, 5, 97
Huysmans, J. K., 12, 97
Hyman, Stanley Edgar, 2, 123, 129
   West, essay on, 2

**I**

*I Stole a Million*, 14
"Imposter, The," 93
*It Can't Happen Here* (Lewis), 71

**J**

James, Henry, 11
James, William, 19, 63–65
Jarry, Alfred, 93
Jewish-American writers, 87, 108
"Jim Baker's Bluejay Yarn" (Twain), 130
Johnson, Samuel, 120
Josephson, Matthew, 93
*Journal of Balso Snell, The, see Dream Life
   of Balso Snell*
Joyce, James, 12, 76, 78, 93, 96–97
*Jurgen* (Cabell), 12
*Justine* (de Sade), 45
   *Cool Million, A*, and, 45–64
Juvenal, 51

**K**

Kabbalah, 1
Kafka, Franz, 132
Keats, John, 76
kenoma, 4
   *see also* gnosticism
King, Alexander, 14
Knopf, 91
Kober, Arthur, 90

**L**

*La Bas* (Huysmans), 97
*Last Puritan, The* (Santayana), 64
Lawrence, D. H., 4
Lewis, Sinclair, 71
*Liber Brunensis*, 13
Liebling, A. J., 19, 76
Light, James F., 18
Liveright, Horace, 14
*Lonely Years, The* (Babel), 119

Lucilius, 5

**M**

Machen, Arthur, 12
"Mademoiselle Coeur-Brise," 15
Magritte, René, 161
Mailer, Norman, 1
Malamud, Bernard, 1, 87
*Maltese Falcon, The,* (Hammett), 13
*Man Who Died, The* (Lawrence), 4
Martin, Jay, 115, 130
Marx, Karl, 65
Marxism, 34
Marxists, 67
masochism, 2
Mathieu, Beatrice, 97
Maugham, Somerset W., 4
McKenney, Eileen, 15
McKenney, Ruth, 15
Melville, Herman, 4
*Merzbilder,* 158
*Merzkunst* (Schwitters), 92
*Messianic Idea of Judaism, The,* (Scholem), 1
    comment on *Miss Lonelyhearts,* 1
*Metamorphosis, The* (Kafka), 132
Milton, John, 6
*Miss Lonelyhearts,* 1–4, 13–15, 31, 61, 65, 69–71, 75, 86, 98–99, 111–18, 129, 130, 134–36, 142, 145–56, 165, 167
    adaptations of, 15
    allegory, 19
    American literature and, 27
    Bellow and, 1
    characters, 19–20
    comic book technique, 124
    critics and, 66
    *Day of the Locust* and, 31, 39
    feminine masochism, 2
    Fitzgerald and, 61
    Freud and, 64
    greatness, 27
    homosexuality, 23–24
    humor, 148–49
    idyllic scene, 20
    imagery, 26–27, 38
    irony, 148
    language and, 145–56
    love and, 78
    Malamud and, 1

narrator, 154
negations, 2
Oedipus complex, 24
pace, 26
play, 15
plot, 19
popular, 119
psychosexuality, 2
religious, 2
rhetoric, 3, 20, 25
sales, 15
Sophoclean irony, 19
suffering and, 22, 24
theme, 21
tone, 24, 27
*Ulysses* and, 80
verbal economy, 2
violence, 24–25
"Miss Lonelyhearts and the clean old man," 26
"Miss Lonelyhearts and the lamb," 25
"Miss Lonelyhearts in the Dismal Swamp," 4, 136
*Moon and Sixpence* (Maugham), 4
Moore, George, 158
morality, 51
Morgan, John P., 66
"My First Goose" (Babel), 123
"My Sister Eileen," 15, 105

**N**

Nabokov, Vladimir, 120
Nathan of Gaza, 8
*Nathanael West: The Ironic Prophet,* 129
naturalism, 61
Nero, 162
*New Masses, The,* 62, 66–67
*New York Times, The,* 8–9, 119
*New Yorker, The,* 66
Nietzsche, Friedrich, 12
nihilism, 2, 7–8
*Notes from the Underground* (Dostoevski), 43

**O**

Odets, Clifford, 130
Odo of Cluny, 18
Oedipus complex, 24
*Omoo* (Melville), 4
"One Eye, Two-Eyes, and Three-Eyes" (Grimm), 167

*Onward and Upward* (Alger), 137
Ozick, Cynthia, 1

**P**

*Parlor, Bedlam and Bath* (Perelman), 97
parody, 4, 17, 114
    *Cool Million* and, 27, 82, 137
Perelman, S. J., 12–13, 62, 66–67, 90,
    97, 106, 139, 158
Persius, 51
Petronius, 51
Picasso, Pablo, 93, 160
*Pilgrim's Progress* (Bunyan), 65, 94
*Plumed Serpent, The* (Lawrence), 4
Pope, Alexander, 51, 160
*Portrait of the Artist as a Young Man, A*
    (Joyce), 96
Pound, Ezra, 96
*Psychology of Religion* (Starbuck), 63
Pynchon, Thomas, 1

**R**

RKO Radio, 14
*Red Cavalry*, 124, 126–28
"Redemption Through Sin" (Scholem), 1
Reid, Randall, 111, 146
Republic Studios, 14
*Révolution Surréaliste, La*, 93
Reynolds, Quent, 90
Rilke, Rainer Maria, 96
Rimbaud, Arthur, 12, 97
Rockwell, Norman, 29, 66
Roman Catholic mysticism, 17
Roth, Philip, 1
Rourke, Constance, 95
Ryder, Thomas, 49

**S**

Sabbatian movement, 2, 7
Sackett, Stanley, 90
Sade, Marquis de, 45, 93, 96
sadomasochism, 42
*Sanctuary* ( Faulkner), 1
Santayana, George, 64
*Saturday Evening Post*, 29
*Saturday Review*, 16
*Satyricon* (Petronius), 51
    *Day of the Locust, The*, and, 51
Scandinavian novels, 61
Scholem, Gershom, 1
Schwitters, Kurt, 92–93, 158–59

Screen Writers Guild, 15
Seager, Allan, 37–38
Seldes, Gilbert, 129
sexuality, 4, 39
Shakespeare, William, 43, 162
Shepard, Alice, 14
Sibon, Marcelle, 15
sin, 64–65
Singer, Isaac B., 75
*Sink or Swim* (Alger), 137
Snow White, 166, 168–69
Socialist Realism, 62
"Some Notes on Miss Lonelyhearts," 19,
    24, 111, 120, 125, 127
"Some Notes on Violence," 36
*Sound and the Fury, The* (Faulkner), 1
Soupault, Philippe, 15, 158
*Spirit of Culver*, 14
Stein, Gertrude, 63
Stern, Maurice, 11
Stewart, Ogden, 66
stock market crash, 13–14
*Strictly from Hunger* (Perelman), 66
structure, 157
*Sun Also Rises, The* (Hemingway), 1,
    27
    *Miss Lonelyhearts* and, 1, 27
surrealism, 158
Swift, Jonathan, 51, 82, 161
symbolism, 45, 54–55
    in *Dream Life of Balso Snell*, 162
    in *Miss Lonelyhearts*, 31, 38

**T**

*Tale of a Tub* (Swift), 51
*Tarzan* (Burroughs), 166
"Tattered Tom," 66
Thorpe, T.B., 130
*Through the Fallopian Tubes on a Bicycle*
    (Perelman), 97, *see Parlor,*
    *Bedlam and Bath*
Tolstoy, Leo, 11, 63, 65
totalitarianism, 29
Tracy, Lee, 15
Trotskyites, 66
*True Story*, 97
Twain, Mark, 130
    and tall talk, 131
Twentieth Century-Fox, 14
*Typee* (Melville), 4
Tzara, Tristan, 164

**U**

*Ulysses* (Joyce), 78, 134
    Molly Bloom soliloquy, 78, 134
Universal-International Pictures, 14

**V**

Van Gogh, Vincent, 18
*Varieties of Religious Experience* (James), 19,
    63–64
    *Miss Lonelyhearts* and, 19
Venus, 53
Verlaine, Paul, 12
Villon, François, 160
violence, 8, 43, 128
Voltaire, 137, 139

**W**

*Waiting for Lefty* (Odets), 139
Ward, Lynd, 129
Weinstein, Anna Wallenstein, 11, 13
Weinstein, Laura, 11–12, 14
Weinstein, Lorraine, *see* Laura
Weinstein, Max, 11
Weinstein, Nathan, *see* West, Nathanael
Weinstein, Nathan von Wallenstein, *see*
    West, Nathanael
Weinstein, Nathan, 12
West, Nathanael, 2–4, 6, 11–13, 15, 36,
    43, 54, 62, 85, 93, 115, 119–28
    American life, condemnation of, 54
    anti-Semitism, 13
    biography, 115
    characters, 36, 43
    disease and, 43, 54–55
    credo of, 6
    cripples in, works of, 42, 45
    critics and, 85
    death, 1, 15
    education, 11–13
    fascism and, 35

    humor, 3–4, 62, 66
    Jewishness, 6, 12
    letters, 3
    library, 12
    life in works by, 75
    literary craftsman, as, 43
    Marxism and, 34
    moralist, as, 51
    name, 106
    parables, 43
    Perelman and, 66–68
    personal life, 11–16, 89–91
    plays, 15
    position in American literature, 15,
        16, 119
    publication, 14–16, 18
    scholarly articles on, 15
    screenplays, 14
    vision of self, 38
    work, acclaim, 129
    economy of names in, work of, 31
    endings, 42, 75, 85
    language of, 17
    work, movies of, 130
    satire in works by, 43, 54–55, 57,
        62, 65, 68, 143
    work, violence in, 43
    world, and the, 42
Weston, Jessie, 114
Whitman, Walt, 2, 8
Williams, William Carlos, 13–14, 63,
    91–92, 97
    review of *Miss Lonelyhearts*, 146
Wilson, Edmund, 63
*Winesburg, Ohio* (Anderson), 160
"With Old Man Makhno" (Babel), 120
*Women and Angels* (Brodkey), 2

**Y**

Yeats, William Butler, 96